I0810077

IMAGES
of America

RUIDOSO
THE CARMON PHILLIPS COLLECTION

On the Cover: Although a comparatively small waterway, the Rio Ruidoso provides anglers with good trout fishing. This photograph, taken in the Upper Canyon, appeared in a brochure about Ruidoso's attractions that was printed in the early 1950s. The caption encouraged one to "Fish for trout from your back door." (Courtesy of the Carmon Phillips Collection.)

IMAGES
of America

RUIDOSO
THE CARMON PHILLIPS COLLECTION

Lyn Kidder

ARCADIA
PUBLISHING

ISBN 978-1-4671-3185-8

Published by Arcadia Publishing
Charleston, South Carolina

Printed in the United States of America

Library of Congress Control Number: 2013957660

For all general information, please contact Arcadia Publishing:
Telephone 843-853-2070
Fax 843-853-0044
E-mail sales@arcadiapublishing.com
For customer service and orders:
Toll-Free 1-888-313-2665

Visit us on the Internet at www.arcadiapublishing.com

To everyone who loves Ruidoso

Contents

ACKNOWLEDGMENTS

Deepest thanks to the Hubbard Museum of the American West for the monumental task of scanning and cataloging thousands of negatives, with special thanks to David Mandel, Ray Pawley, and Phillip Collins. And thanks to Delana Phillips Clements for hanging on to her father's collection, in spite of having no idea what she would do with them. Thanks to photographers Herb Brunell and Frederic Moras for their help with the images in this book. And a final thank-you to everyone who shared their stories with me.

Unless otherwise noted, all photographs are courtesy of the Carmon Phillips Collection at the Hubbard Museum of the American West, Ruidoso Downs, New Mexico.

INTRODUCTION

Legends from many cultures include stories of heroes who went to the mountains, or a specific mountain, to face challenges, receive wisdom, or perform heroic deeds. Mountains are the mysterious homes of gods, monsters, and the unknown and are powerful symbols in the human imagination.

Ordinary mortals are also drawn to the mountains—for healing, for enlightenment, for escape. For the Mescalero Apaches, the canyons of the Sacramento Mountains provided safety, and the legend of their mountain gods tells of a wounded warrior whom they heal in a cave on the slopes of Sierra Blanca (Spanish for "white mountain"), the highest peak.

On a more prosaic level, people come to the mountains for escape from their everyday lives and, in the Southwest, from the oppressive heat of summer in the desert. In the 1880s, it was a hard three-day trip from El Paso, but the *El Paso Times* described Ruidoso as "the most popular resort for camping out in all the country for 200 miles about El Paso, a grassy mountain valley surmounted by a dense forest in which earthly mortals from the city may hide themselves for a few weeks of rest and relaxation."

In 1907, a primitive road was graded from Alamogordo to Roswell, making the Ruidoso area accessible by automobile. Families camped along the banks of the Rio Ruidoso (Spanish for "noisy river") or rented primitive cabins. Some families spent the entire summer in the mountains, with the weary fathers making the long trek for a weekend of relaxation. Many families eventually built cabins of their own, and generations of children enjoyed summers in the pine forests.

The town experienced an economic boom during World War II, when off-duty servicemen and women came from bases in Roswell, Alamogordo, and El Paso. Although Ruidoso's population nearly doubled between 1940 and 1950, there were still only some 2,000 full-time residents at mid-century.

Among those residents were Carmon and Leona Mae Phillips. Carmon took on the challenge of making a life for himself and his family in a small mountain town. He restored an abandoned adobe mill, operated a photography business, and continuously promoted his new town. Over the next 50 years, he took more than 6,000 photographs of every possible subject. He carefully cataloged the negatives, but after his death, they sat in cardboard boxes on shelves in the mill. In 2011, his daughter, Delana Phillips Clements, donated the collection to the Hubbard Museum of the American West, where the negatives were scanned. This book is but a small sampling of the portrait of Ruidoso that Carmon Phillips created.

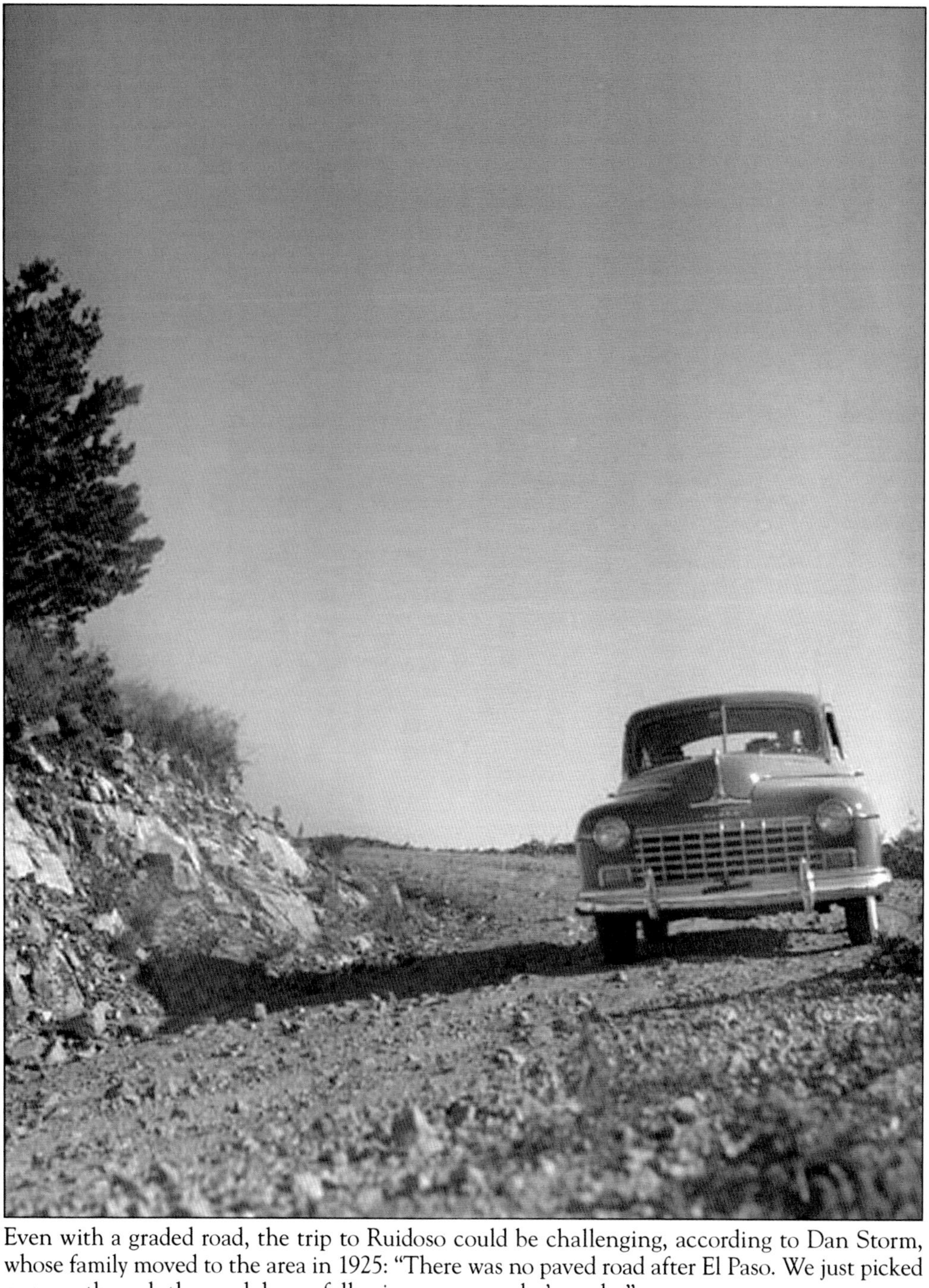

Even with a graded road, the trip to Ruidoso could be challenging, according to Dan Storm, whose family moved to the area in 1925: "There was no paved road after El Paso. We just picked our way through the sand dunes, following someone else's tracks."

One

The Road to Ruidoso

William Carmon Phillips was born in Erick, Oklahoma, in 1913. Like many Oklahomans of the era, necessity taught him lessons in self-reliance. During the Depression, he traveled the country, sometimes by train, looking for work. It was on one such trip that he first came to Ruidoso.

"I first saw Ruidoso in 1936, when I was on a bus on my way to California," Philips later said. "The bus pulled up in front of the Wingfield house, and there were people who had set up a couple little stands, selling cherry cider and food to the passengers and other visitors." Ike Wingfield, who built the house in 1929, had been born in the adobe mill that would later be a part of Carmon Phillips's life in Ruidoso. The enterprising Wingfield family ran a dairy, general store, and post office, and their children collected nickels in exchange for opening the pasture gate for automobiles headed to the Upper Canyon.

Phillips found no work in California, but he did get a job with the Lyceum Theater Circuit (and, later, the Griffith Amusement Company), renovating and promoting movie theaters in small towns in New Mexico and Texas. Phillips was a tireless promoter, organizing publicity events that had some connection with the films that were being shown or that simply got people into the theater.

After a theater was successfully reestablished in a community, the company sent him to another town. While working in Clovis, New Mexico, he met Leona Mae. They married in 1938 and continued their gypsy lifestyle until World War II, when they moved to Dallas, Texas, where Carmon worked for Lockheed Martin. While in Dallas, he also found time to attend classes in photography and painting.

After the war, he had the opportunity to move to California and continue working for the company. But he had fallen in love with a small New Mexico mountain town during the vacations he and Leona Mae had managed to take by saving their gas rationing coupons. Leona Mae was reluctant to make the move—she had spent her childhood there, and to her, Ruidoso life meant hauling water and using an outhouse. Carmon promised indoor plumbing. They moved to Ruidoso in 1945.

To make a living in a town whose winter population was only a few thousand people, Carmon drew on his experience in promoting movie theaters in similar small, less-than-prosperous towns. He had been successful in this former career, receiving letters of recognition from Metro-Goldwyn-Mayer, Columbia Pictures, and Walt Disney.

In 1939, the *Theater Partner*, a trade publication for movie theater owners and managers, described Phillips's "bunch of explosive stunts that had the whole town talking." The article concluded with a prophetic description of the life he would live in Ruidoso:

> He makes them [the townspeople] want to come to the Lea Theater. He doesn't let them forget he's there. Best of all, he has made friends with everyone in town through these promotional stunts. He is on good terms with the civic organizations, the merchants know and like him, the newspaper cooperates wholeheartedly and the whole town supports his theater.

That's showmanship.
And that was Carmon Phillips.

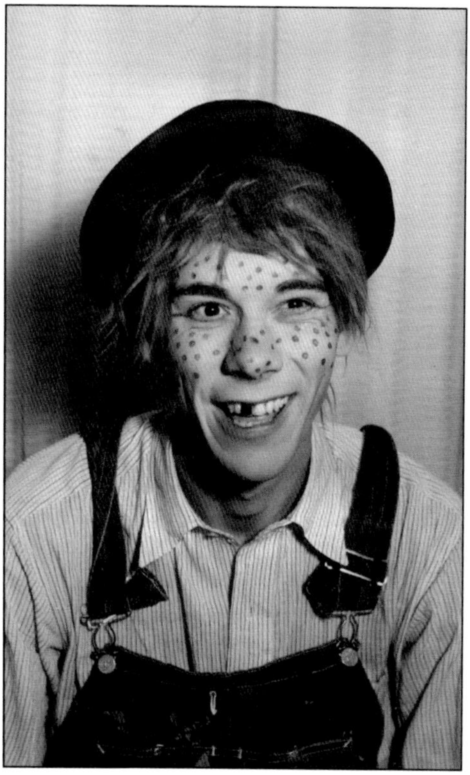

Phillips created the character Tobias X. Frothingham, also known as "Toby," writing scripts for him in the style of vaudeville and minstrel show comedy. Toby appeared at local events, leading goat-milking contests, serving as emcee, and playing his trumpet. This photograph appeared in the *Deming Graphic*, of Deming, New Mexico, in 1938.

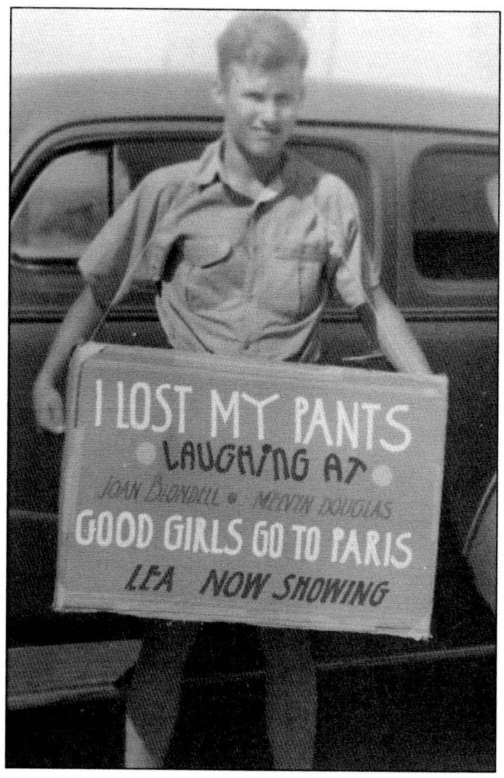

Carmon Phillips had a way of persuading people to do things, as seen by this publicity stunt for the Lea Theater in Eunice, New Mexico, in 1939. Phillips also organized beauty contests, movie star look-alike contests, Easter egg hunts, kite flying, model airplane building, and diaper-pinning contests, as well as "womanless weddings" in which all the participants were local men. The prizes for every contest included tickets to his movie theater.

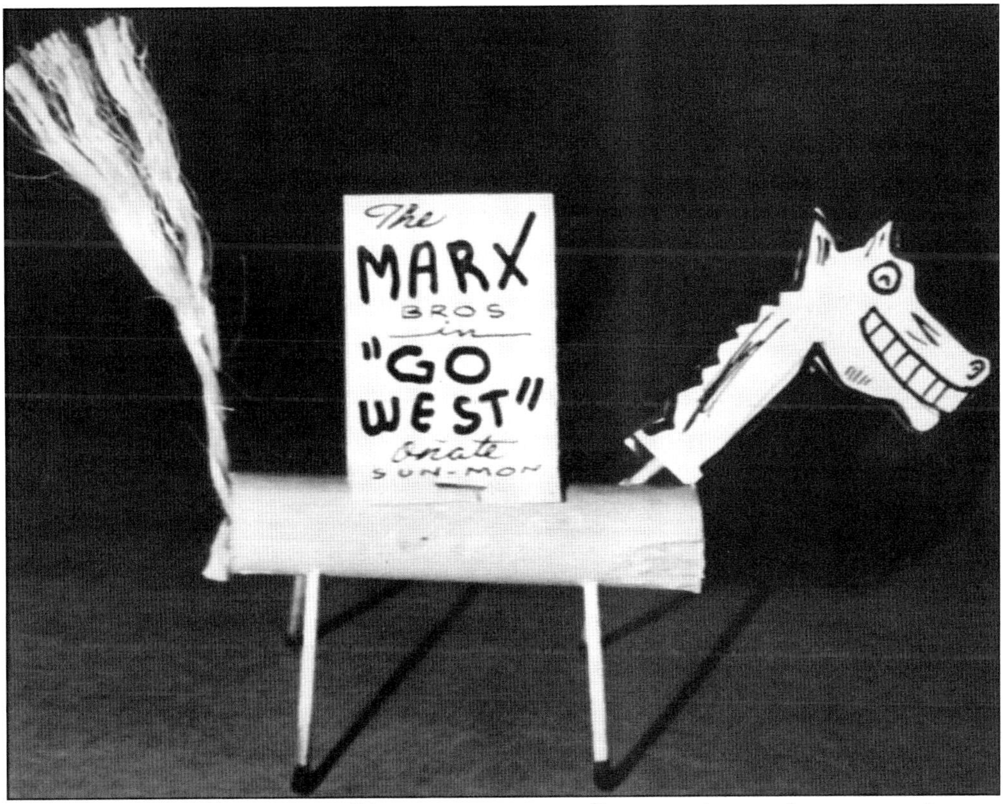

In 1941, Carmon made these small horses using pieces of broomsticks, matches, rope, and paper. He placed them on counters, desks, and tables in public places around Belen, New Mexico, to promote the Marx Brothers movie *Go West*.

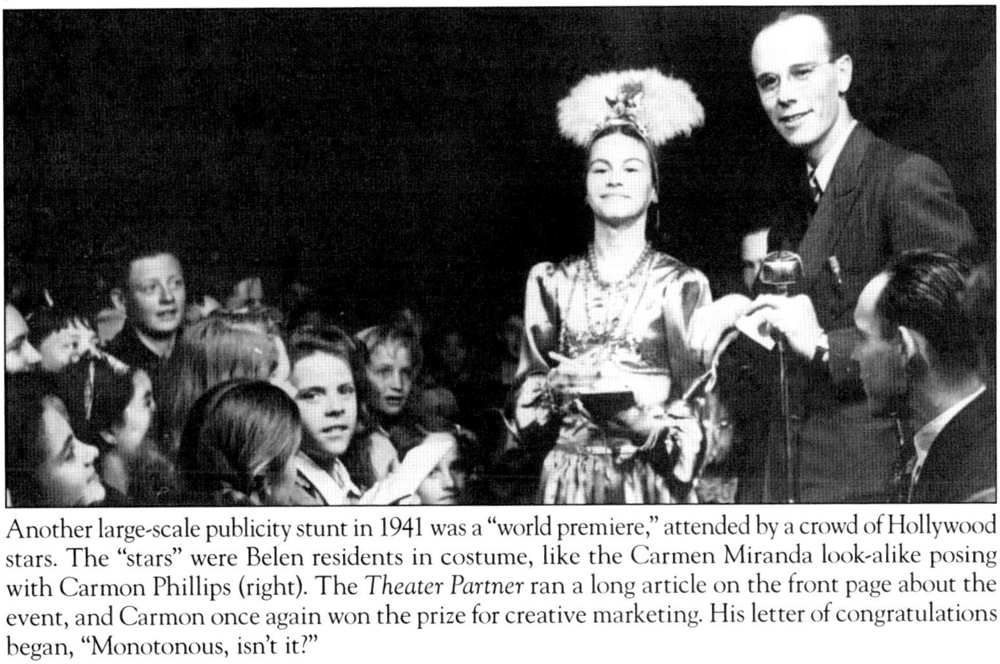

Another large-scale publicity stunt in 1941 was a "world premiere," attended by a crowd of Hollywood stars. The "stars" were Belen residents in costume, like the Carmen Miranda look-alike posing with Carmon Phillips (right). The *Theater Partner* ran a long article on the front page about the event, and Carmon once again won the prize for creative marketing. His letter of congratulations began, "Monotonous, isn't it?"

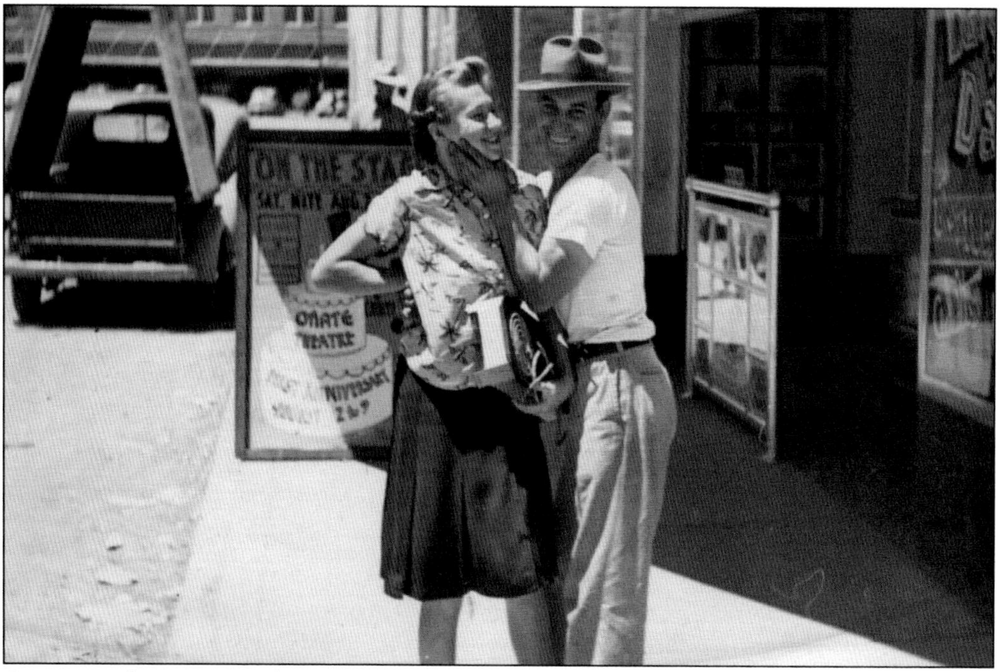

Carmon and Leona Mae clown around in front of the Onate Theatre in Belen, New Mexico.

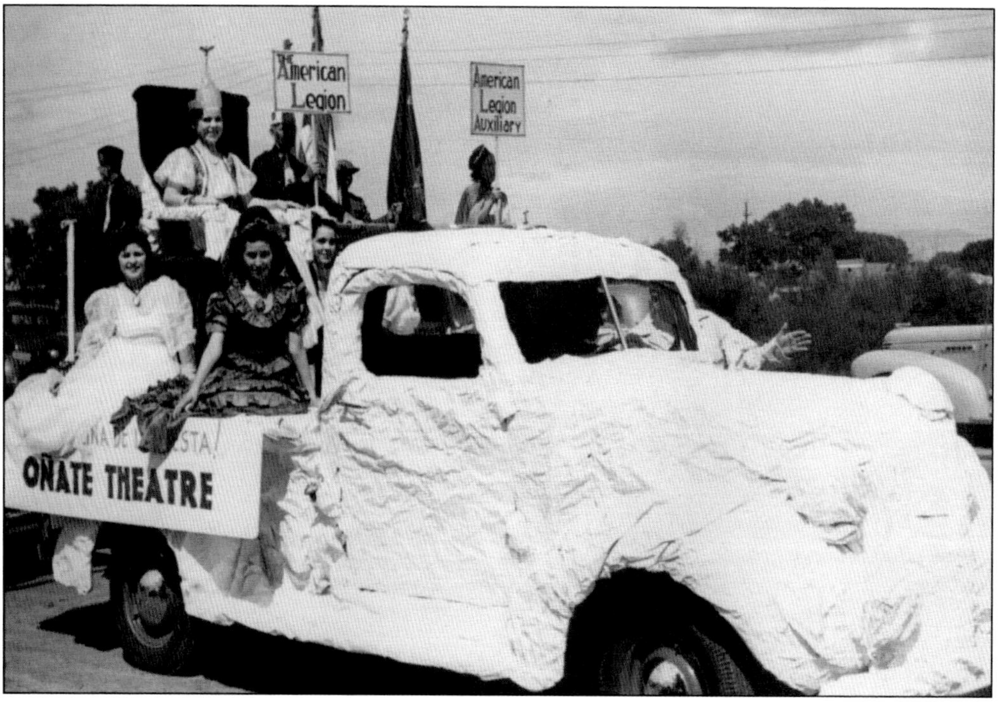

The town of Belen held an annual fiesta for 147 years without selecting a fiesta queen, a situation that Phillips sought to remedy in 1941. He got local businesses to sponsor the 27 contestants, and townspeople voted for their favorites. Moviegoers had extra chances to vote. The winner received $10 and a pass to the Onate Theatre, good for one month. The chamber of commerce thanked him for his originality and ability in achieving an "unusual success."

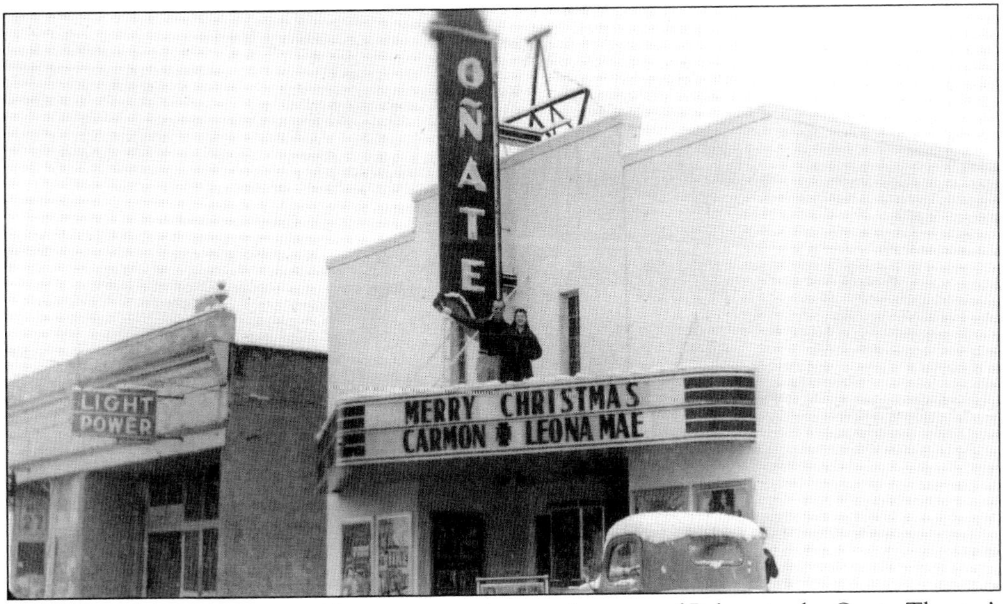

Carmon and Leona Mae sent Christmas greetings to the town of Belen via the Onate Theatre's marquee in 1941.

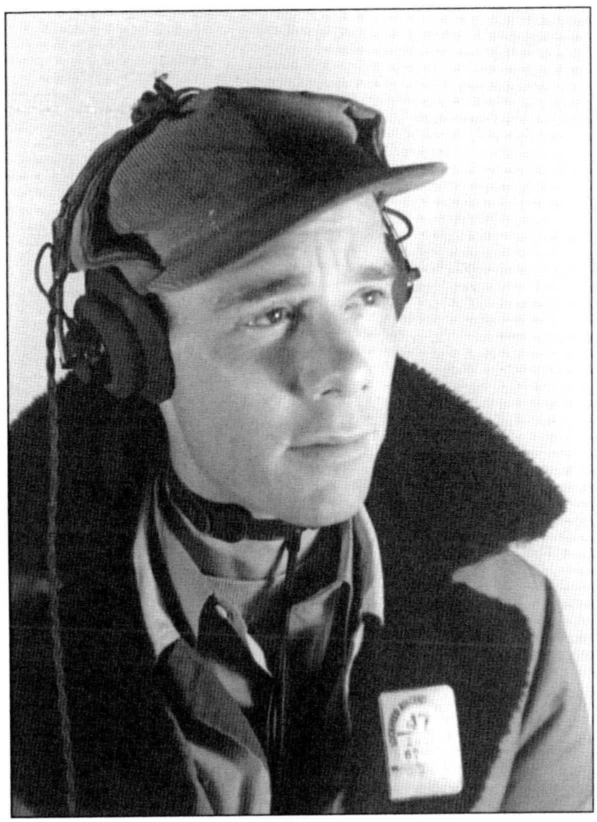
During World War II, Carmon installed radar equipment in airplanes for Lockheed Martin in Dallas, Texas. Radar was a new technology, and the work was so secret that he could not even tell Leona Mae about it.

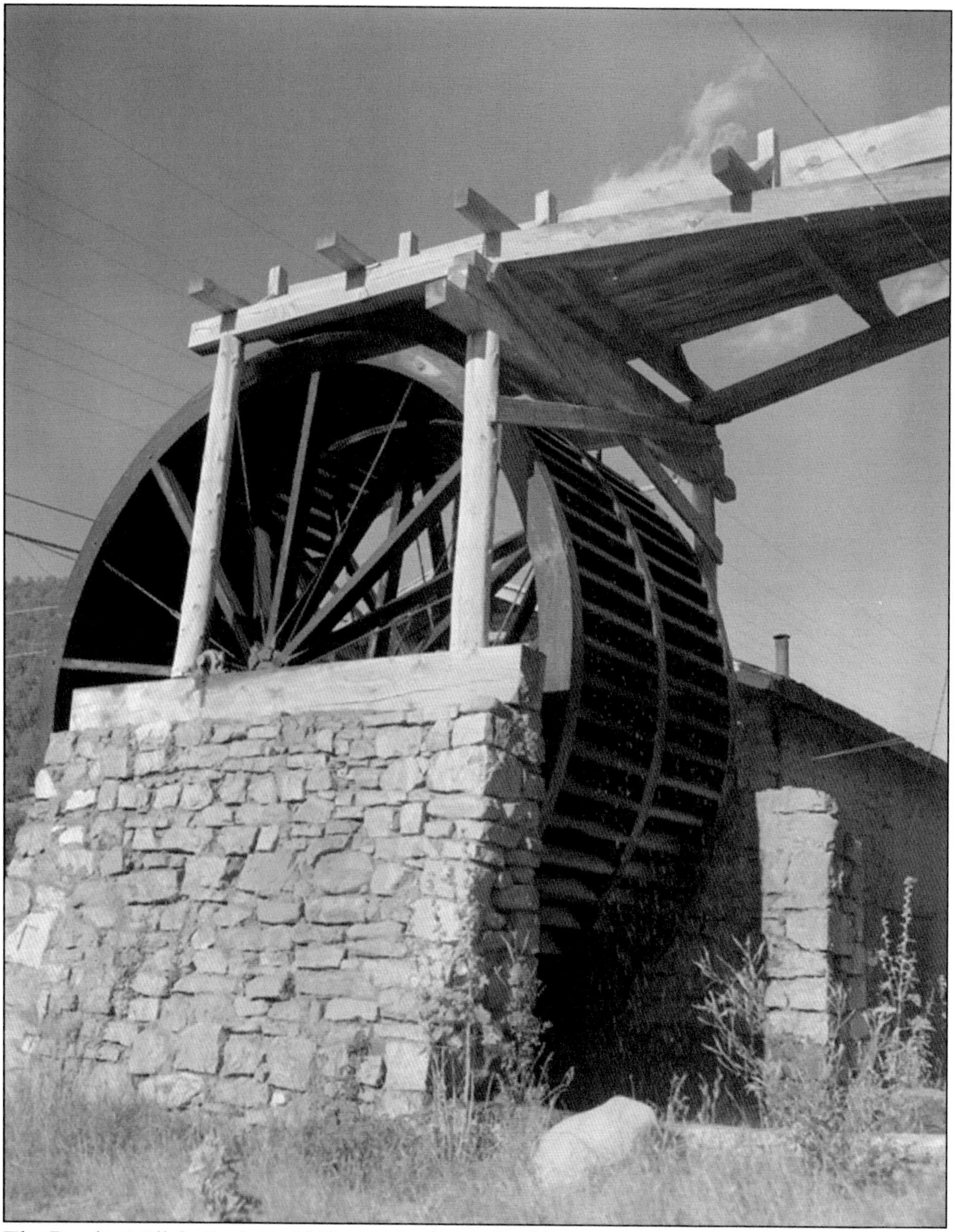

The Dowlin Mill, built about 1868, was the largest building in the area, serving as a social center and a stopping point for travelers between El Paso, Roswell, Fort Stanton, and the Indian agency at Mescalero. Annie Lesnett, one of the mill's early occupants, claimed to have hosted both Billy the Kid and Mescalero Apache chief Geronimo.

Two

The Old Mill

One of the most prominent buildings in Ruidoso was an adobe mill, built by Paul Dowlin, who had served in the Army at nearby Fort Stanton about 1868. Paul and his brother Will Dowlin constructed a three-mile wooden flume that brought water to power the large wooden mill wheel from farther upriver, a place that became known as Flume Canyon.

Paul Dowlin was killed in 1877, shot by Jerry Dillon, a disgruntled employee. He died in the front yard of the mill the day before the new owners, Frank and Annie Lesnett, arrived from Chicago. The Lesnetts, apparently undeterred by this violent act, raised their family and operated the post office in the mill until 1904.

They sold the mill in 1887 to James Cree, a wealthy owner of a whiskey distillery in Edinburgh, Scotland, who invested in land in Lincoln County. After the death of Lord Cree's son, the land was sold to the White Mountain Development Company in the 1940s.

The land included what was left of the Dowlin Mill. Phillips bought a lot next to the mill with a 500-foot frontage on what was then Main Road for $500, and he and Leona Mae constructed a small building. White Mountain Development Company then hired Phillips to repair the mill's wooden wheel.

"The shaft had broken and the wheel was just sort of squatting there," Phillips later said. He salvaged pieces of redwood from an abandoned water tank at Parsons Mine and painstakingly rebuilt the wheel. After leasing the mill since 1946, he bought it in 1950.

"It was in deplorable condition," he remembered. "People had kept cows in there during the winter, so I hauled out dirt and cow patties a foot deep. There was a lot of old junk that people had stored there. The newspaper ran a story asking them to come and claim their property, but nobody did. The only thing in there of any value was a leather bound dictionary printed in 1886, which I kept."

In the small building that Carmon and Leona Mae had constructed, they sold curios, souvenirs, and film from a store in the front. In the darkroom at the back of the structure, they developed film, offering overnight service. During the busy summers, processing, cutting, drying, and packaging the photographs could keep them working late into the night. The couple also lived in the structure, which became more crowded with the birth of their daughter Delana in 1950. The growing family was perhaps an additional motivation to renovate the mill, where the gift shop was moved in 1951.

In addition to the usual souvenirs, the Phillips family sold film, postcards, and prints from Carmon's photographs. A large advertisement in the *Ruidoso News* in 1946 urged readers, "Live a lifetime in one evening. You can have real pleasure looking at snapshots of days gone forever. Keep your album to date. You'll be happy you did." The advertisement went on to explain the one-day photograph-finishing service available at the Old Mill.

Phillips later recalled, "Most of my time in Ruidoso was spent just trying to make a living."

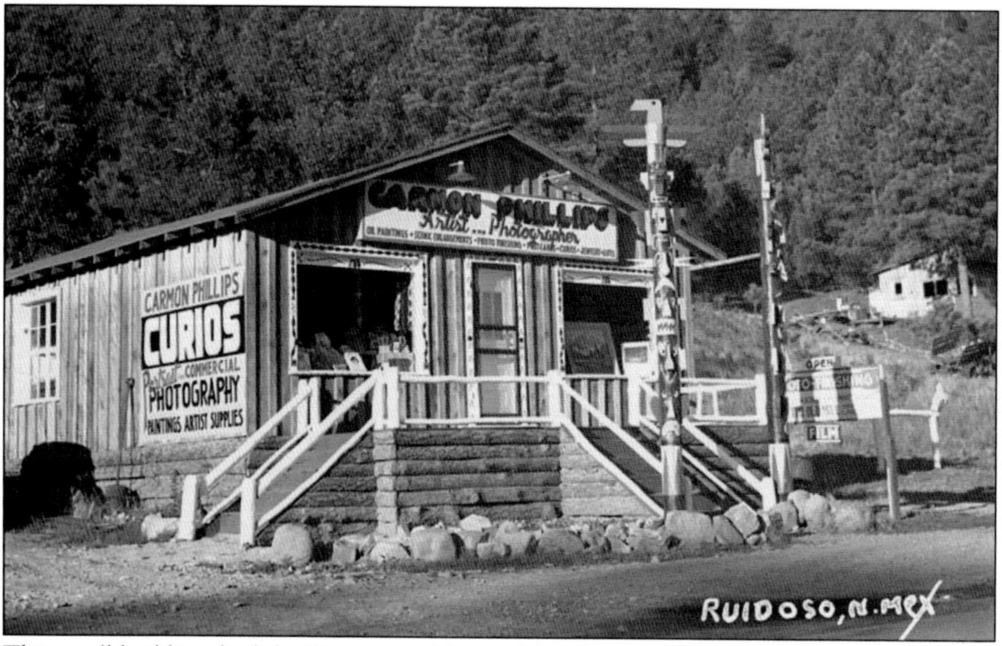

This small building, built by Carmon and Leona Mae, held the first gift shop, Carmon's studio and darkroom, and their living space. Carmon carved the totem poles. In 1947, the *Ruidoso News* noted, "Carmon Phillips's 'Totem Looking Poles'—that's what he calls 'em—are startling when you come around that curve and down the hill by the old mill. I predict they will attract plenty of attention."

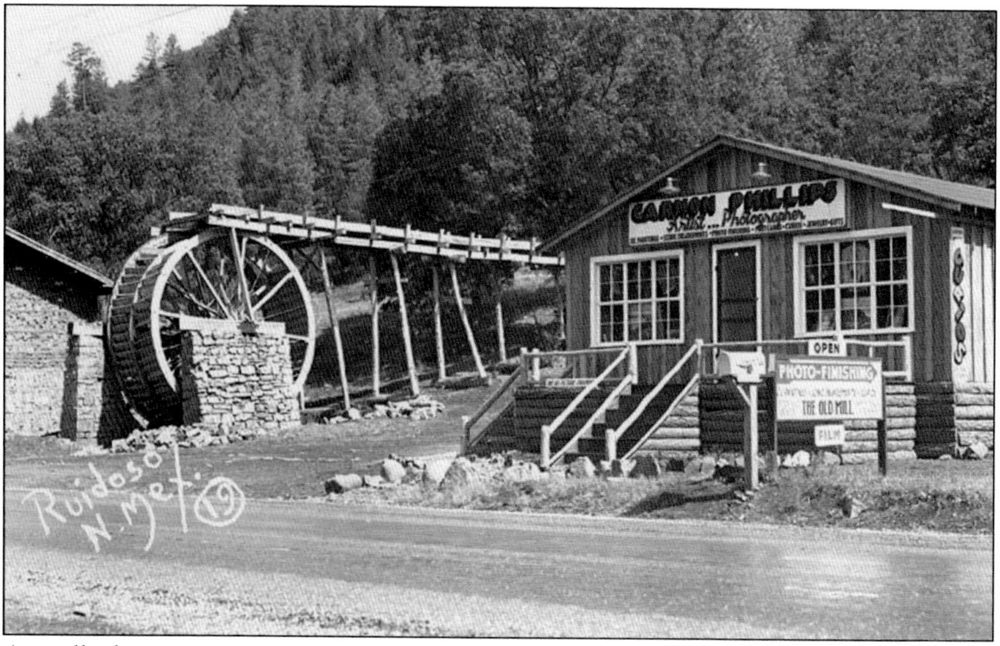

A small advertisement appeared in the May 17, 1946, edition of the *Ruidoso News*. Next to a drawing of a sailor with a telescope, it said, "Take a Look, We're Open Now, Carmon Phillips Artist & Photographer, By the Old Mill." In this earlier photograph, the totem poles are absent, and the wheel has not yet been repaired.

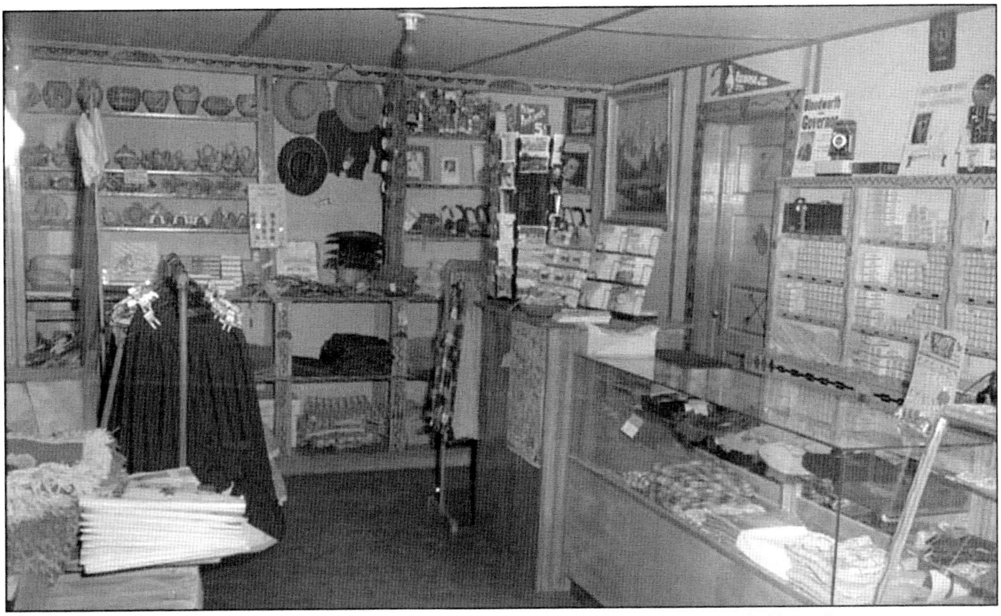

In March 1947, a writer for the *Ruidoso News* gushed, "The Carmon Phillips shop is getting so full of attractive merchandise that the urge is to buy everything you see," and "Many of the lovely Fiesta skirts and blouses being worn here come from the Carmon Phillips shop." Carmon made most of his shelving and display units, as seen by the film cabinets at right. Phillips worked with a perfume manufacturer to develop fragrances like "Ruidoso Rain" and "Turquoise Night." In addition to offering watch repair, he also sold cameras and records for learning Spanish.

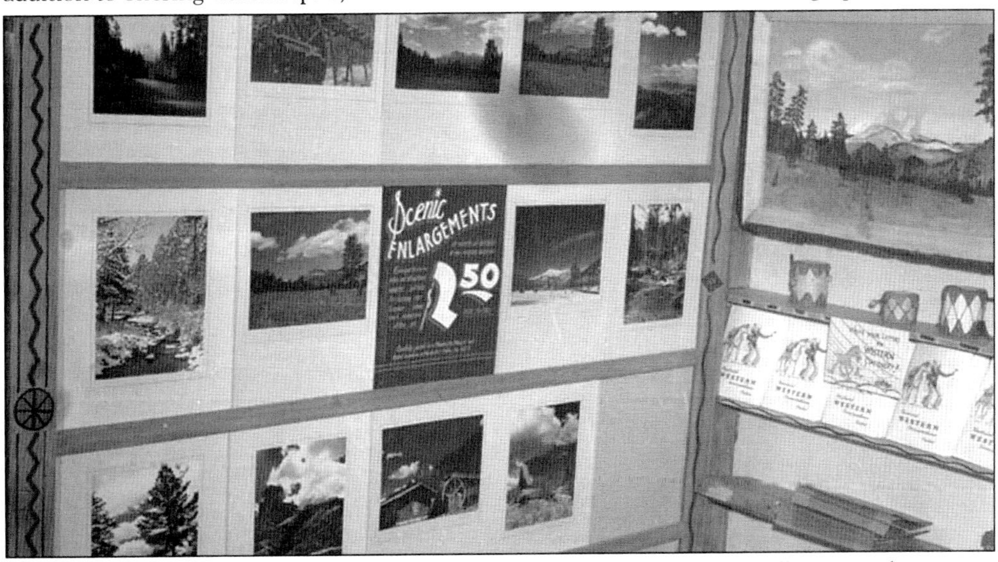

The January 26, 1951, headline of the *Ruidoso News* announced, "Carmon Phillips moves business to Old Mill." The article noted, "Carmon Phillips, successful businessman and artist and photographer of renown throughout the Southwest recently moved his gift and curio shop from the small building where he started to the building known throughout the Southwest as the Historical Old Mill in Ruidoso. Mr. Phillips has spent considerable time and effort in restoring the old landmark to keep every detail as historically accurate as possible while making it into a suitable place for his business."

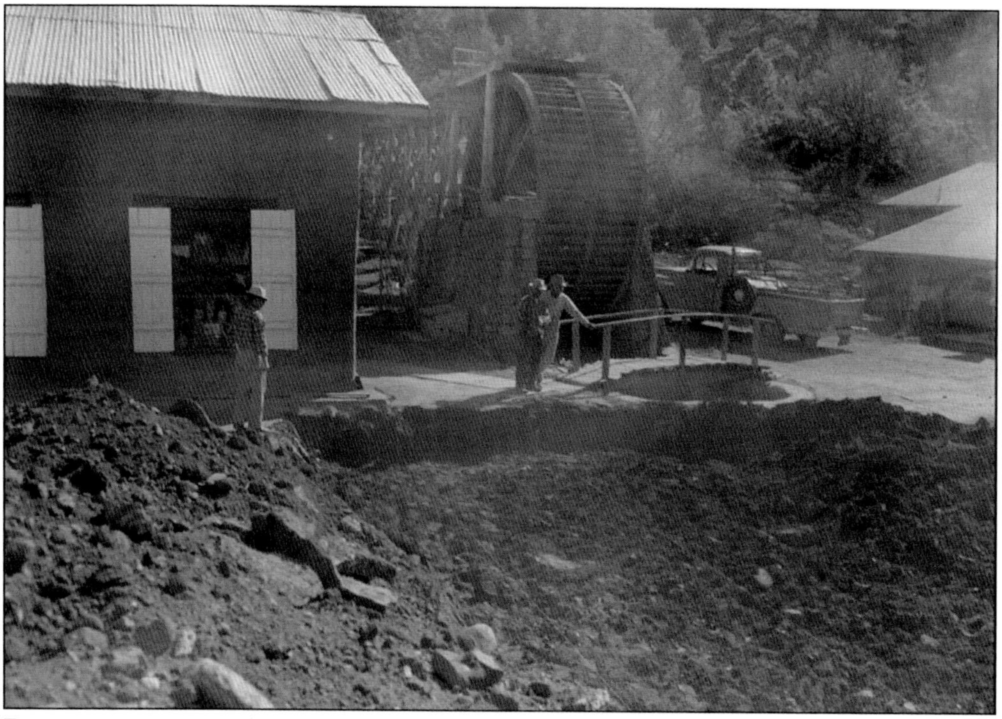

Every improvement to the primary road into Ruidoso raised the roadbed, giving the impression that the mill had been built in a hole. Proper drainage is an engineering challenge in a town of steep hillsides and sudden torrential rains. Below, the totem poles that Carmon carved have been moved to the front of the mill.

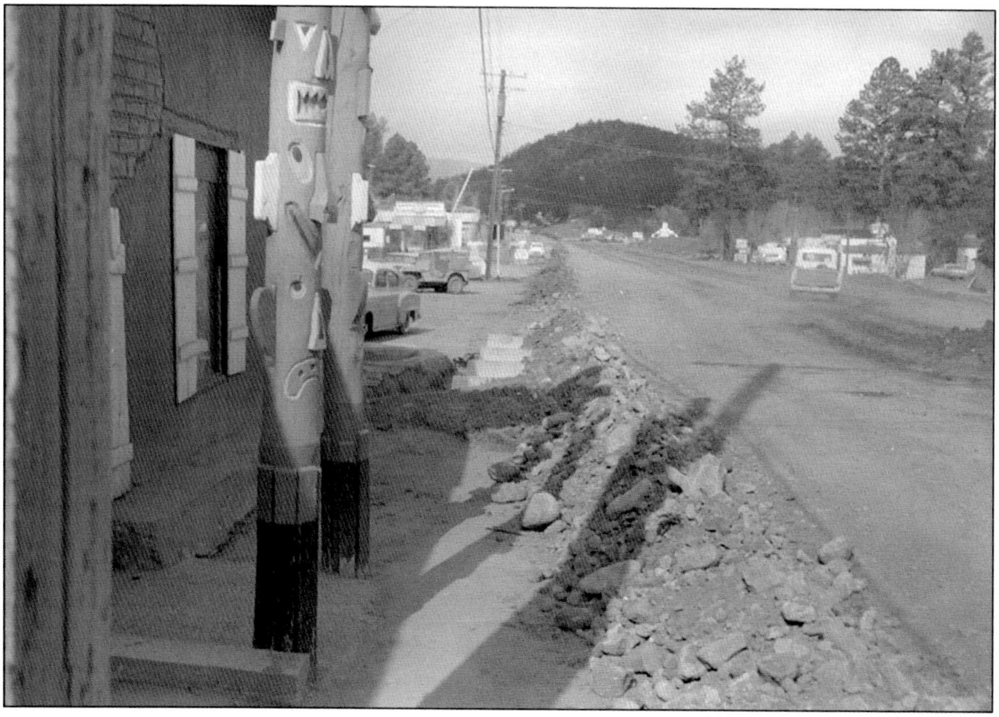

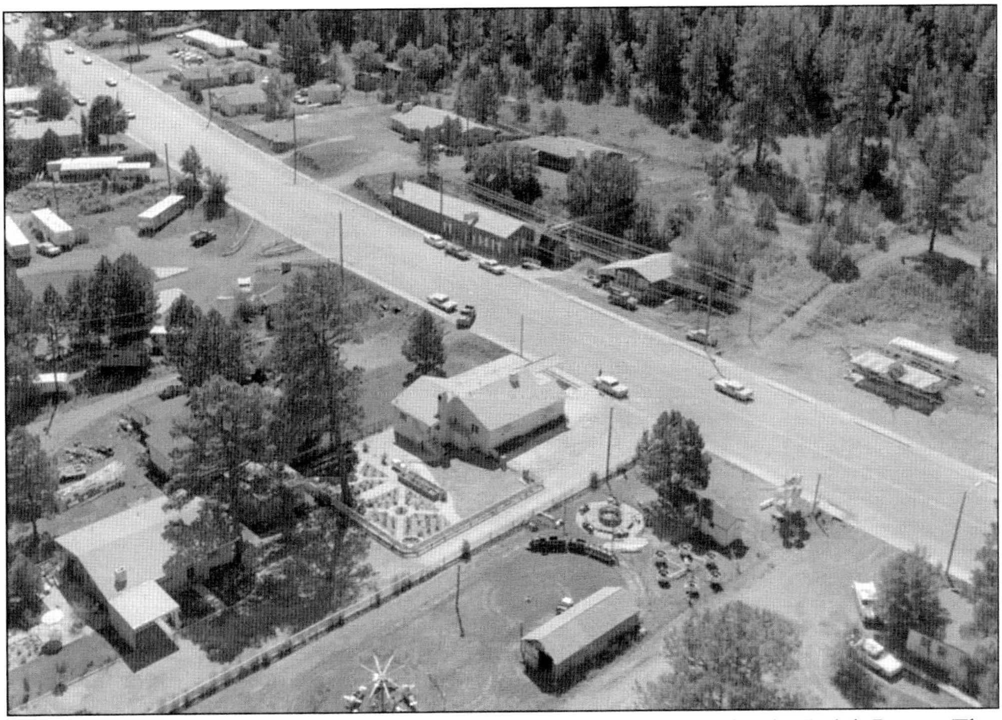

Carmon loved flying and took many aerial photographs while aloft with pilot Ralph Brown. This one shows the mill on the left and the house and original shop on the right. The little building in the lower right is the Burger Trolley, with a small children's amusement park across the street. Delana remembers going there to buy snow cones. The photograph was taken after 1960, when the road was widened to four lanes.

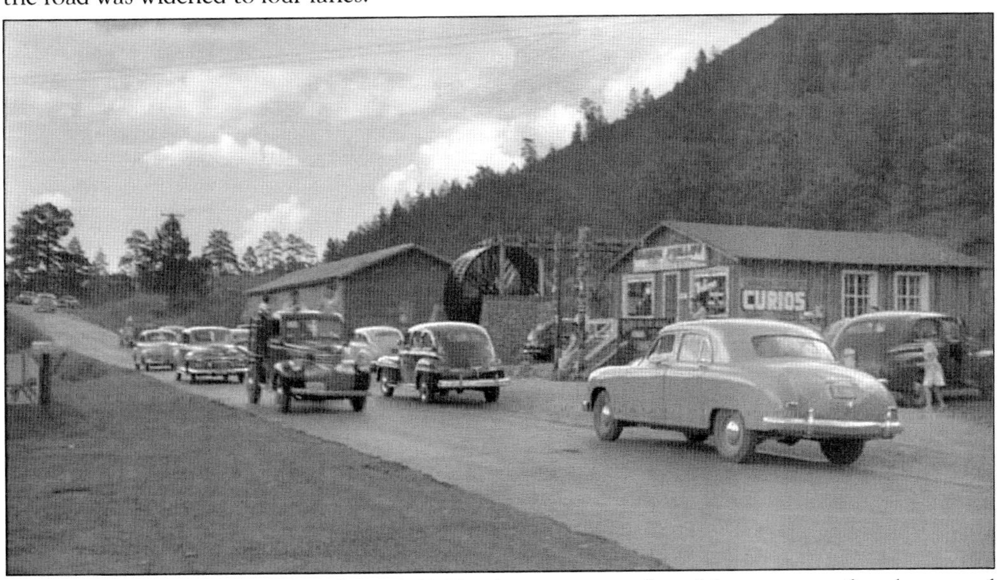

Sudderth Drive was Main Road until 1960, when it was widened from two to four lanes and renamed for John Sudderth, the state highway commissioner. In the early 1950s, the mill was still relatively isolated. Older Ruidoso residents remember when the entire area, from the mill to Carrizo Canyon, was a pasture.

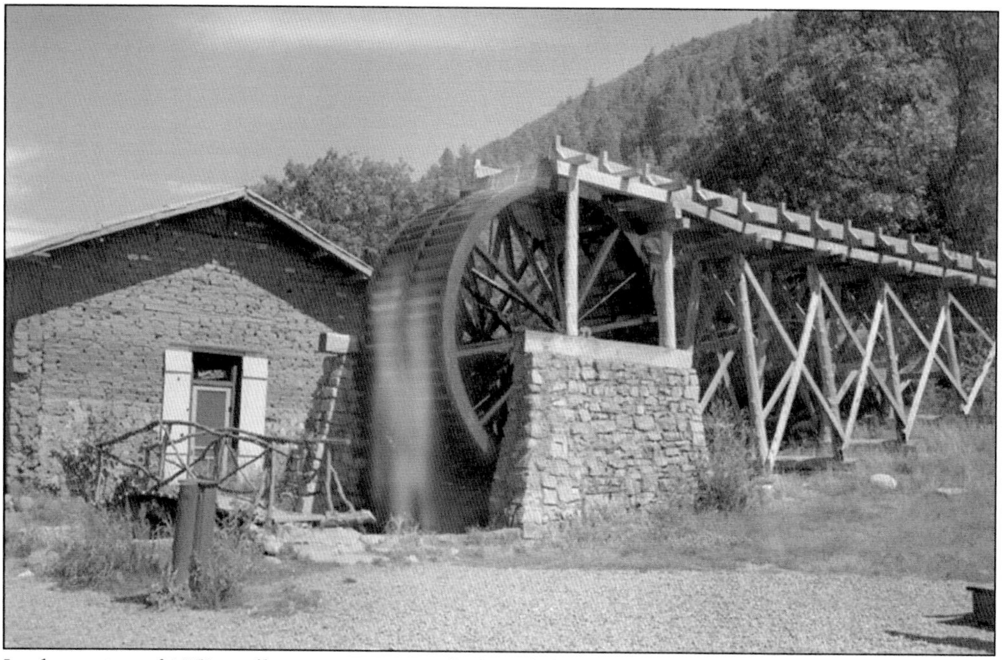

In the spring of 1952, millstones were installed, and the turning mill wheel ground whole wheat flour for the first time in many decades. Phillips reported that the flint stones were "at least 100 years old." Flour and, later, cornmeal were packaged and sold in paper sacks, with bread recipes attached to the bags.

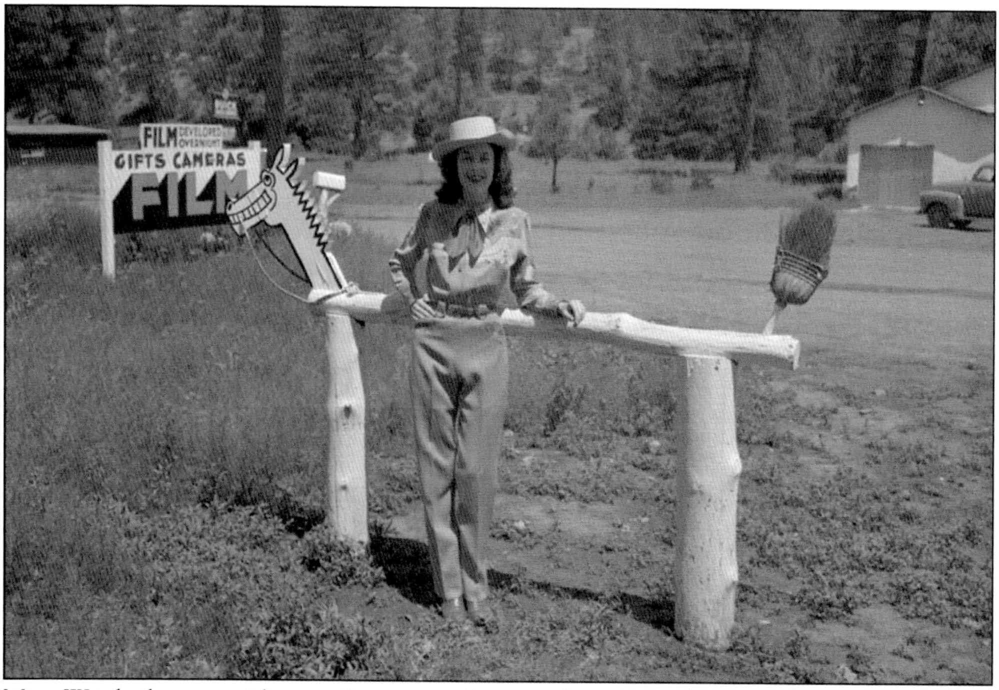

Mary Wimberly poses with a wooden cartoon horse in front of the shop. This was a larger version of the promotional device that Phillips created for the Marx Brothers movie *Go West* while managing a movie theater in Belen, New Mexico.

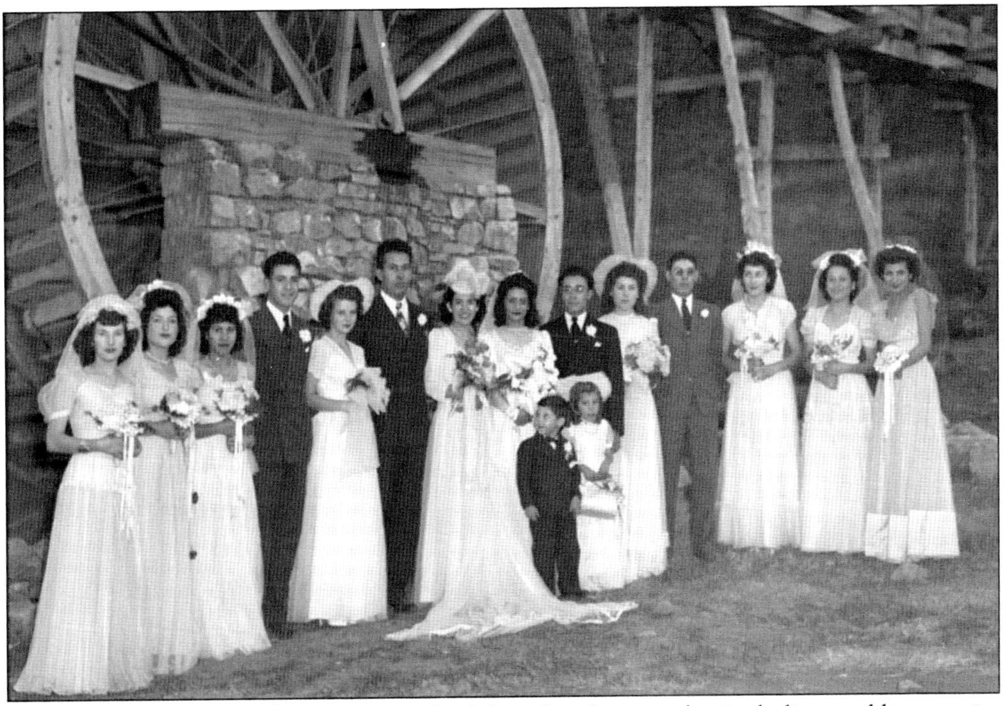

The mill wheel remained a convenient backdrop for photographs, including wedding parties and the day's catch. In the photograph above, bride and groom Nora Nunez and Albert Salcido celebrate their wedding.

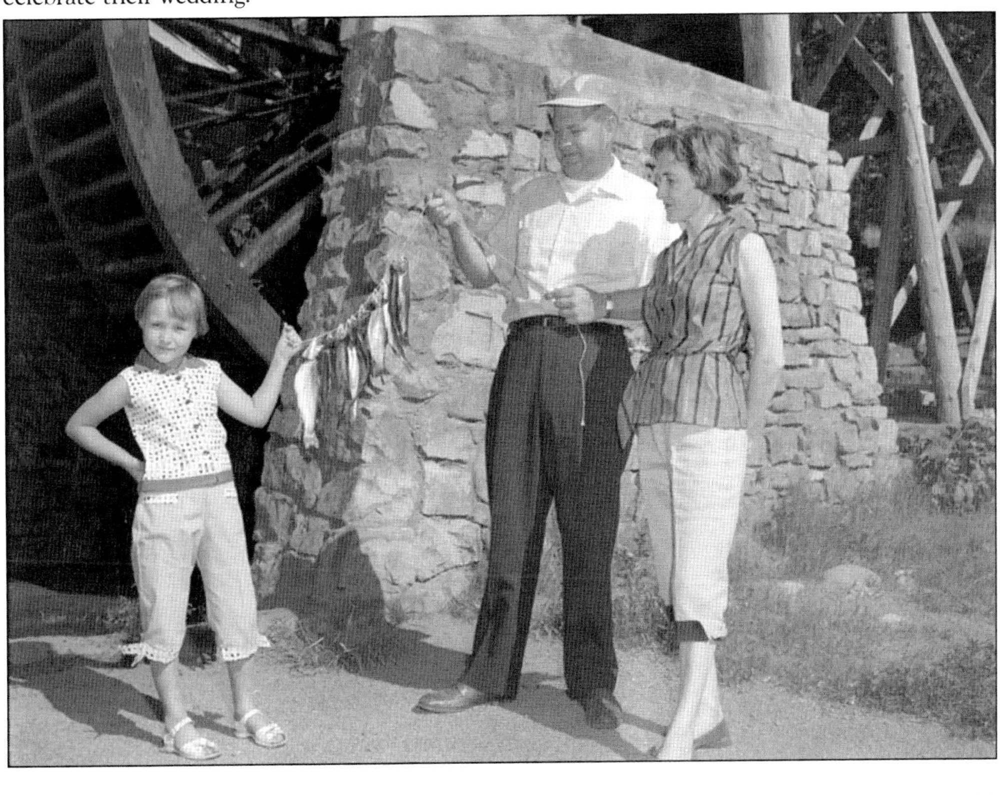

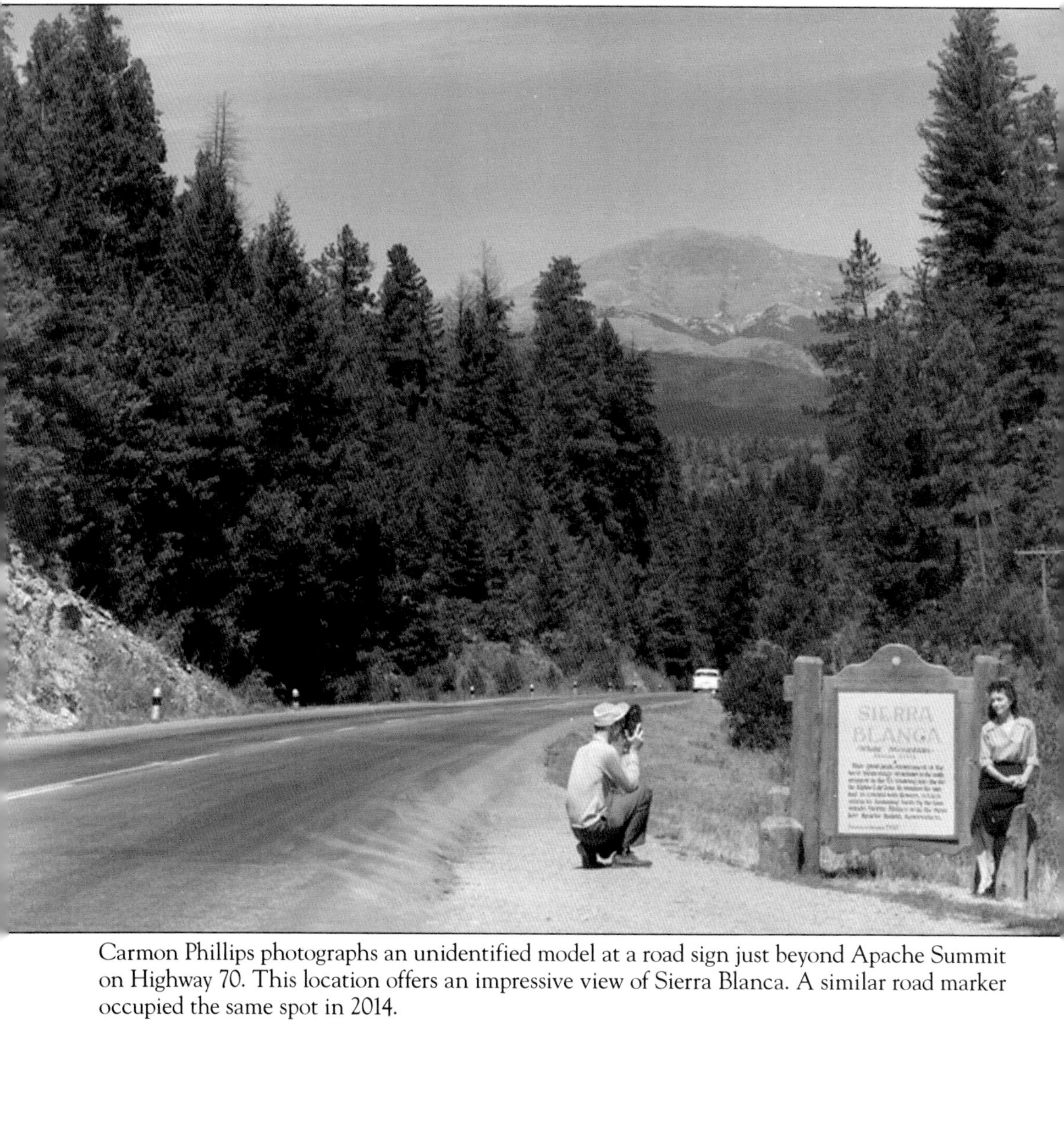

Carmon Phillips photographs an unidentified model at a road sign just beyond Apache Summit on Highway 70. This location offers an impressive view of Sierra Blanca. A similar road marker occupied the same spot in 2014.

Three

The Year-round Playground of the Southwest

Carmon Phillips arrived in Ruidoso just as the town, along with the rest of the country, was riding a euphoric wave of optimism. The village was incorporated in 1945, and the fledgling town embarked on an impressive campaign of civic improvements, including the town's first water system and jail, as well as trash collection (a job that was initially handled by the Women's Chamber of Commerce). Work began on a public water system, diminishing the need to haul water from springs and the Rio Ruidoso. New businesses opened, and the *Ruidoso News*, started in 1946, loudly beat the drum for anything that promoted Ruidoso.

Phillips seems to have assigned himself the task of photographing everything in the area. He soon became involved with the Lions Club and the chamber of commerce, for which he was elected president of the former and a director of the latter in 1947. He set about publicizing the area's many attractions.

In addition to the excellent summer climate, visitors came to Ruidoso for horse racing, which began informally in a large pasture owned by Fountain and Alice Miller in what is now Ruidoso Downs.

In a 1974 article in the *New Yorker* magazine, writer John McPhee described the racetrack and Ruidoso:

> The setting is a small race track in big dry mountains that rise up to eleven and twelve thousand feet. Ruidoso is a linear town, stretched out along miles of highway in creases of the mountains, its wide streets lined with flaky plastic. Curio bins. Drive-in burgers. The same versatile hand that painted Las Vegas into the desert may have painted Ruidoso into the mountains. One has only to get on a horse and go sidewise, though, up into a canyon or on to a mesa, to see what beautiful country it was built in and why the town is the retreat and playground of, primarily, Texans. Ruidoso is where Texans cool off. It is the nearest mountain range to the plains of West Texas and Texans have been going to Ruidoso in big numbers for many decades.

Ruidoso's other big attraction in its early days was gambling. Although it was illegal, there were slot machines everywhere, including restaurants and grocery stores, and games of poker and roulette were found in most bars, which also provided bands and dancing.

Outdoor activities included horseback riding, hiking, golf, and fishing, as well as amusements like shooting galleries, roller skating, bowling, and "carpet golf" (later, miniature golf). Summer visitors could travel south to the nearby Mescalero Apache Reservation for bonfires and ceremonial dancing. Winter visitors skied and tobogganed at Cedar Creek.

Over the years, Phillips published *Pictorial Ruidoso*, a magazine that came out "every now and then," according to his daughter Delana. The first issue appeared in summer 1948, selling for 35¢ a copy. By 1963, its size had increased to 72 pages and the price to 75¢. His work also appeared in regional and national magazines.

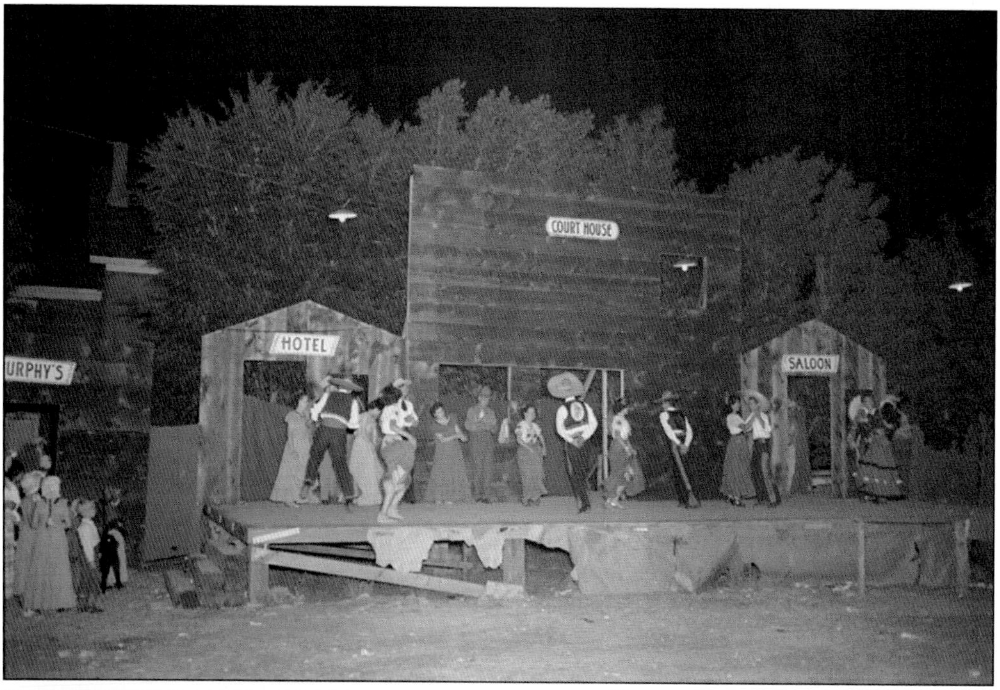

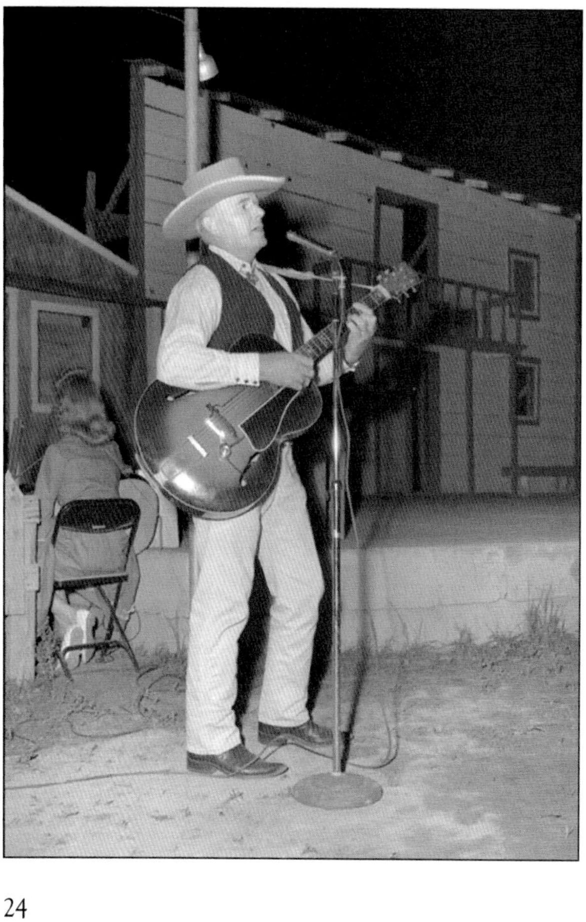

Beginning in 1940, Old Lincoln Days featured the pageant *The Last Escape of Billy the Kid*, with artist Peter Hurd playing the role of Billy the Kid. Other than a few interruptions during World War II, the pageant has been staged every year in early August.

Marcus Storm, brother of Dan Storm, wrote a ballad about Billy the Kid, which is played every year during the pageant at Old Lincoln Days. This photograph dates from 1962.

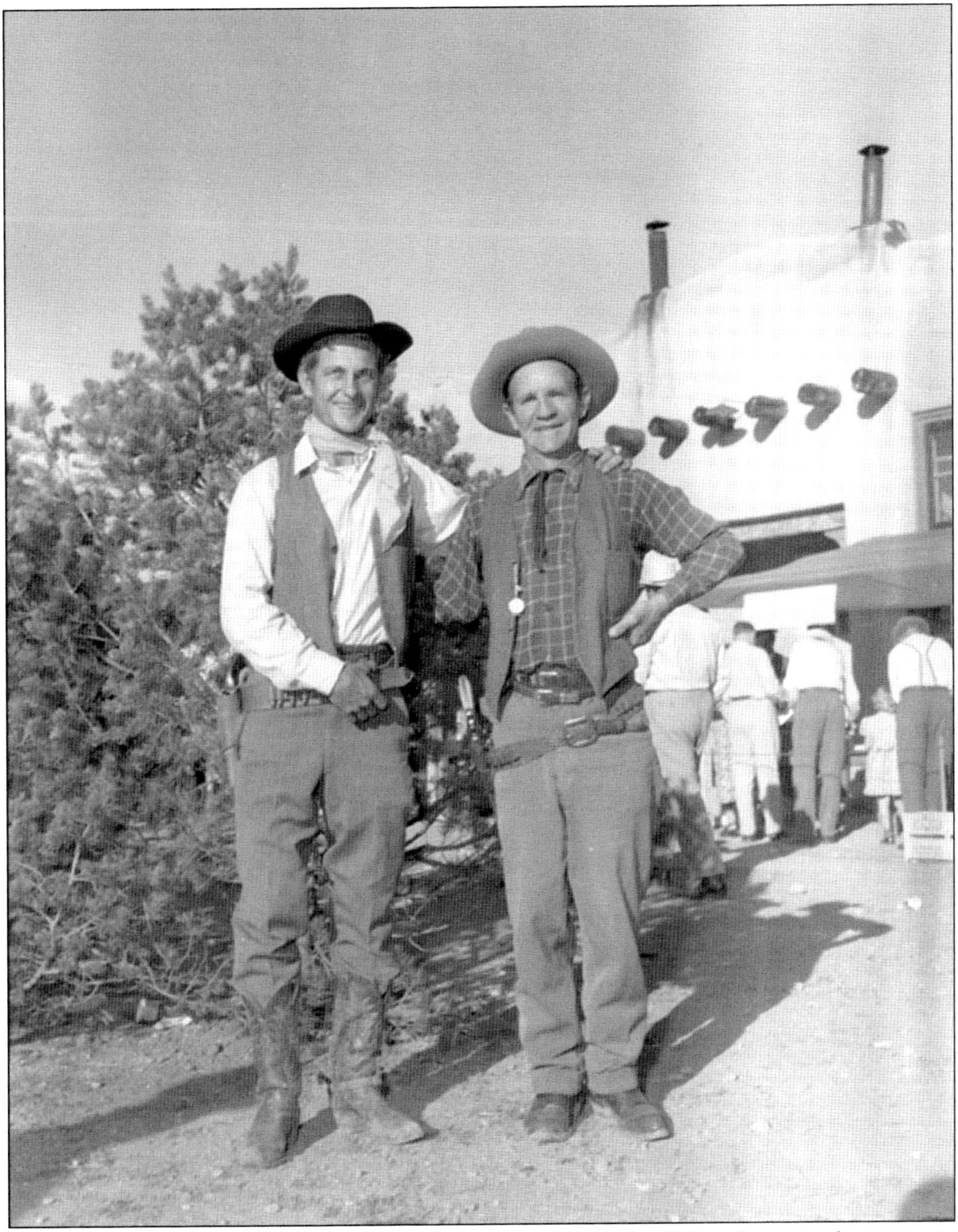

In 1949 and 1950, John Davis (left) played the part of Billy the Kid in the annual pageant in Lincoln. Dan Storm (right) played Buckshot Roberts every year until his death in 1999. The building to the right is the Lincoln School.

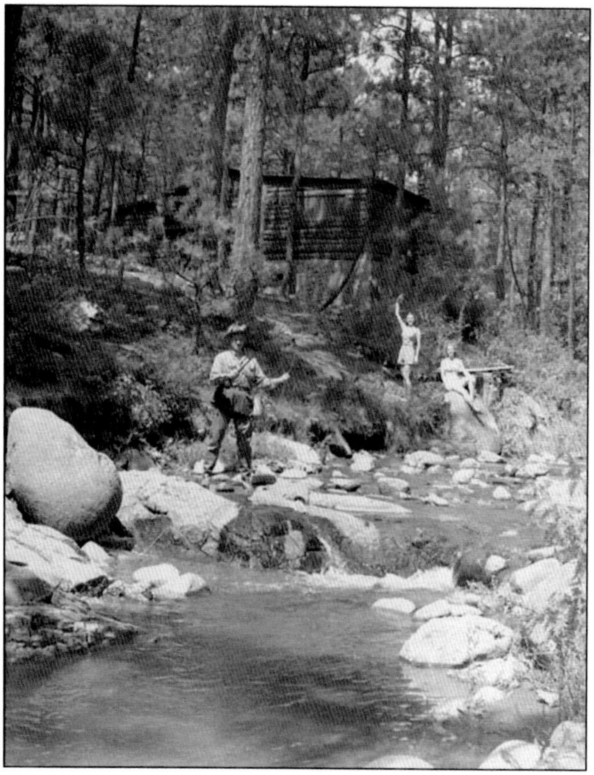

A fisherman and his two companions pose on the Rio Ruidoso in Upper Canyon, below the Mescalero Apache Reservation line. A *Ruidoso News* headline in May 1946 stated, "Ruidoso's Lady Anglers Catch the Whoppers and Leave the Little Ones." According to the article, Mary Farus and Martha Graves "have caught trout up to 18 inches long in said noisy stream." Said to "live from one fishing season to another," Farus took a taxi at 5:00 a.m. on opening day, fishing in Upper Canyon above the reservation line, where she would catch her limit before noon.

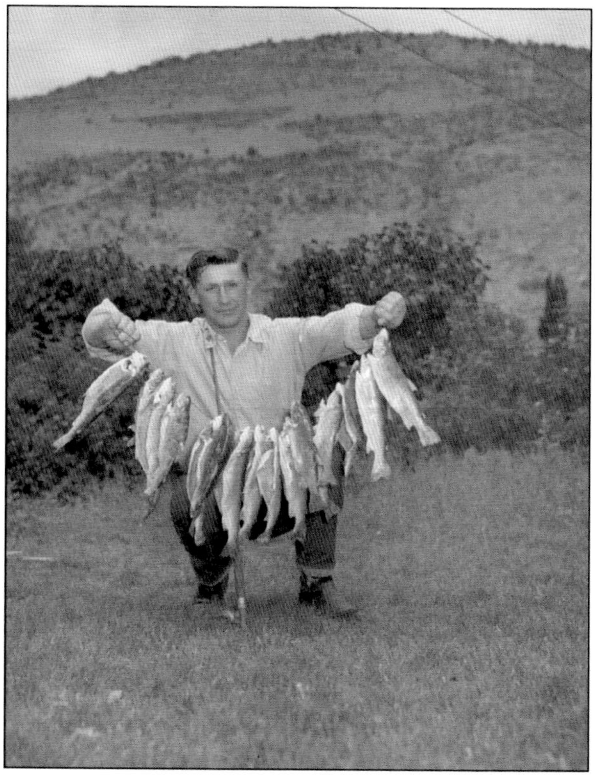

Wayne Estes poses with a string of fish in 1948.

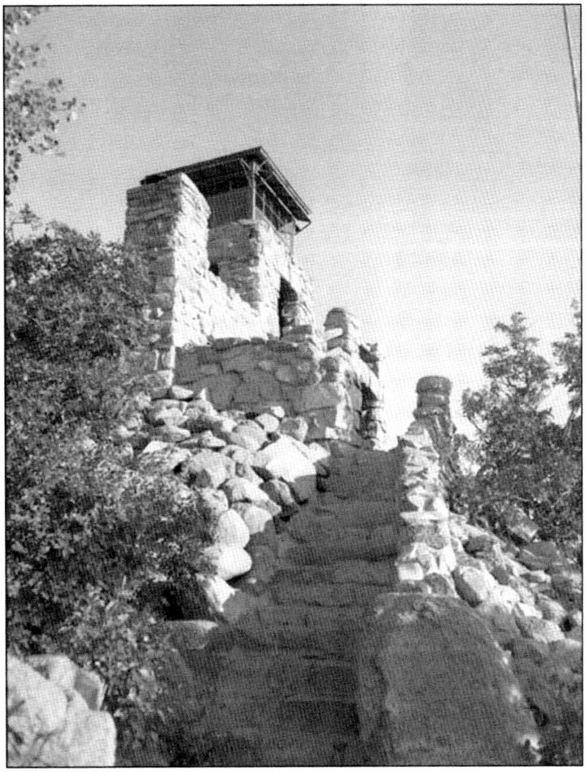

The Civilian Conservation Corps built the stone Monjeau Lookout Tower in the 1930s. During the extremely dry summer of 1945, an unidentified man, on fire watch in the tower, saw a strange, intense light in the west on the morning of July 16. It was later learned that the test of the first atomic bomb had taken place at Trinity Site.

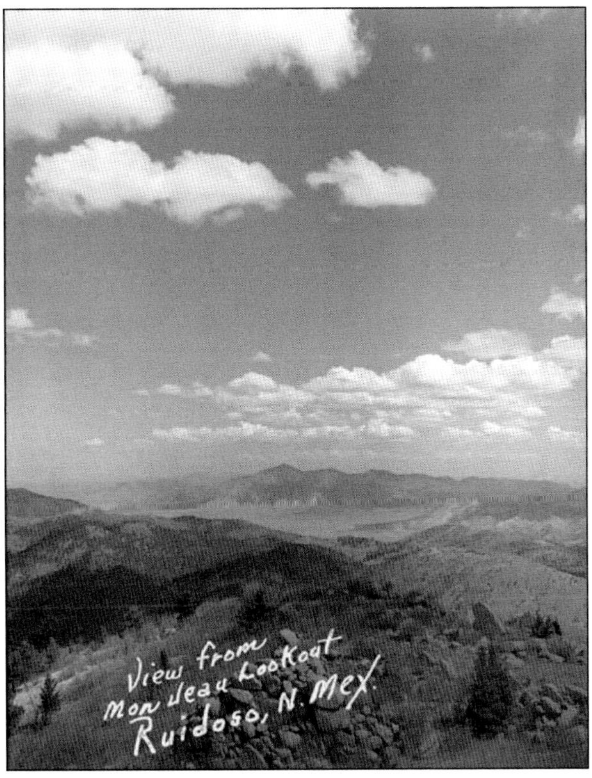

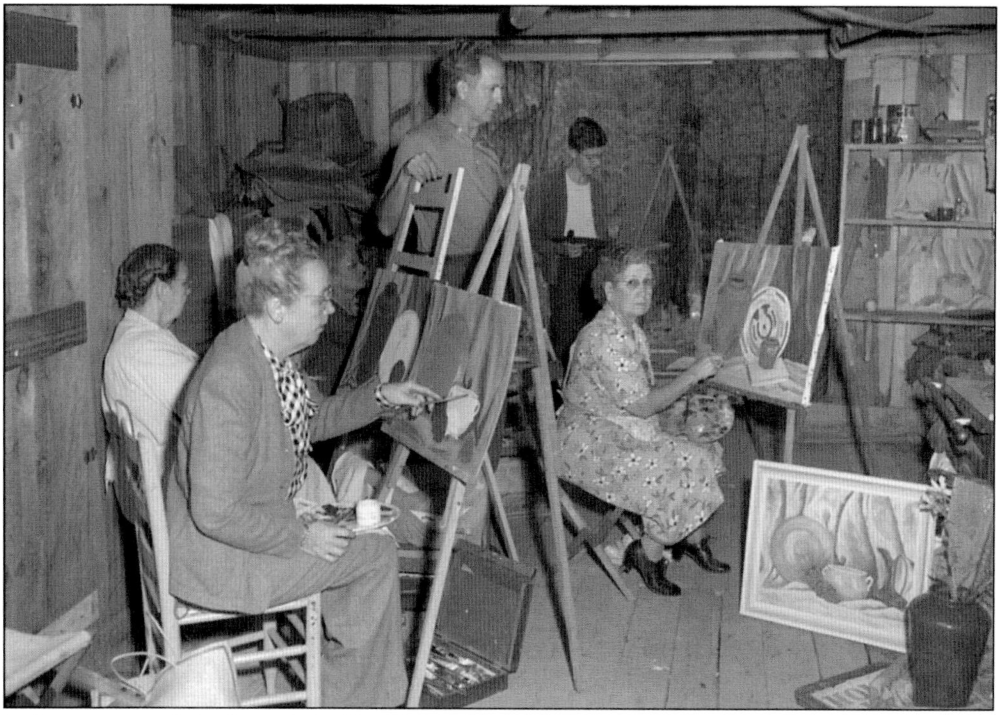

In the summer of 1948, Dr. and Mrs. Donald MacKay of El Paso opened the Arts Colony of the Southwest in the Carrizo Lodge. Art classes were held in the former stable. Many summer "art colonies" came and went over the years, including the Robinwood Art School in a building behind the 1947 post office and the High Bank Arts Center, run from the home of artist Kathryne Hail Travis.

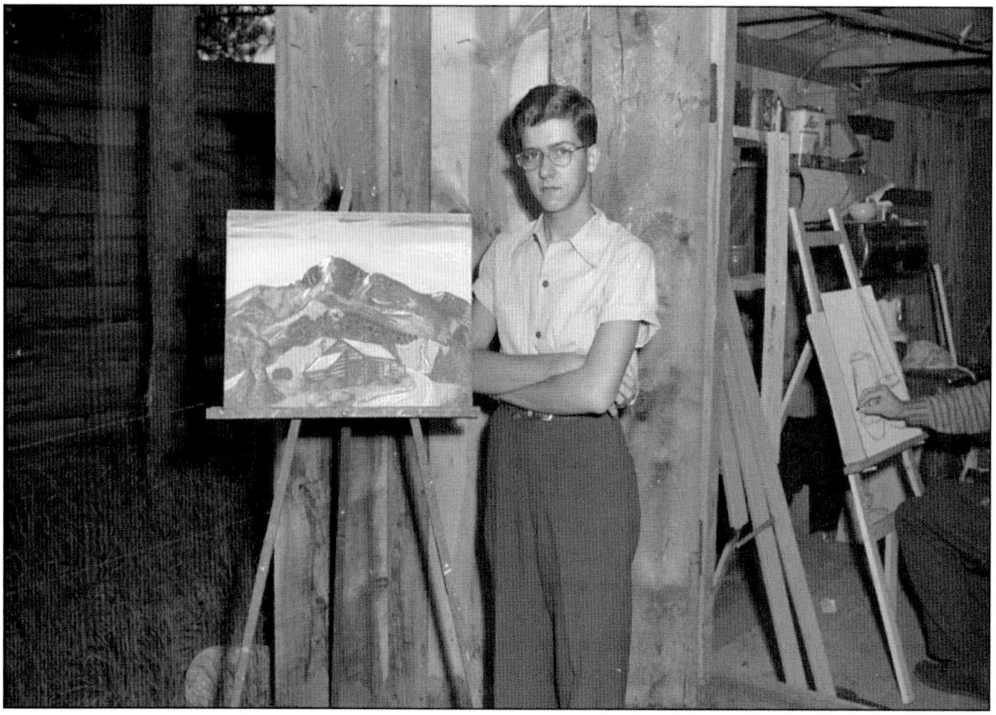

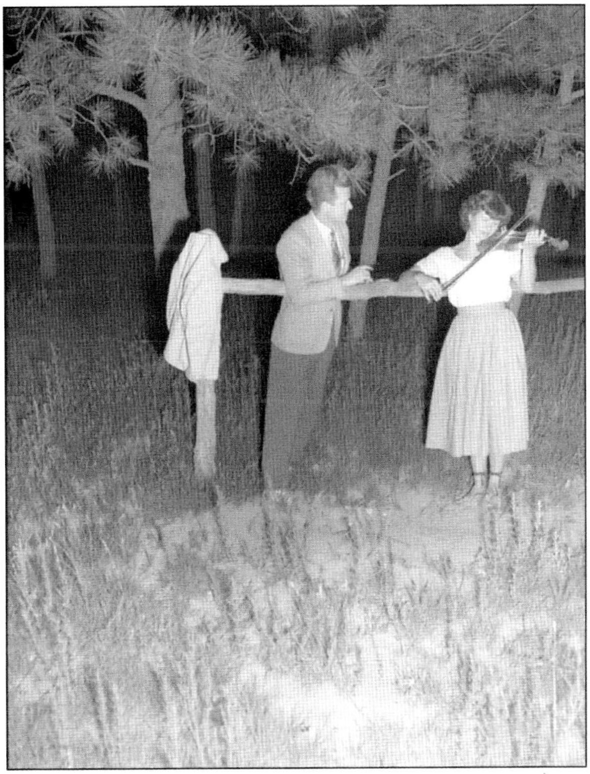

The Arts Colony of the Southwest also offered classes in music and dance. A local theater group performed the comic farce *The Arrival of Kitty*, which takes place in a resort in the Catskill Mountains.

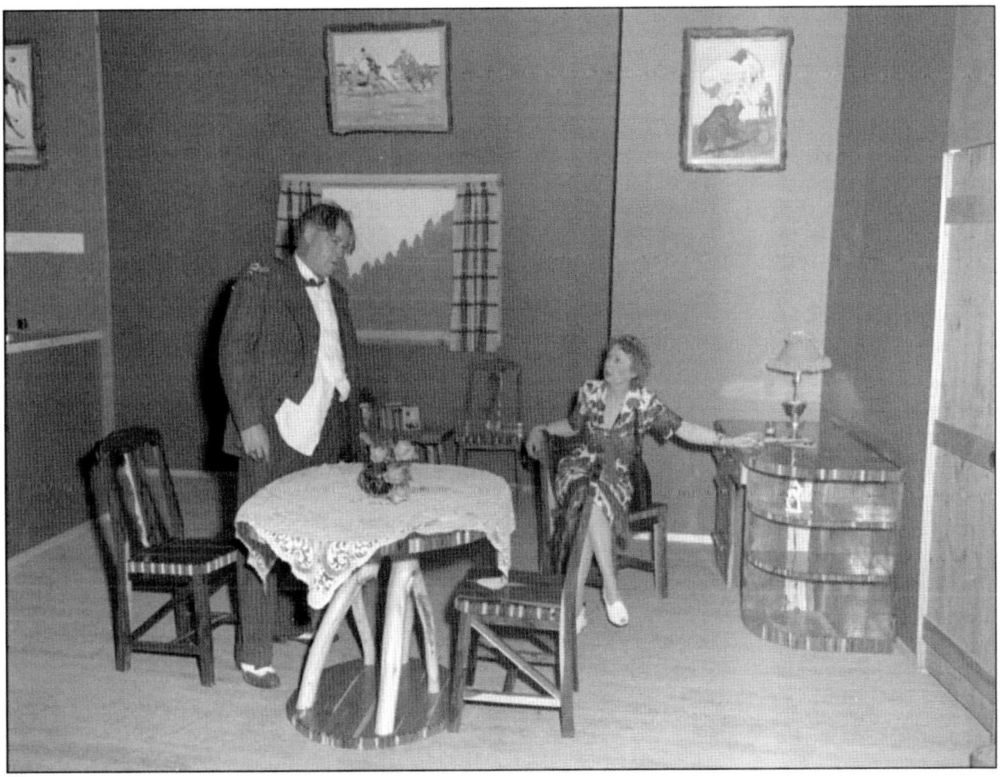

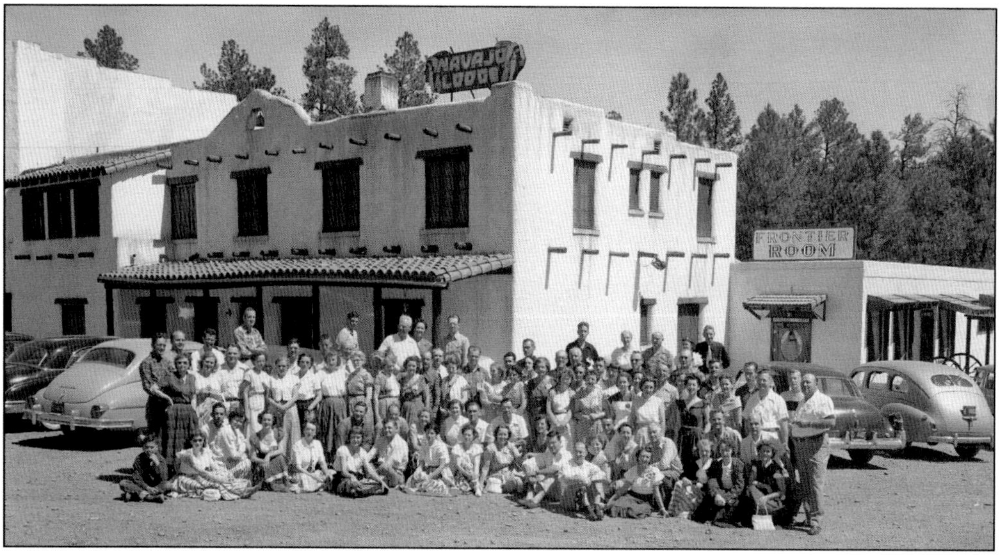

Known for its casual elegance and excellent food, the Navajo Lodge was the social center of Ruidoso during the 1930s, 1940s, and 1950s. Bob and Edith Boyce opened the first Navajo Lodge, a collection of log cabins and a dining hall, in 1924. Construction on the "new" three-story adobe Navajo Lodge began in 1938. The Pueblo Revival architecture featured vigas and kiva fireplaces.

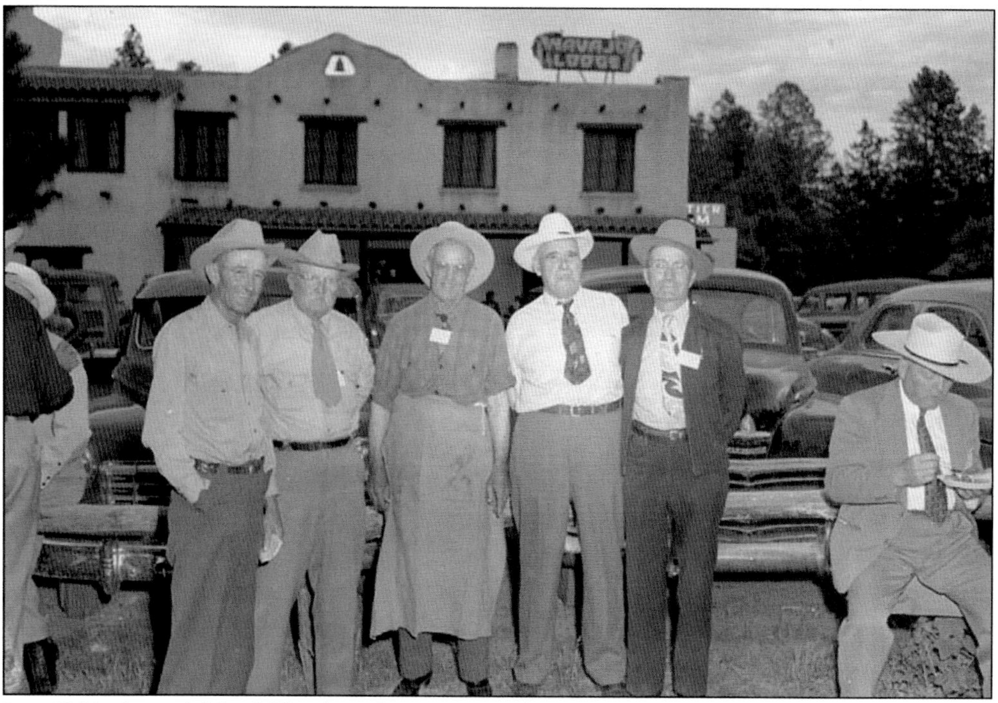

In a 1946 editorial, Lloyd Bloodworth wrote, "Ruidoso is the most delightful convention city in New Mexico and I can't understand why all the conventions are not held here." Edith Boyce, owner of the Navajo Lodge, agreed, remembering, "Just before the war I had at least one convention every month coming to the lodge." Groups of all kinds—square dancers, cotton growers, bakers, bankers, broadcasters, insurance professionals, and beverage distributors—met for conventions at the Navajo Lodge.

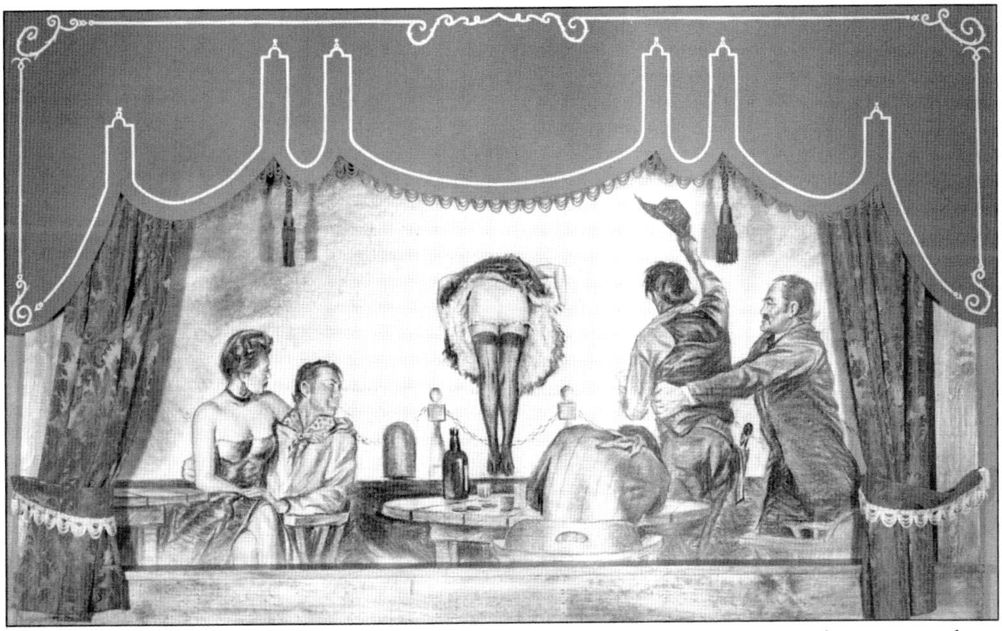

Artist Reynolds Jones lived with his family in the Navajo Lodge for a year after moving from California to Ruidoso. His painting of Ruidoso residents as Wild West saloon habitués hung in the Buffalo Room. The people in the painting are, from left to right, Irene Nosker, Ken Nosker, Bonnie Jones (wife of the artist), unidentified, Ralph Bonnell, and unidentified.

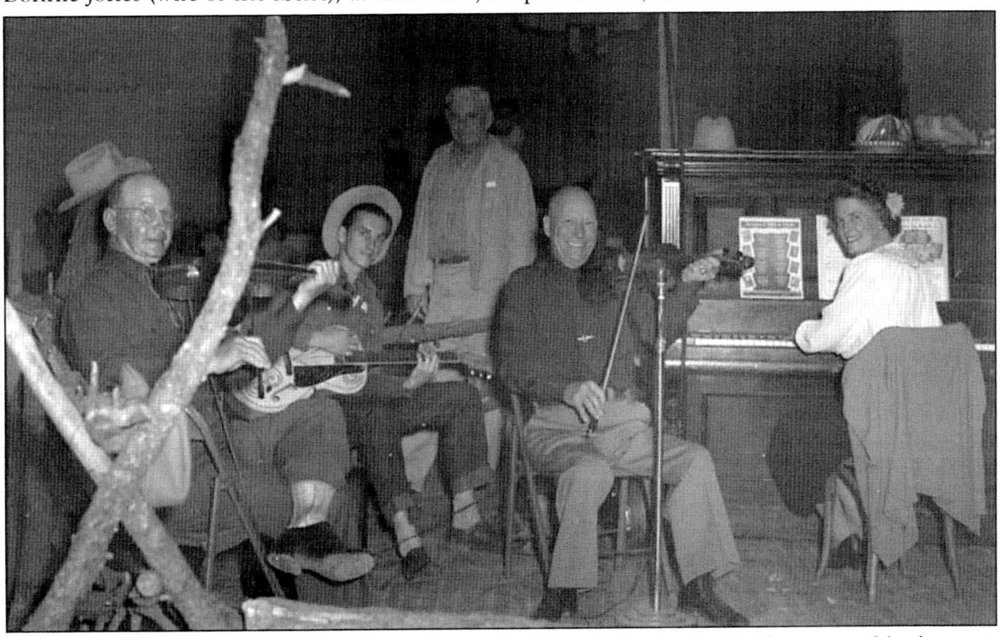

The *Roswell Record* noted, "Saturday night in the Navajo Lodge in Ruidoso a weekly dance is held in which couples come from a radius of 100 miles away. Many of the dancers are not aware that the pretty young woman presiding at the piano is a state senator." From left to right are Will T. Coe, Dan Storm, unidentified, Wilbur Coe, and Louise Coe, the first woman elected to the state legislature, in 1927. This photograph, however, was taken in 1948 in the Ruidoso school gymnasium.

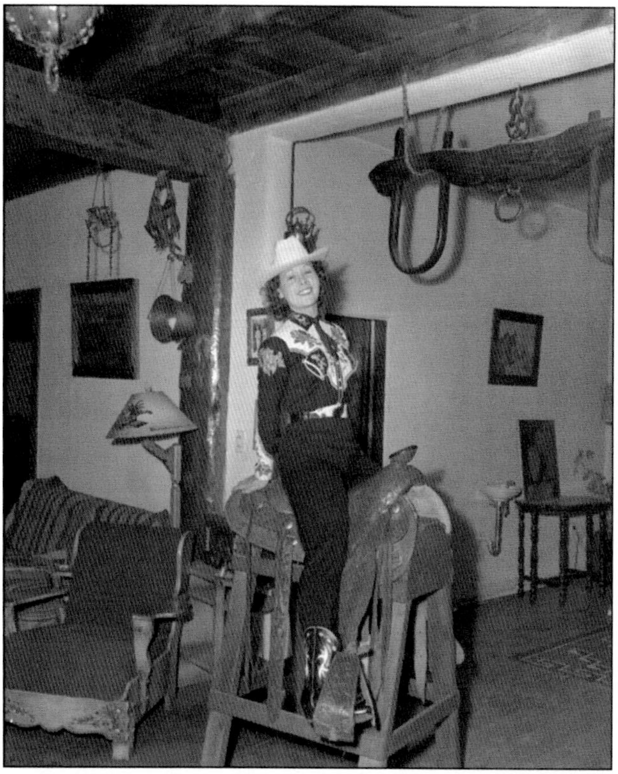

Helen Barajas poses on a stool made from a saddle in the Navajo Lodge. Her father, Frank Barajas, first served as a night watchman before being elected town marshal in 1947.

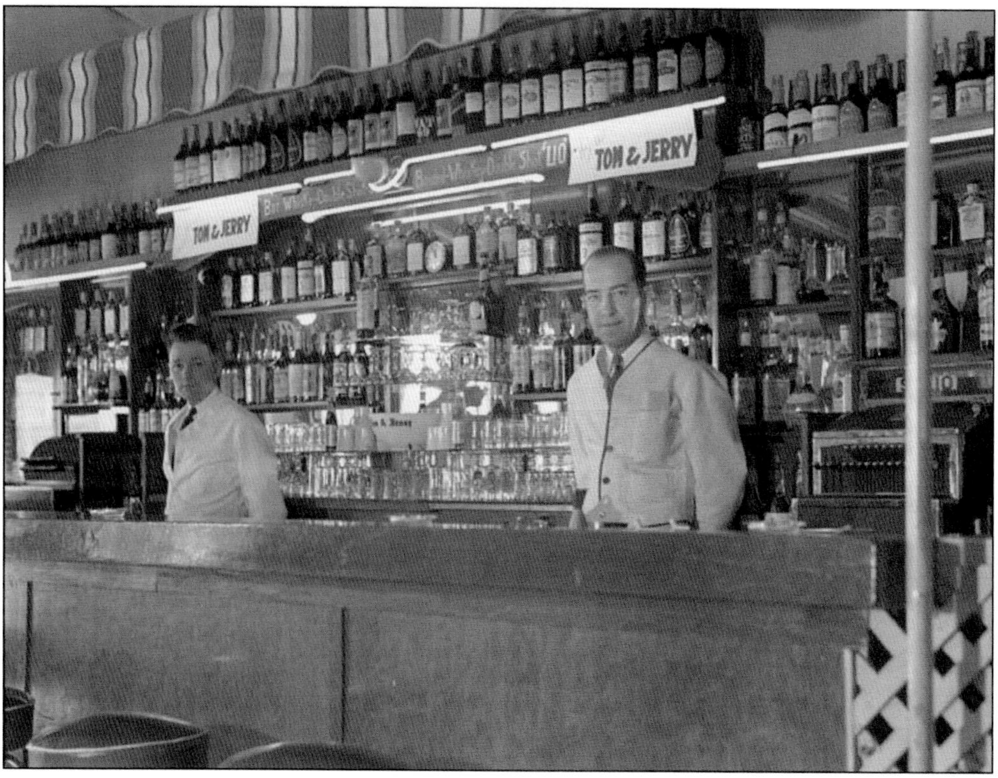

This photograph, taken by Carmon Phillips, appeared in newspaper advertisements for the Mint Bar in 1946. The man on the right was Joe Morton, known simply as "Joe the Bartender." The man on the left is unidentified.

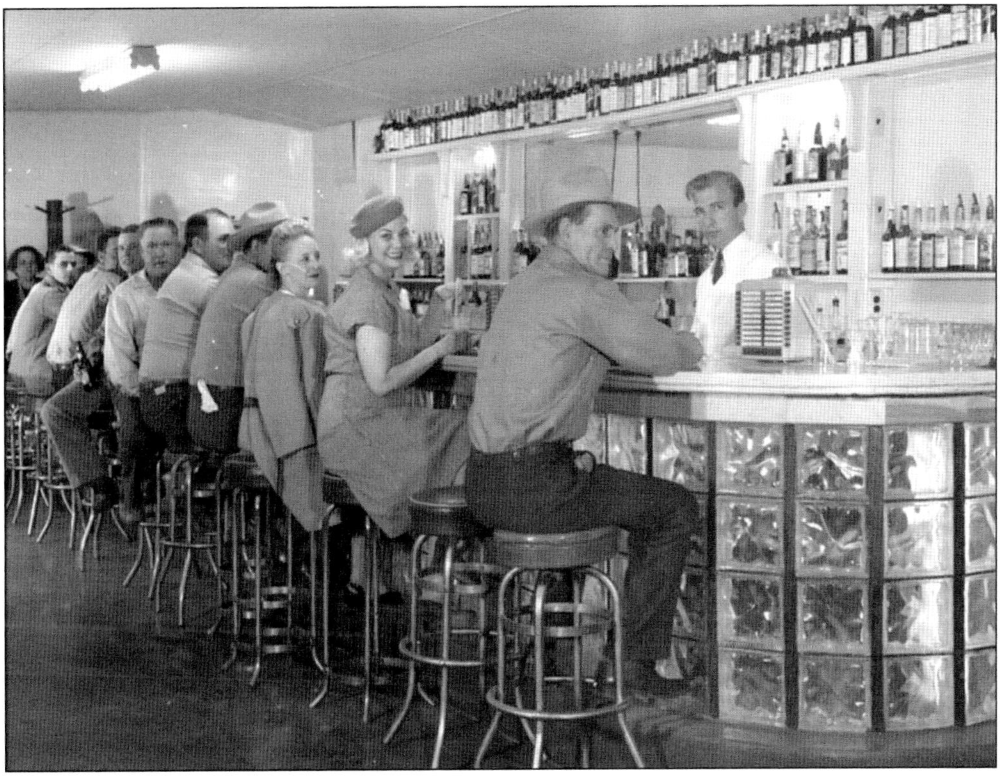

A lively crowd lines the glass block counter of the Central Bar in 1947. Gib Roberson is seated on the first stool. Both the Mint Bar and the Central Bar were destroyed by fire in 1953.

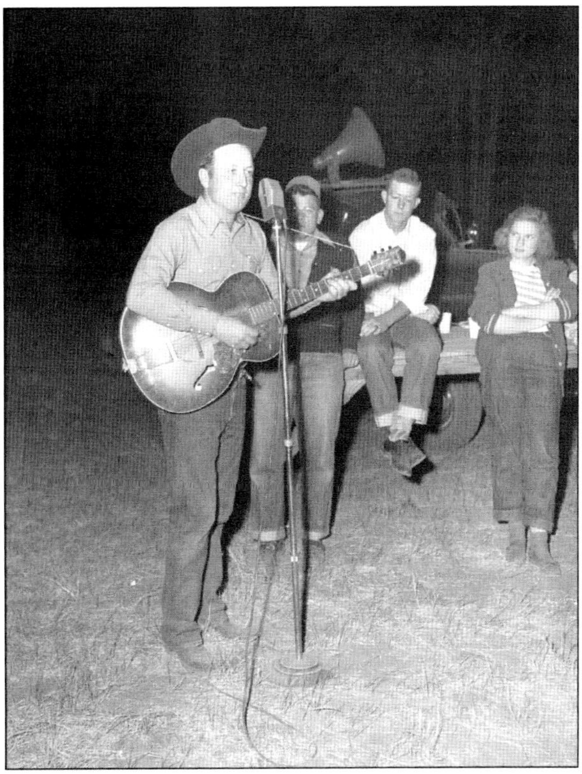

Ray Reed began singing and performing in the 1930s, when he worked as a guide and entertainer in Yosemite Park. He joined the Cross-B Boys band, who had their world premiere at the Navajo Lodge. When the band broke up in 1946, Reed moved to Ruidoso with his family. He continued to perform, often offering trail rides and chuck wagon dinners.

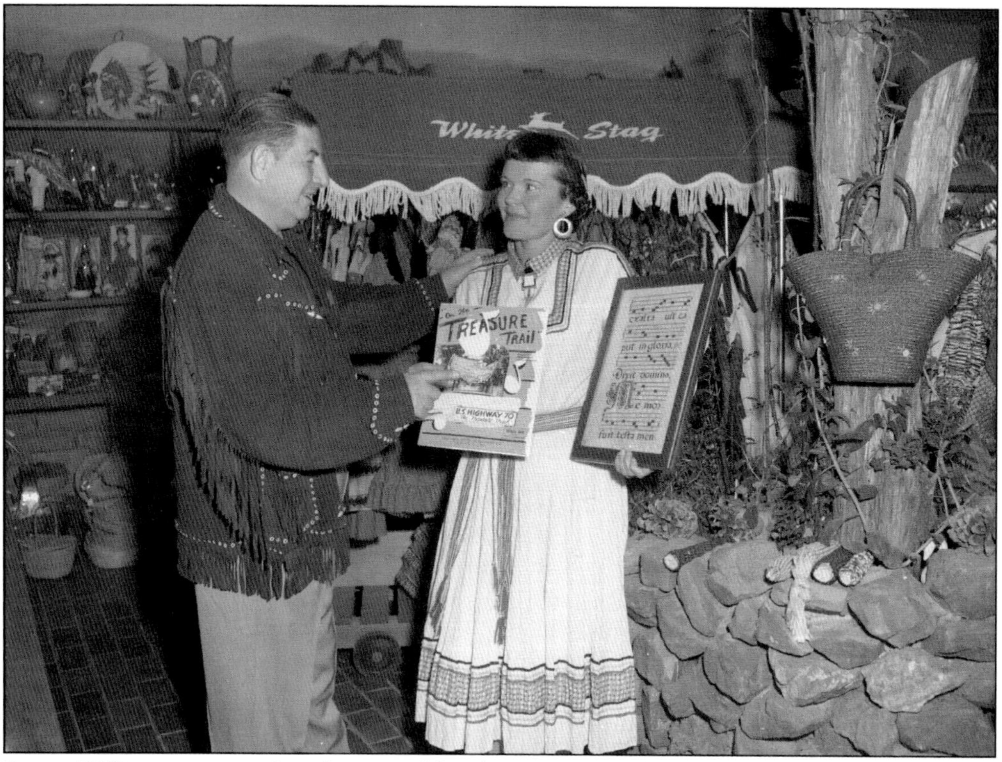

Bernie Williams, a songwriter who wrote "On the Treasure Trail," talks with Marie Rooney, owner of the Adobe Gallery. It was Rooney's custom to wear Indian jewelry and fiesta dresses. A gallery of the same name was located on the same site in 2014.

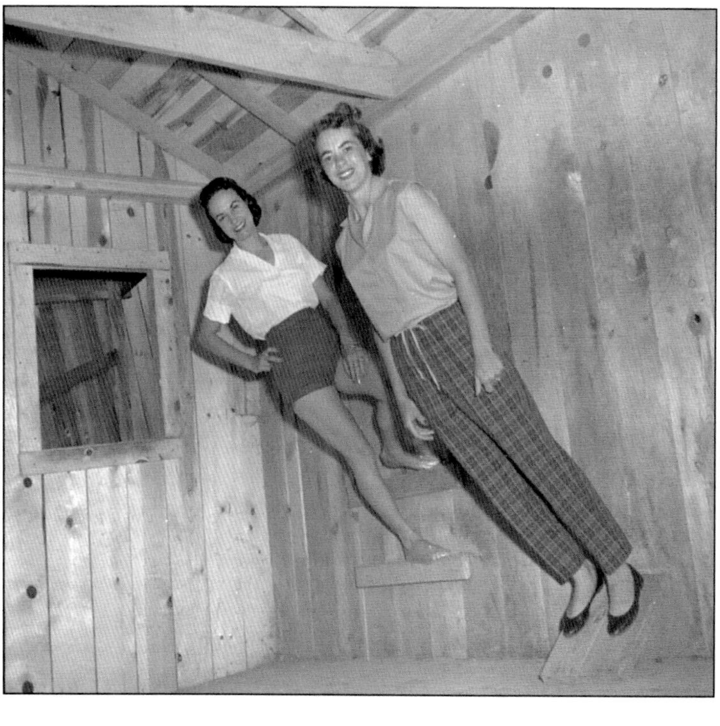

Built as a tourist attraction, the Mystery Spot was a house in Ruidoso Downs that gave the illusion of being tilted. Some claimed it was a mysterious spot in the universe; less fanciful people said that it was just built that way. Everyone agreed that one exited the house in a disoriented state of mind. Barbara Pearson (left) and Mary Lou Gooch posed for this photograph in 1949.

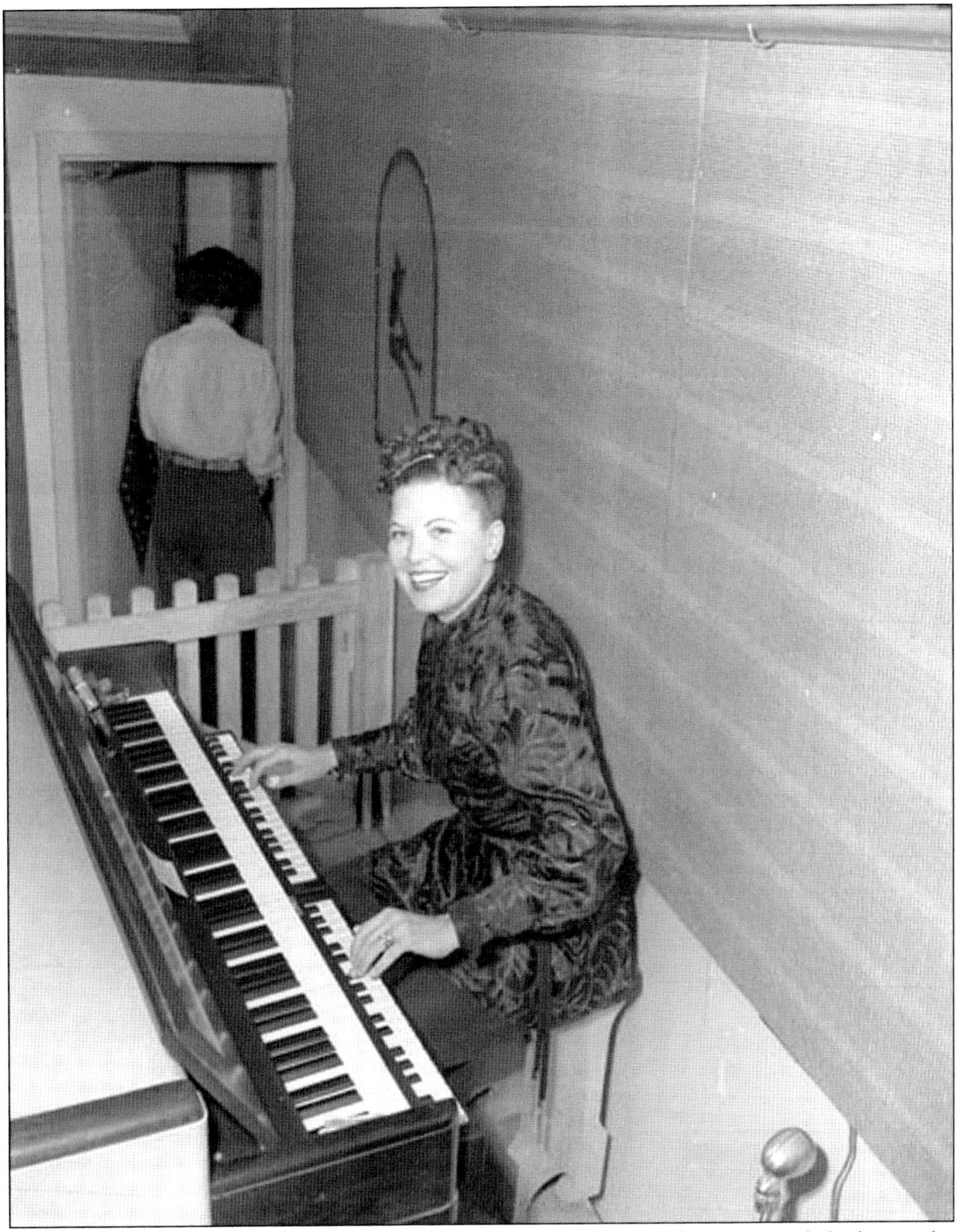

"Boots" Anderson appeared at the Buckaroo, singing and playing the piano nightly during the summer of 1951. Opened in 1946, the Buckaroo was located in the building that later housed the store Candle Power in 2014.

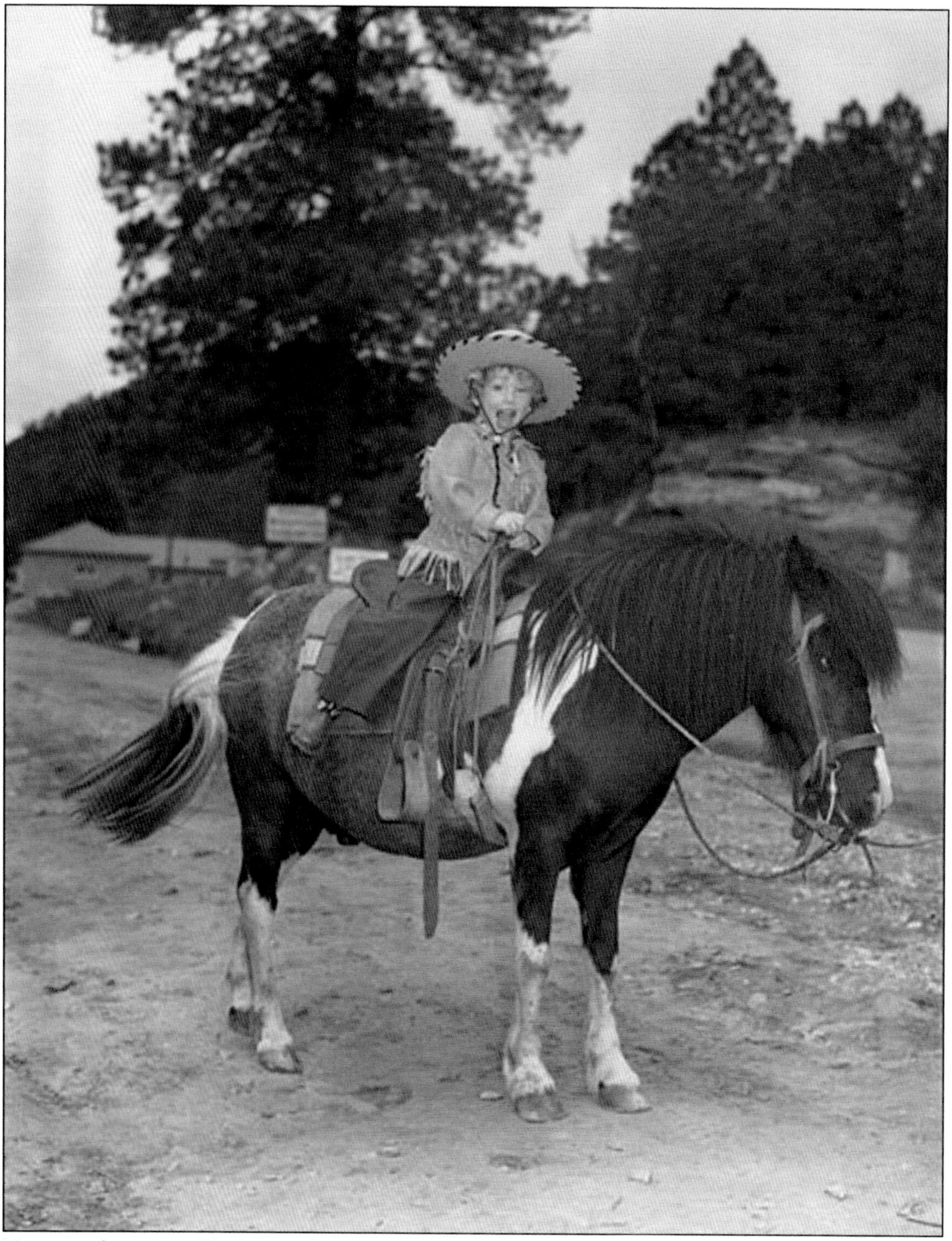

Visitors often rented horses and ponies for a week or more. Local residents, of course, had their own horses. With very few cars on the streets, a horse was a pleasant and convenient means of transportation. Riding stables in town included Sallee's, Weldon's Riding Academy, and Montie's Riding Academy.

A group of horseback riders begins the trek to Sierra Blanca. It was a full day in the saddle, and many inexperienced riders were happy to dismount when they got back to the road in Upper Canyon.

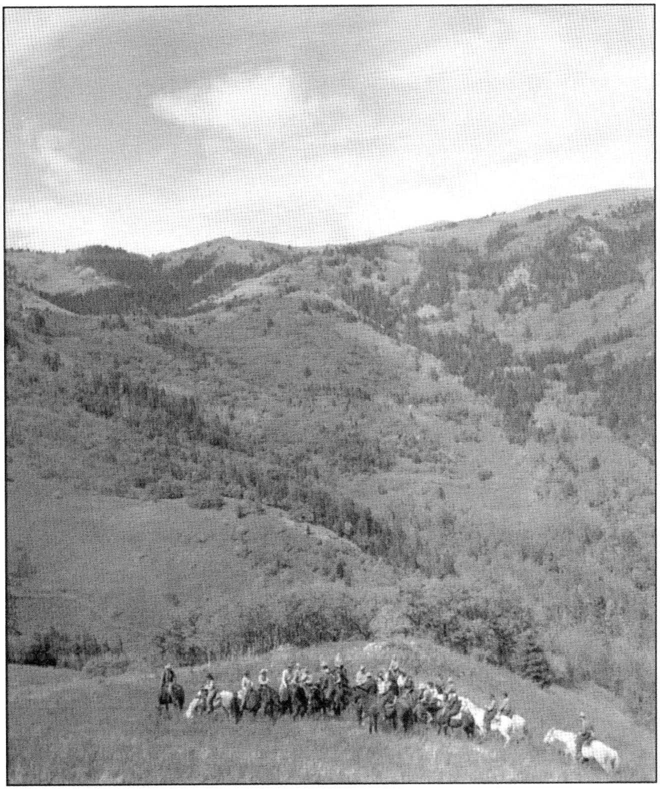

In 1947, John's Riding Academy offered daily trips to Old Baldy and moonlight horseback rides.

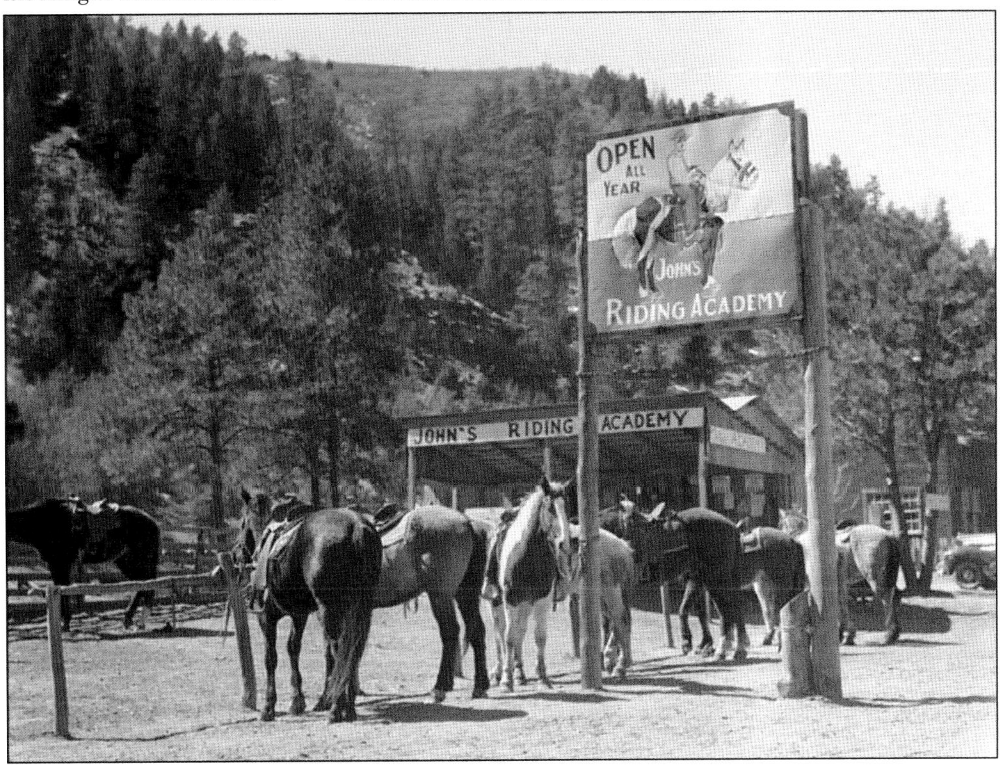

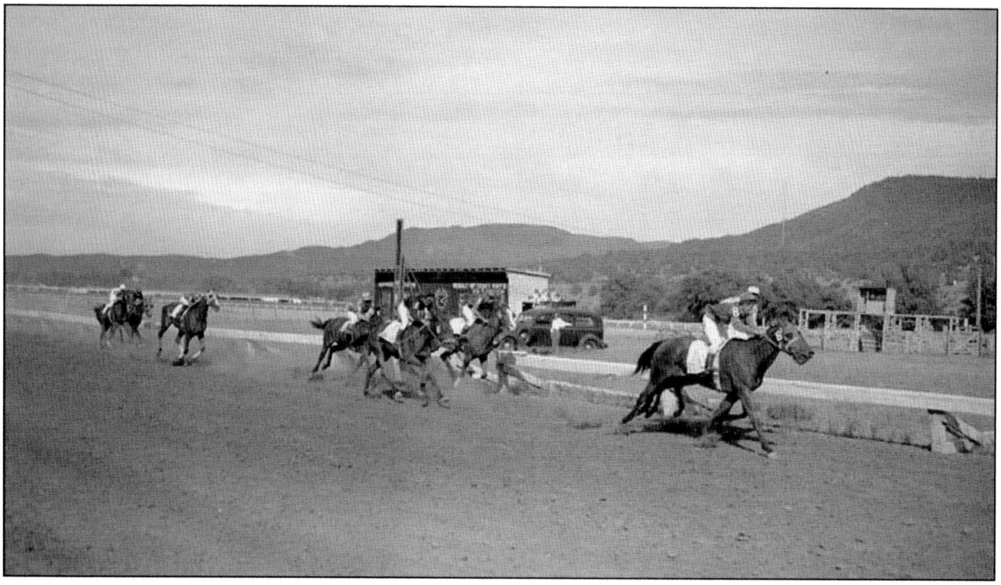

This early photograph of what is now Ruidoso Downs racetrack shows the rodeo stand in the background. Over the years, improvements were made to the primitive track, and Hollywood Park opened in 1947. Gene Hensley bought the track in 1953 and changed the name to Ruidoso Downs. Five years later, the residents of what was then Green Tree voted to change the name of the town to Ruidoso Downs.

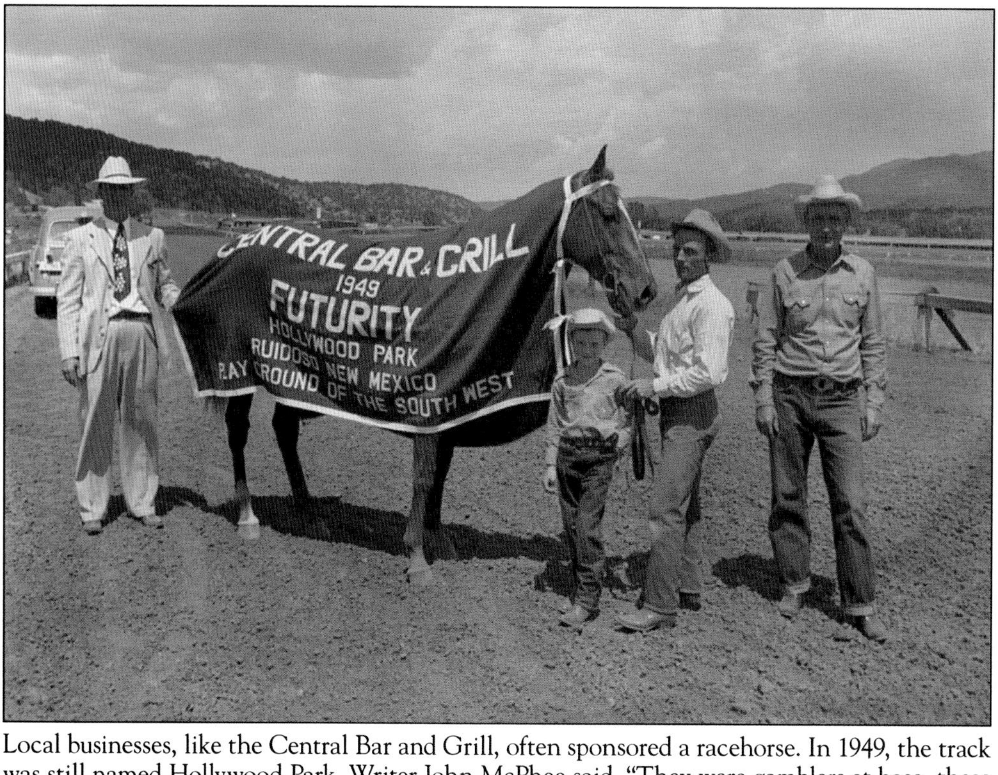

Local businesses, like the Central Bar and Grill, often sponsored a racehorse. In 1949, the track was still named Hollywood Park. Writer John McPhee said, "They were gamblers at base, these vacationing Texans. If they had not had horses to bet on, they would have bet on frogs."

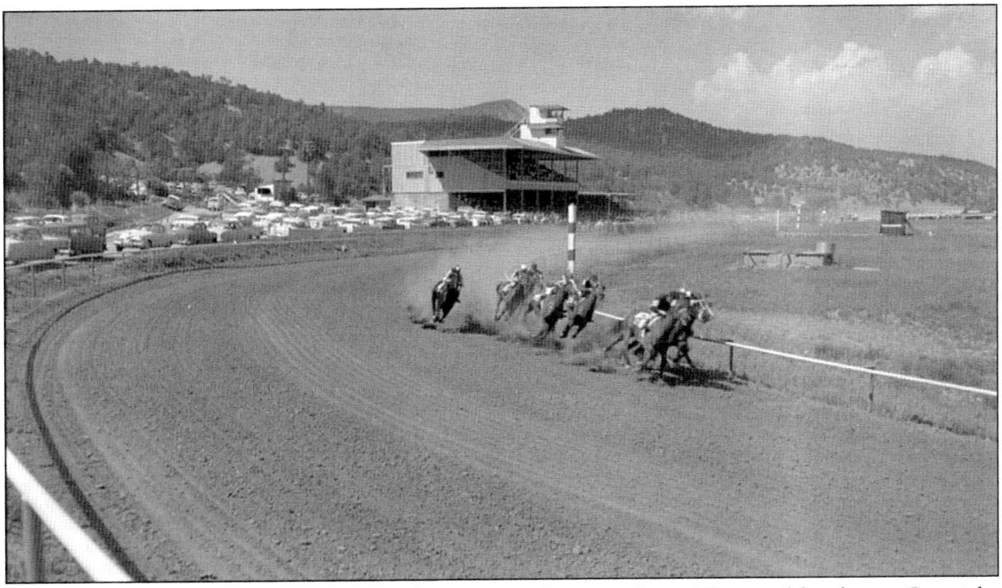

Writer John McPhee described the modern quarter horse as "part Thoroughbred, part Spanish-Arabian, part streak of light." Ruidoso Downs racetrack is home to the Triple Crown of quarter horse racing: the All American Futurity, the Ruidoso Futurity, and the Rainbow Futurity.

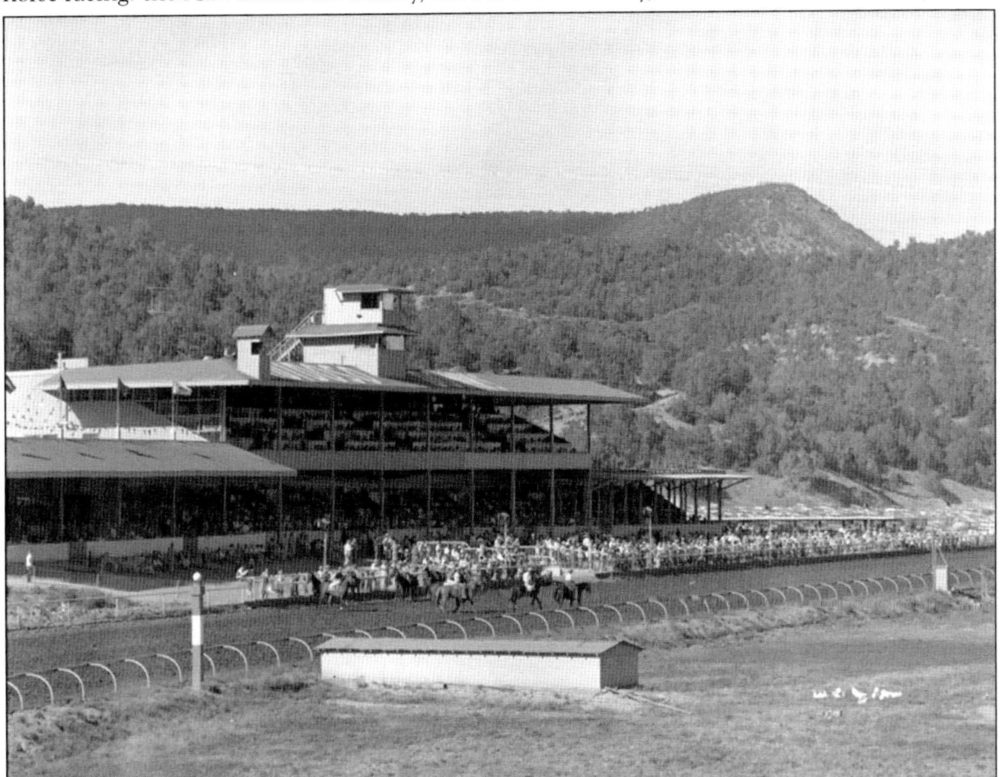

In 1954, new owner Gene Hensley embarked on a $90,000 renovation of the track, adding a second story to the grandstand and creating the private Jockey Club. Movie stars like Robert Mitchum, Chill Wills, and Dale Robertson came to take their chances on the horses.

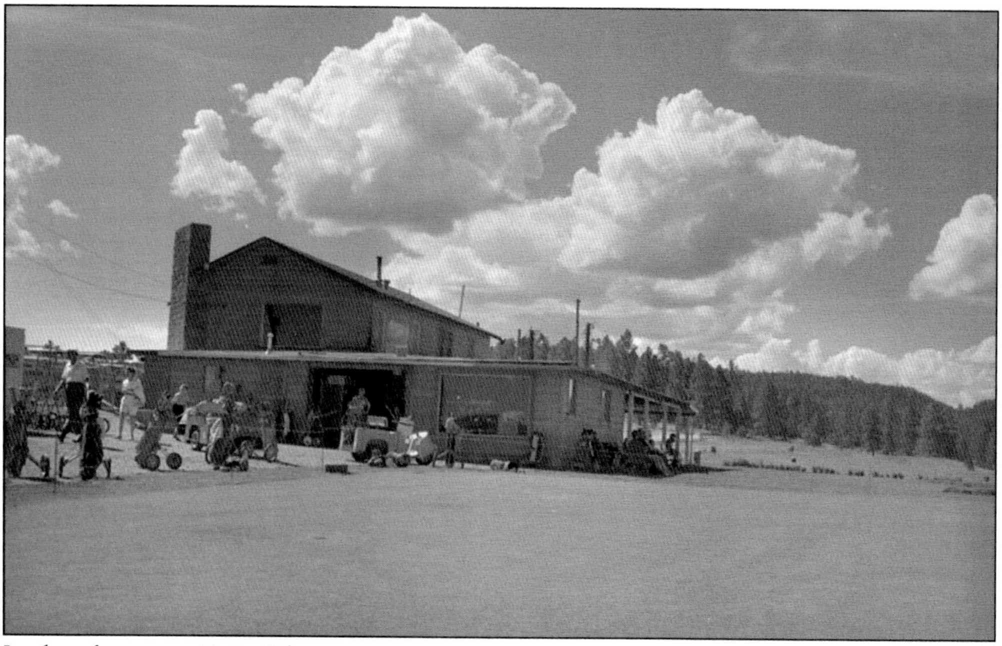

In the of summer 1946, White Mountain Development Company announced the creation of Cree Meadows, a new subdivision and golf course named for James Cree. The owner of a whiskey distillery in Edinburgh, Scotland, Cree bought 9,000 acres of land in Lincoln County in the 1880s. This original clubhouse burned in 1978 and was replaced.

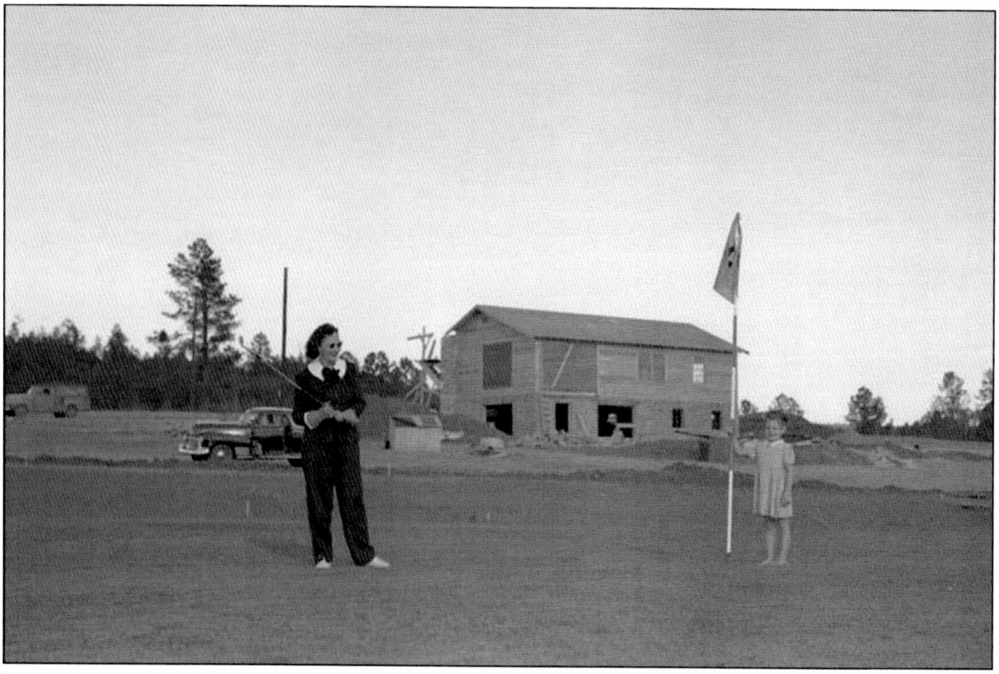

Louise Massey is the first to tee off at the new Cree Meadows Golf Course in July 1947. A well-known singer and songwriter, her song "My Adobe Hacienda," inspired by her ranch in nearby Picacho, had been on the Lucky Strike Hit Parade for 10 weeks at that point. An excellent golfer, Massey pronounced the course "the most beautiful in the Southwest."

Dean Holman worked as a caddy at Cree Meadows in the early 1950s. "We were paid 50 cents a round," he remembered. "If they liked you, they'd tip you a quarter. And those expensive leather golf bags were heavy."

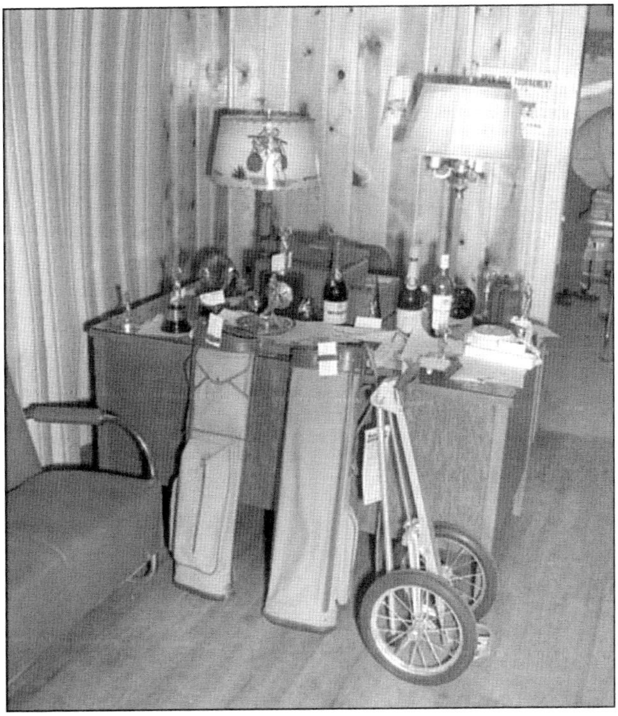

Three women pose with trophies inside the clubhouse. They are, from left to right, Ruby Lee Hardin, unidentified, and Dorothy Palmer.

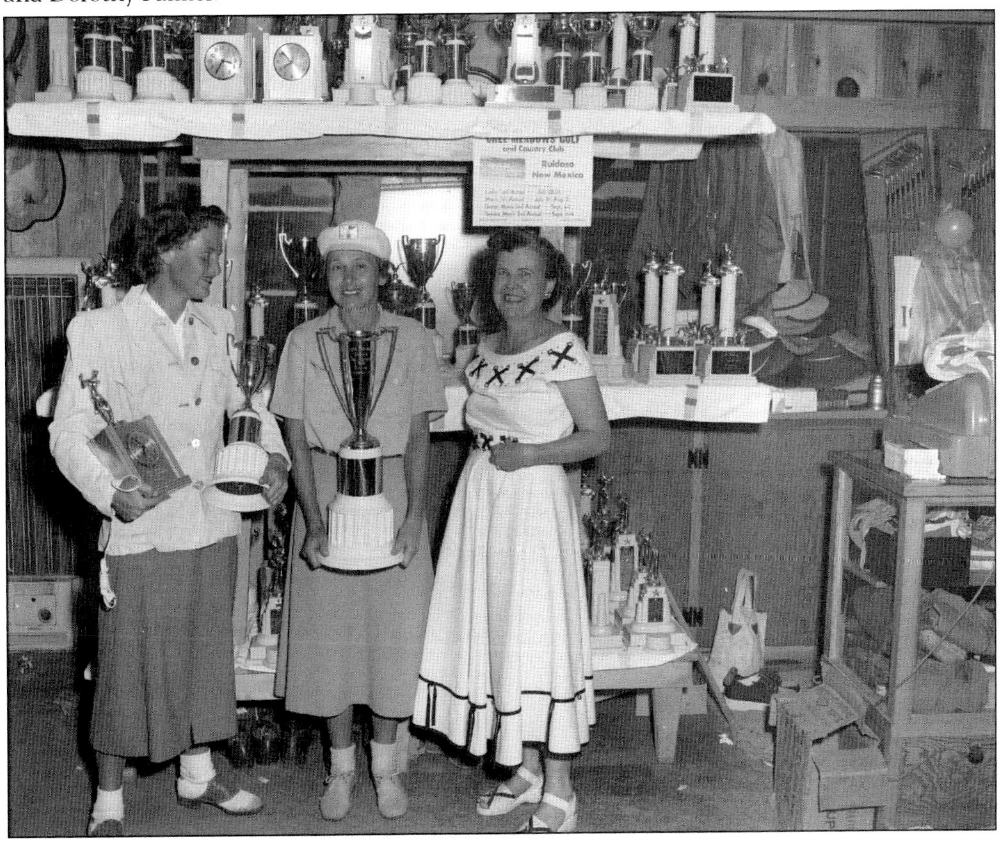

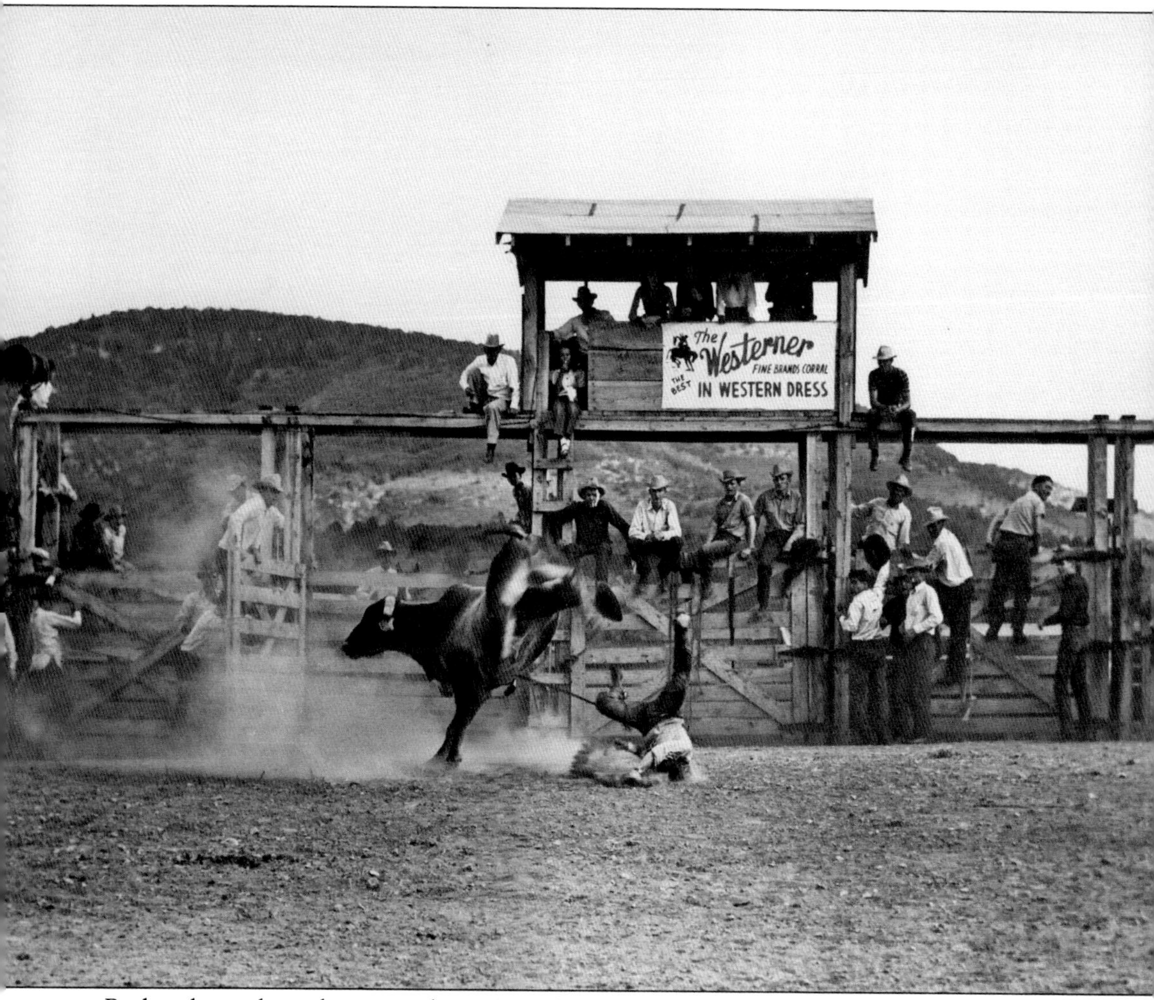

Rodeos have always been popular in Lincoln County. A photograph similar to the one above appeared in *Life* magazine. The rodeo stand stood on the southern side of the racetrack for many years. This advertisement is for The Westerner, a shop that sold high-quality Western wear.

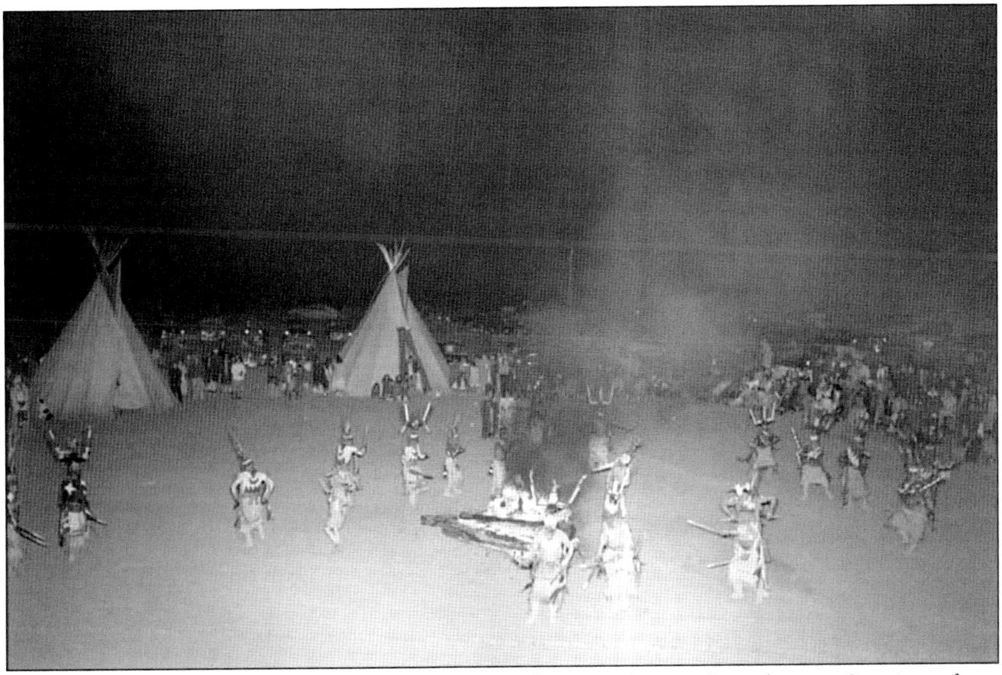

The Mescalero Apache Reservation borders Ruidoso on the south and west. Coming-of-age ceremonies for young Apache women are held every July, with dancing and a huge bonfire.

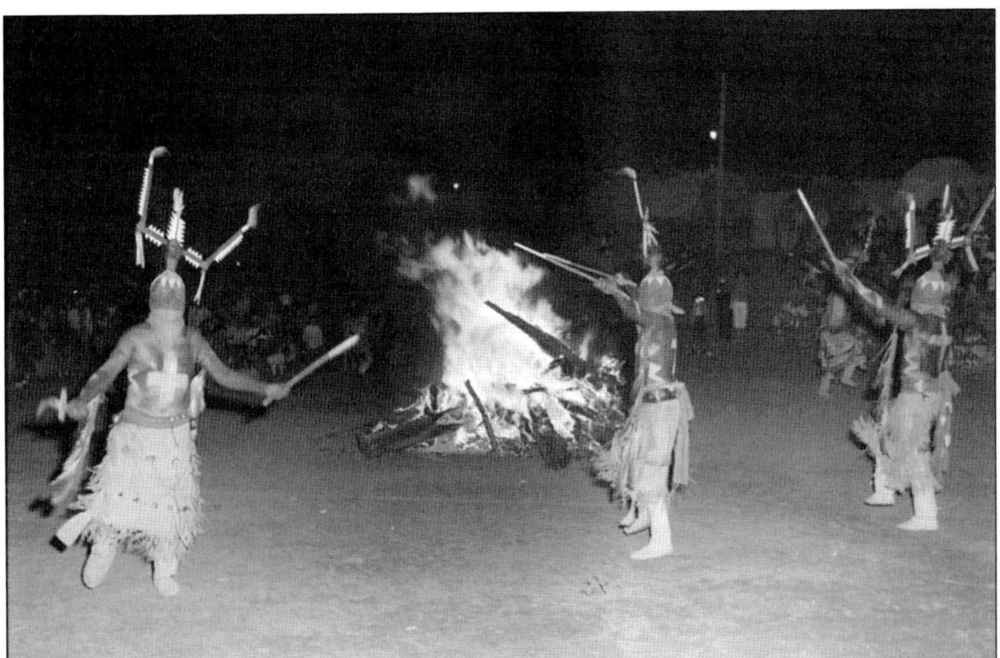

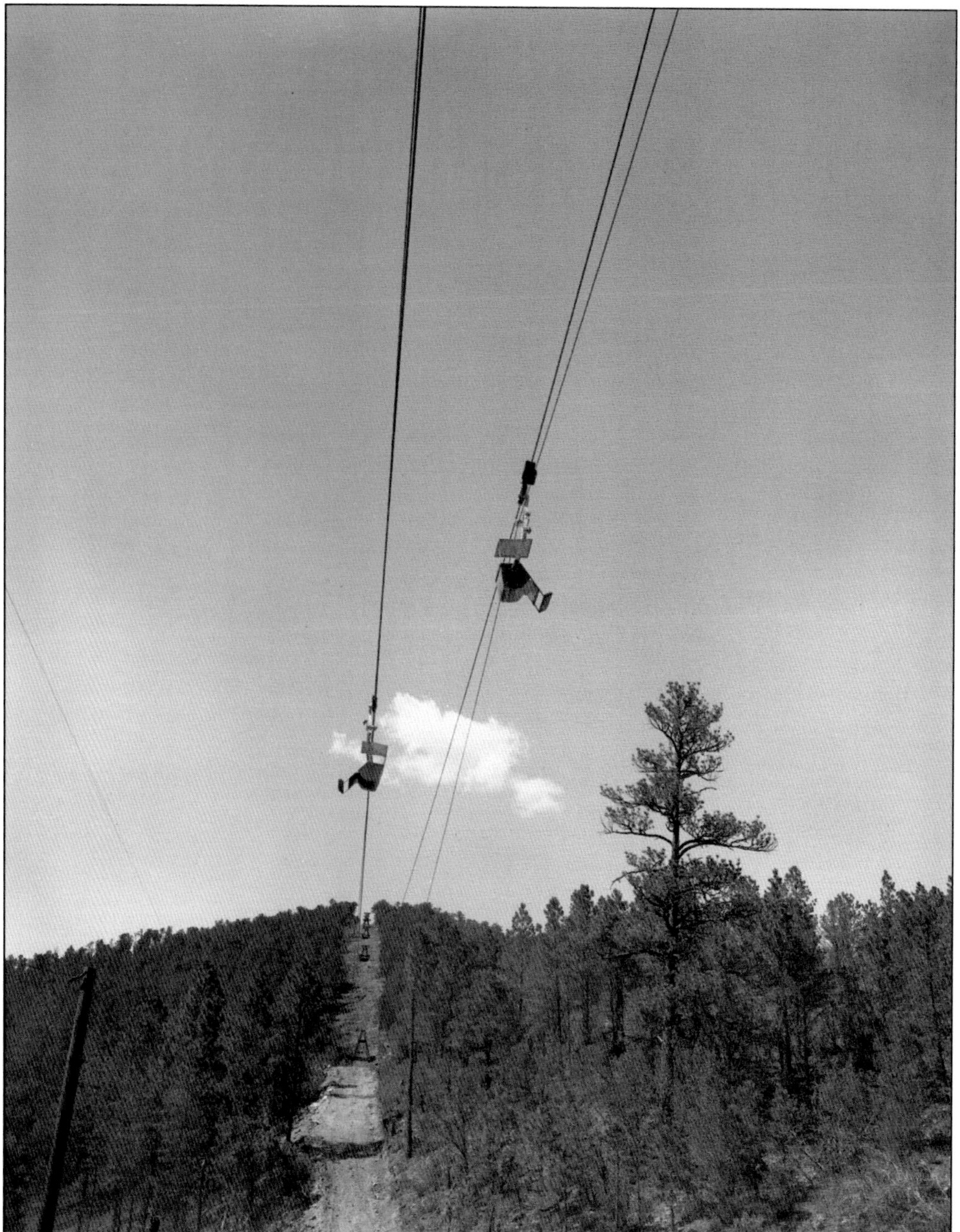

In July 1952, the Ruidoso Sky Ride opened for business. The endeavor was a partnership between Carmon Phillips, Carl DeBord, and Bill Hart. The two-mile-long ride to the top of Moon Mountain was accomplished via machinery that had originally transported ore at the American Mining and Smelting Company in Magdalena, New Mexico. Five towers supported a cable that carried the cars—24 modified ore buckets that were "gaily painted," according to the *Ruidoso News*—sometimes 120 feet in the air. Passengers were assured of its safety—ore weighed more than people, after all.

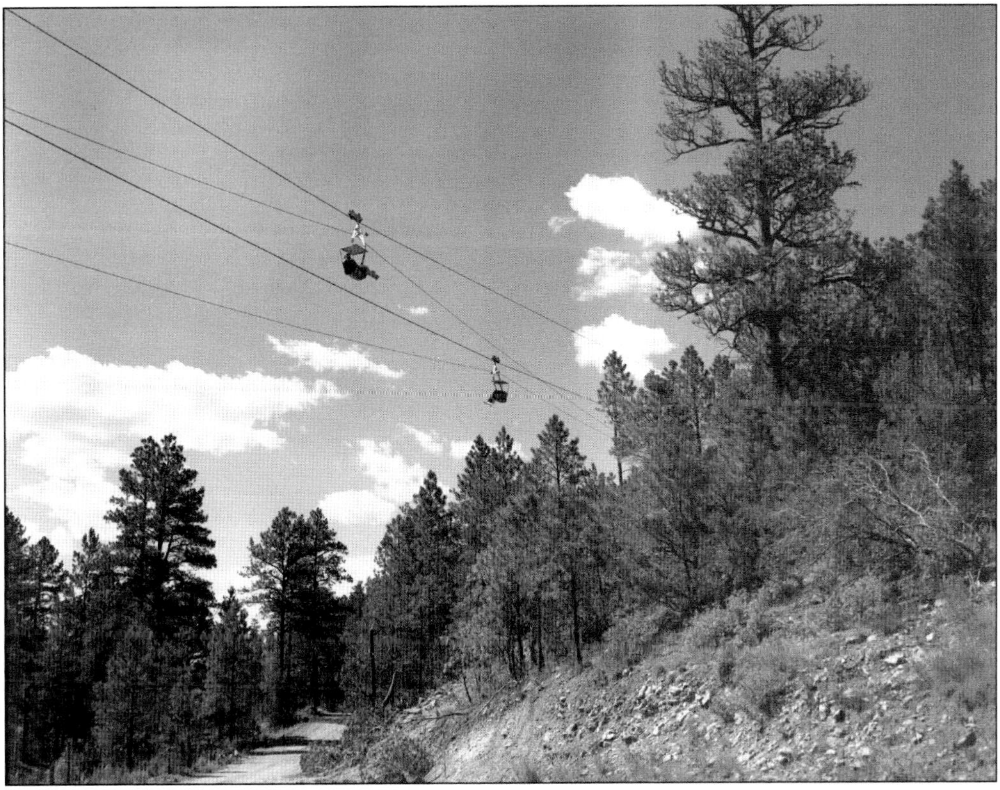

On July 25, 1952, the *Ruidoso News* headline read, "Sky Ride is New Thrill for Vacationers Here." The ticket price was $1 for adults and 50¢ for children. On opening day, 200 people rode it. As one customer said, "It's a $10 ride for $1.50." Plans for the upper terminal included telescopes and picnic tables. Roswell columnist Al Stubbs wrote, "For those people who like to ride high and who enjoy the thrill of being suspended in space, the Sky Ride is just the thing."

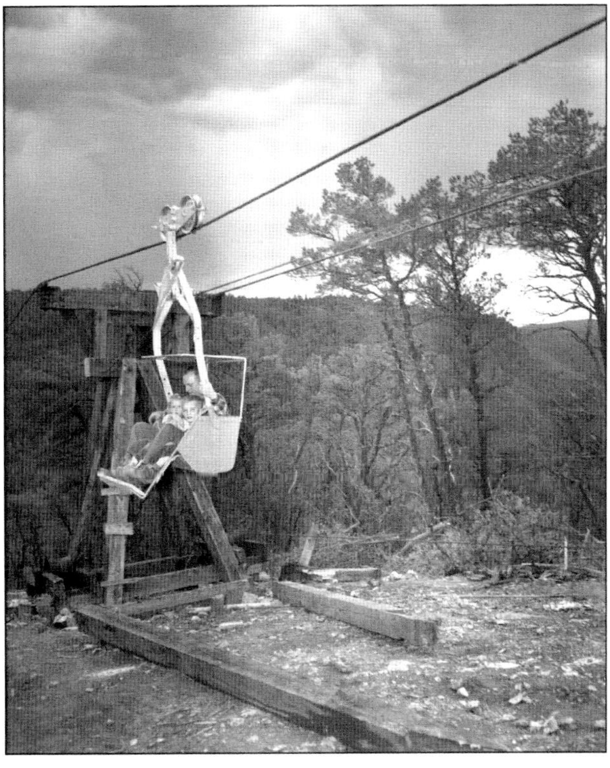

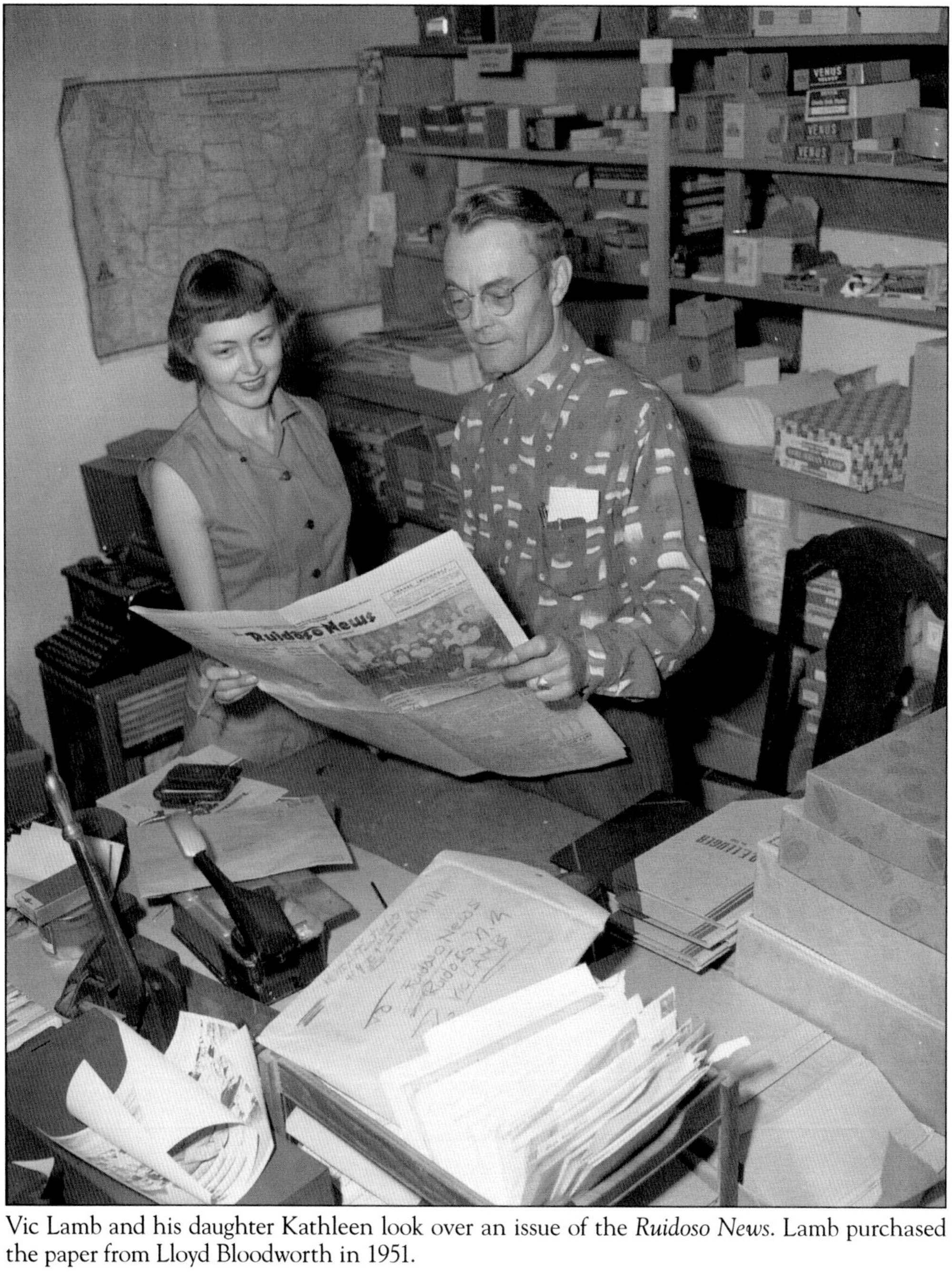

Vic Lamb and his daughter Kathleen look over an issue of the *Ruidoso News*. Lamb purchased the paper from Lloyd Bloodworth in 1951.

Four

THE *RUIDOSO* NEWS

The first publication known as the *Ruidoso News* was a small pamphlet published in the early 1930s by Warren H. Barrett, who owned a small grocery store in Upper Canyon. Published only in the summer, its primary purpose was to promote the area to tourists. It sold for 10¢ a copy.

In 1946, Lloyd Bloodworth began weekly publication of the *Ruidoso News*. The newspaper provided local news, including birth and wedding announcements, and continued to beat the drum for the town's attractiveness as a tourist destination. Regular features during the summer included "Latchstrings," a listing of guests at various lodging establishments, and "Canyon Echoes," which offered a bit more information, as seen in the following excerpts:

> Mrs. F.C. Connor and Lucille Ford of Fort Worth are visiting for the months of July and August. They are staying in the Dan Dee Cabins.

> Mr. and Mrs. P.H. Sammons of Lubbock, Texas, have their little grandson with them on their vacation in Ruidoso. They are in the Autry Cabins.

And with perhaps a gentle dig to those trapped in hotter places:

> Iva Coleman spent last Tuesday in El Paso and said she was glad to get back to the cool climate.

Locals and visitors appeared equally in the news, fostering the sense of belonging that many part-time residents felt, and continue to feel, about Ruidoso. By the end of the first year of publication, the paper was being mailed to subscribers in 18 states. In a June 1946 editorial, Bloodworth wrote, "It is just like a family reunion to see old friends meet. Some of these cabin owners have been coming to Ruidoso for years and their children have grown up together during the summer months. It's really swell up here."

Carmon Phillips lost no time in building a relationship with the local press. He contributed photographs of many events that took place in Ruidoso and passed on newsworthy information about his business and personal life, including the antics of the family cat:

> Carmon Phillips and the missus it seems have a performing cat. The puss and Carmon are both at home in a dark room. Carmon's a photographer and the cat is a cat, so the game—in the darkness—resolves itself into a matter of Carmon's hide and the kitty's seek. Especially when the kitty surprises the artist-photographer with a set of claws athwart the clavicles.

In return, Phillips could count on the paper to provide publicity for any community event that he helped to organize.

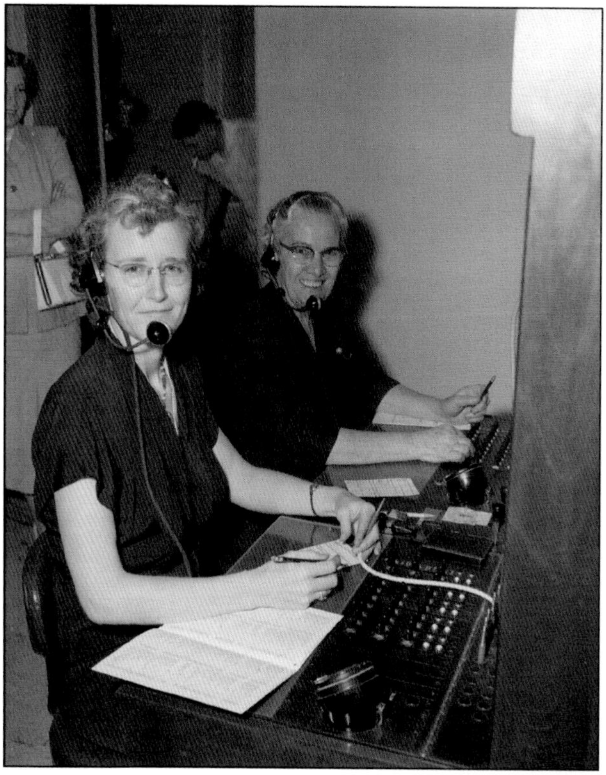

Vera Danning (left) and Mrs. J.V. Hobbie, "veteran operators," try out the new switchboard that brought dial phones to Ruidoso residents for the first time, in July 1954. Deploring the state of the telephone system, a *Ruidoso News* editorial in 1946 quipped, "When a man can hop in his car and drive to Roswell and back in less time than he can get through a long distance call, it's pretty bad." Carmon remembered driving to Carrizozo to make a long-distance call rather than waiting to gain access to the town's single long-distance line.

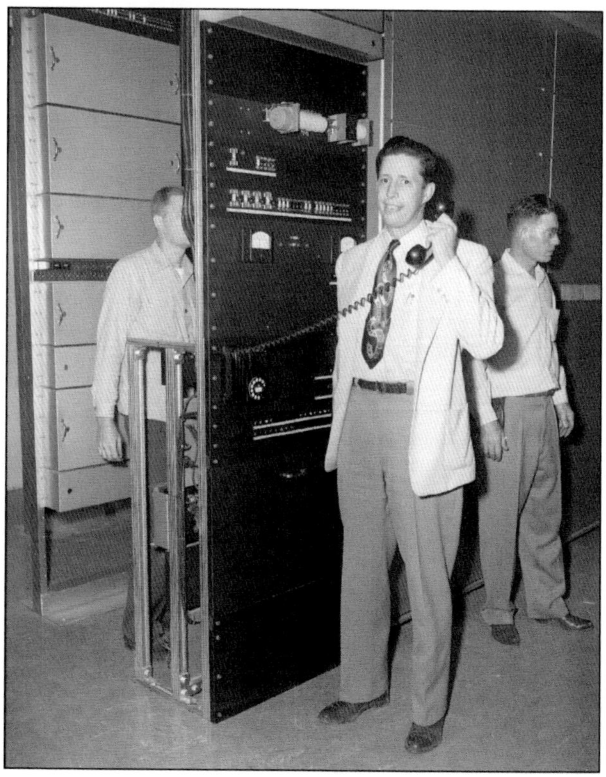

At midnight, Mayor Dan D. Swearingin made the first call, phoning home and talking to his wife. Swearingin's father, a Roswell physician, built the Dan Dee Cabins in 1938 to provide a summer job for his 15-year-old son. The Upper Canyon cabin facility was still in operation in 2014.

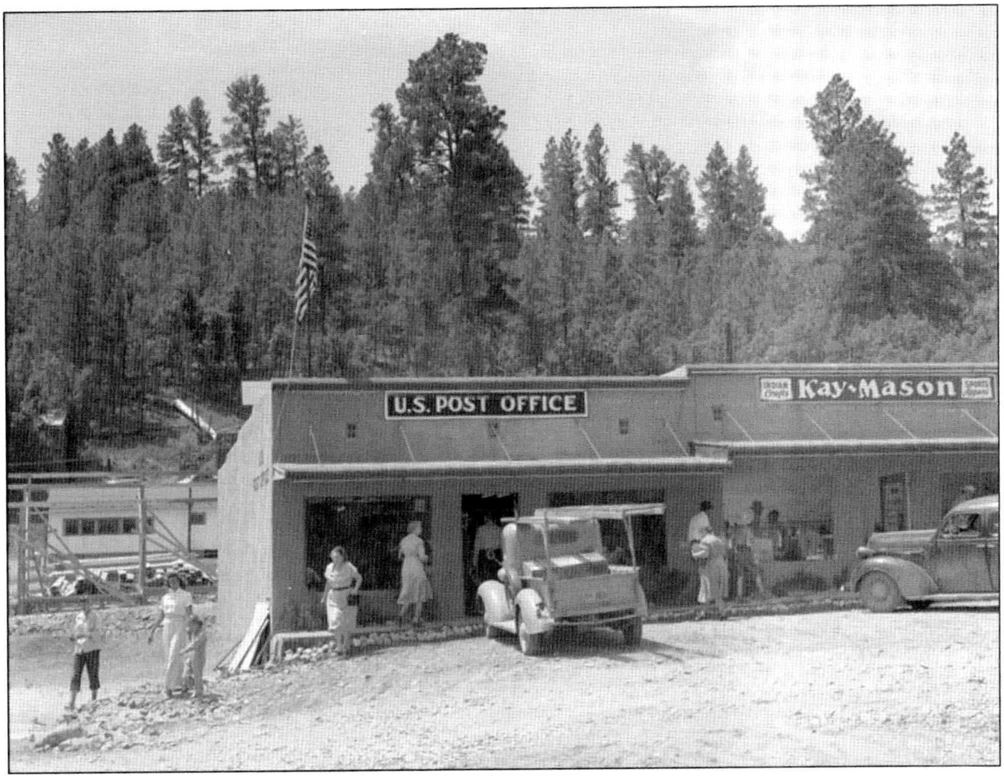

On July 1, 1947, the post office moved to a new building on the southwest corner of what are now Sudderth and Mechem Drives. It was occupied by the Adobe Gallery in 2014.

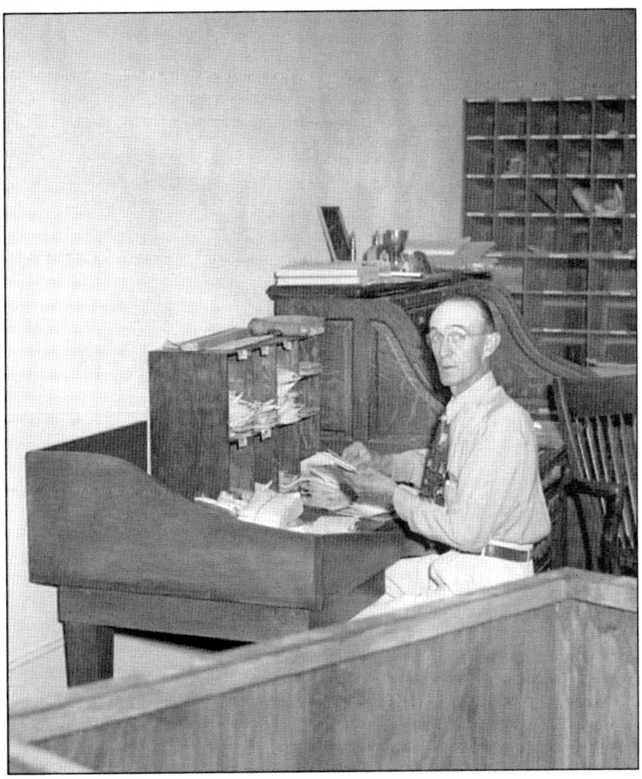

Jack Hull was postmaster when the new post office opened. "When Hull retired in 1957, the office had grown to serve 2500 patrons in the winter and ten times as many during the summer," according to the *History of Lincoln County Post Office*.

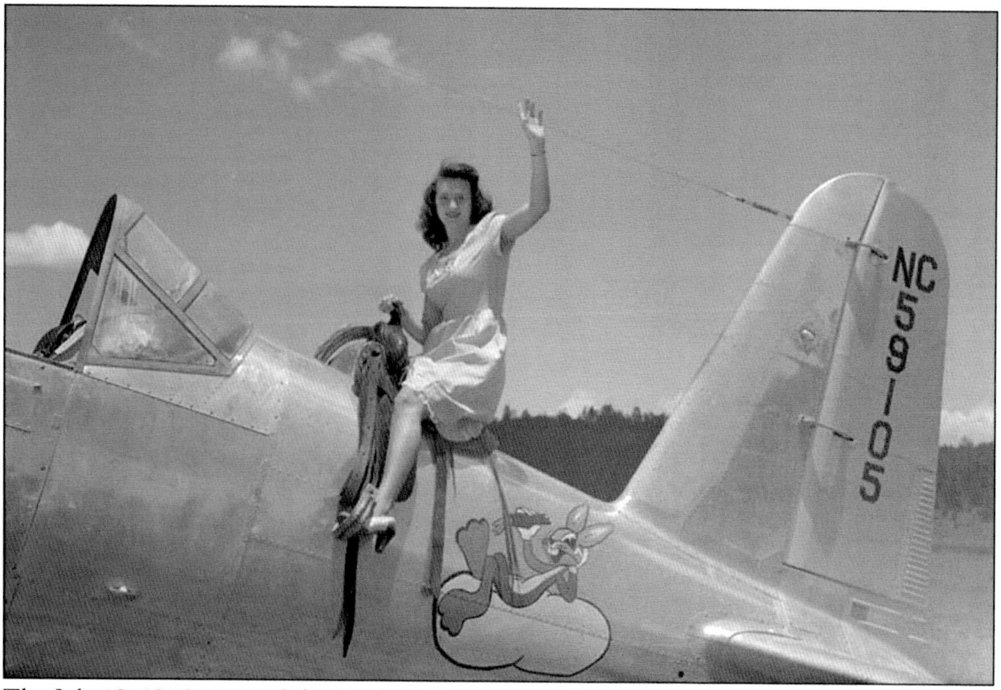

The July 19, 1946, issue of the *Ruidoso News* reported that more than 30 private planes had flown in for an air show and barbecue given by the chamber of commerce and Dewey L. Gann's Ruidoso Flying Service.

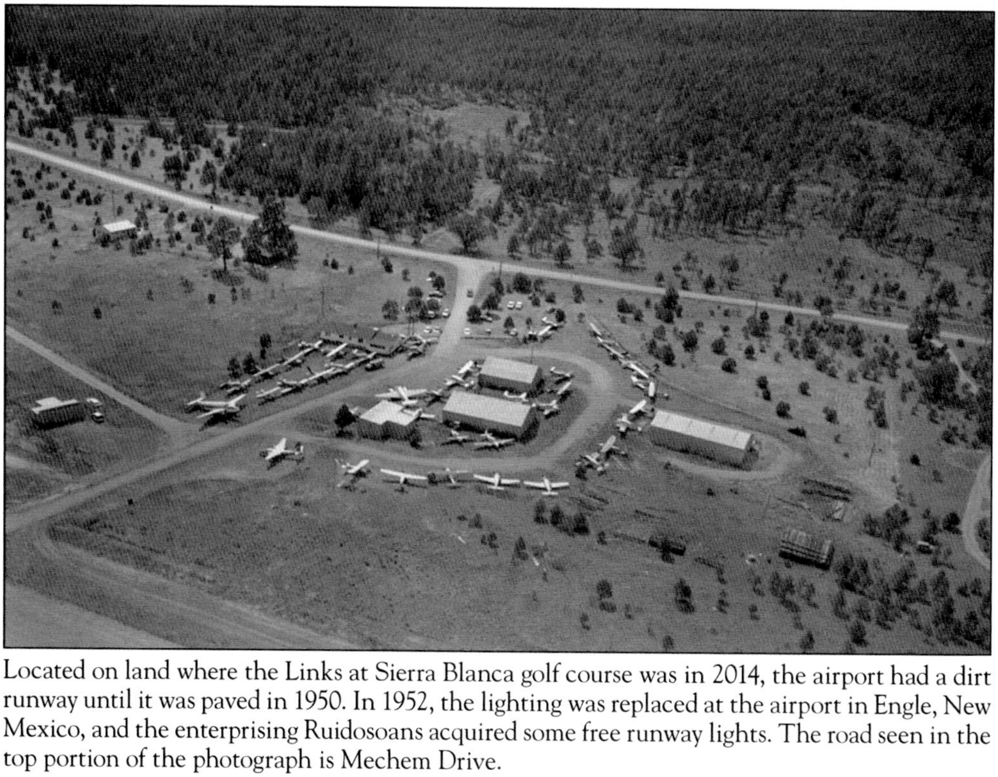

Located on land where the Links at Sierra Blanca golf course was in 2014, the airport had a dirt runway until it was paved in 1950. In 1952, the lighting was replaced at the airport in Engle, New Mexico, and the enterprising Ruidosoans acquired some free runway lights. The road seen in the top portion of the photograph is Mechem Drive.

Lowell B. Morgan (left), aviation student, and Dewey L. Gann, flight instructor, shake hands. Morgan was the first World War II veteran to complete flight training at the Ruidoso airfield. They pose next to a new T-craft flown by Morgan from Carlsbad. Morgan began writing the "Aviation in Our Town" column for the *Ruidoso News* with the intention of encouraging people to fly. But some of the stories—getting lost, running low on fuel, emergency landings in fields—might not have created the desired effect.

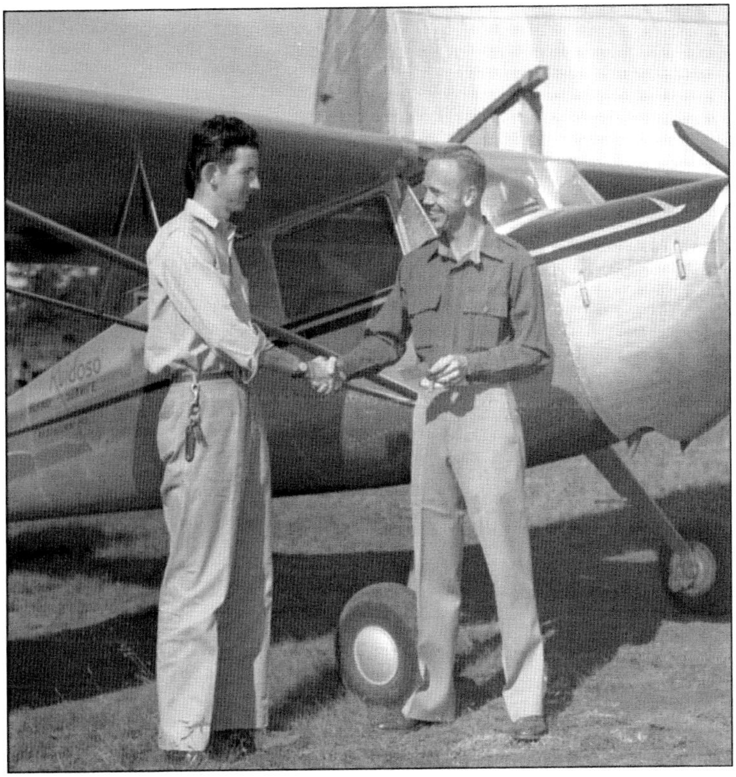

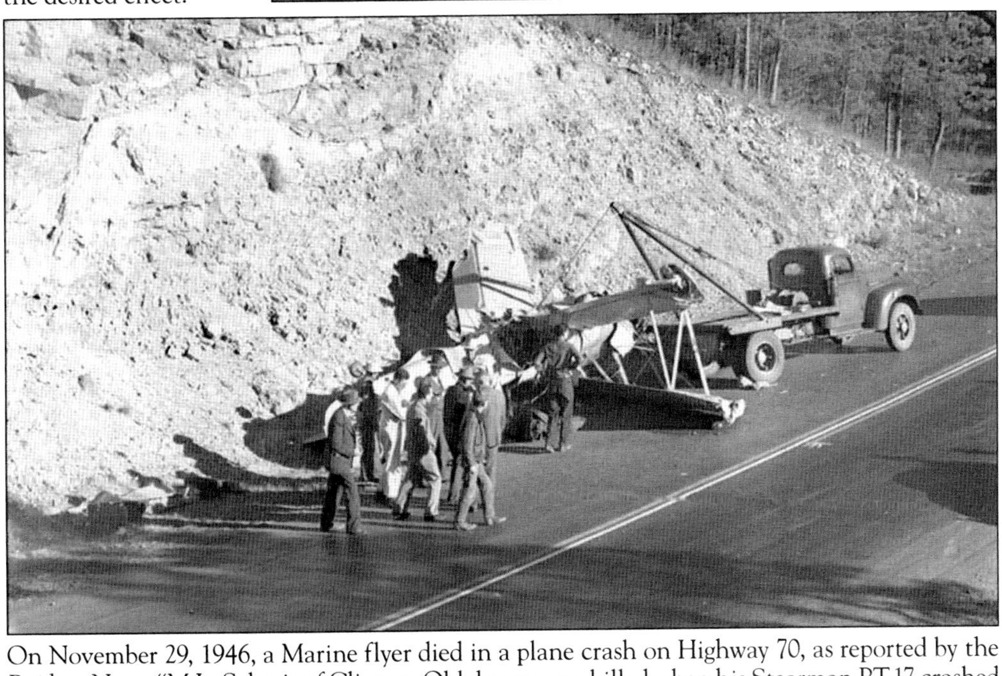

On November 29, 1946, a Marine flyer died in a plane crash on Highway 70, as reported by the *Ruidoso News*: "M.L. Schreir of Clinton, Oklahoma, was killed when his Stearman PT-17 crashed against a bluff adjacent to Highway 70 in Dark Canyon, seven miles west of the Ruidoso Junction." A tow truck from the newly opened Wagon Wheel garage removed the plane. Identified by papers he was carrying, Schreir was a former first lieutenant in the US Marine Corps.

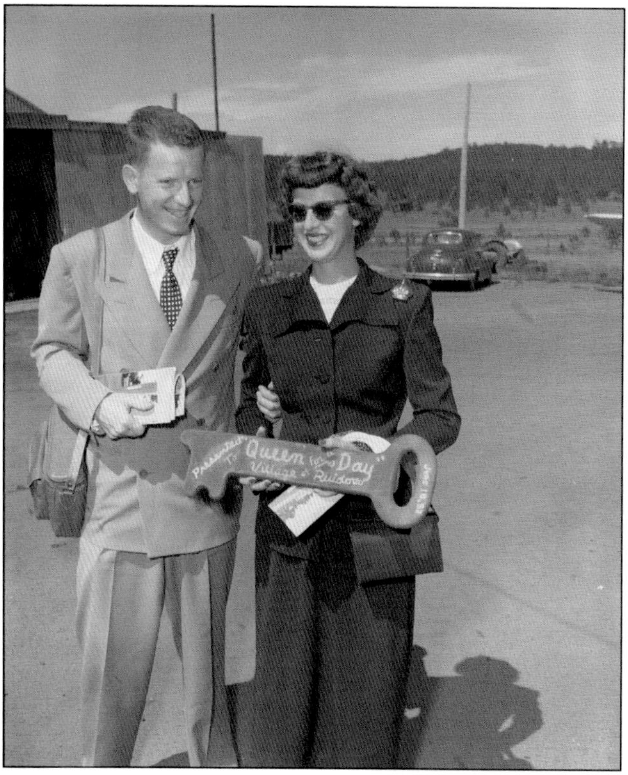

In May 1952, the winning contestant on the popular radio program *Queen For A Day* won a five-day trip to Ruidoso. Ralph Brown's Flying Service flew Ginny Ballance and her husband, Thaxton, of Los Angeles, California, from El Paso, sending (perhaps jokingly) two planes—one for the luggage.

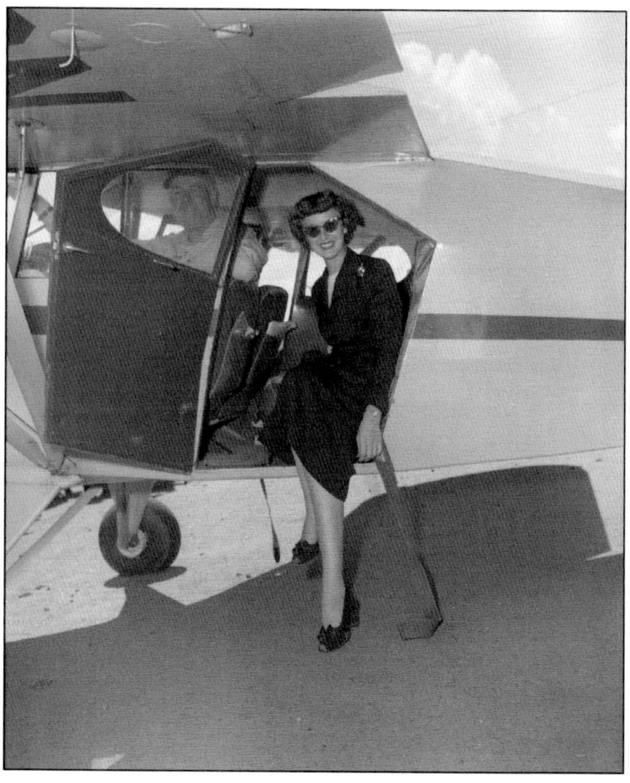

S.K. Kuykendall had written to the popular radio program to offer a stay at his Vaughnland Cabins as a prize. That simple offer grew to include dozens of local businesses that hosted the couple or donated merchandise for the promotion. The couple had private box seats at the opening day of the racetrack. When asked what they thought of the town, the Ballances said, "We'd like to roll it up and take it with us."

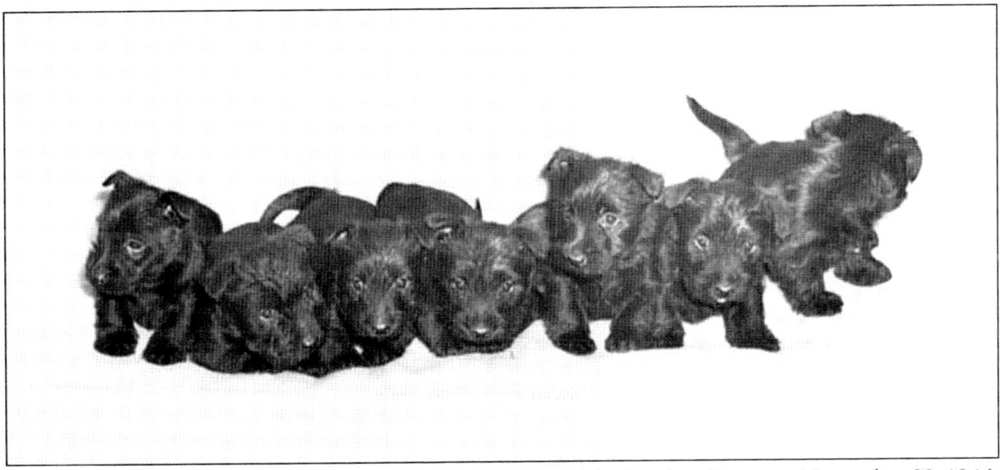

This photograph of puppies appeared on the front page of the *Ruidoso News* on November 29, 1946, presumably a slow news day. The seven Scotties were born on Halloween. Grace Sutton of Ruidoso and Mrs. W.H. Miller of Kansas owned the parents of the pups, which were the "result of a summer romance here," the paper duly reported. The puppy on the right, born at midnight, was named Spooks.

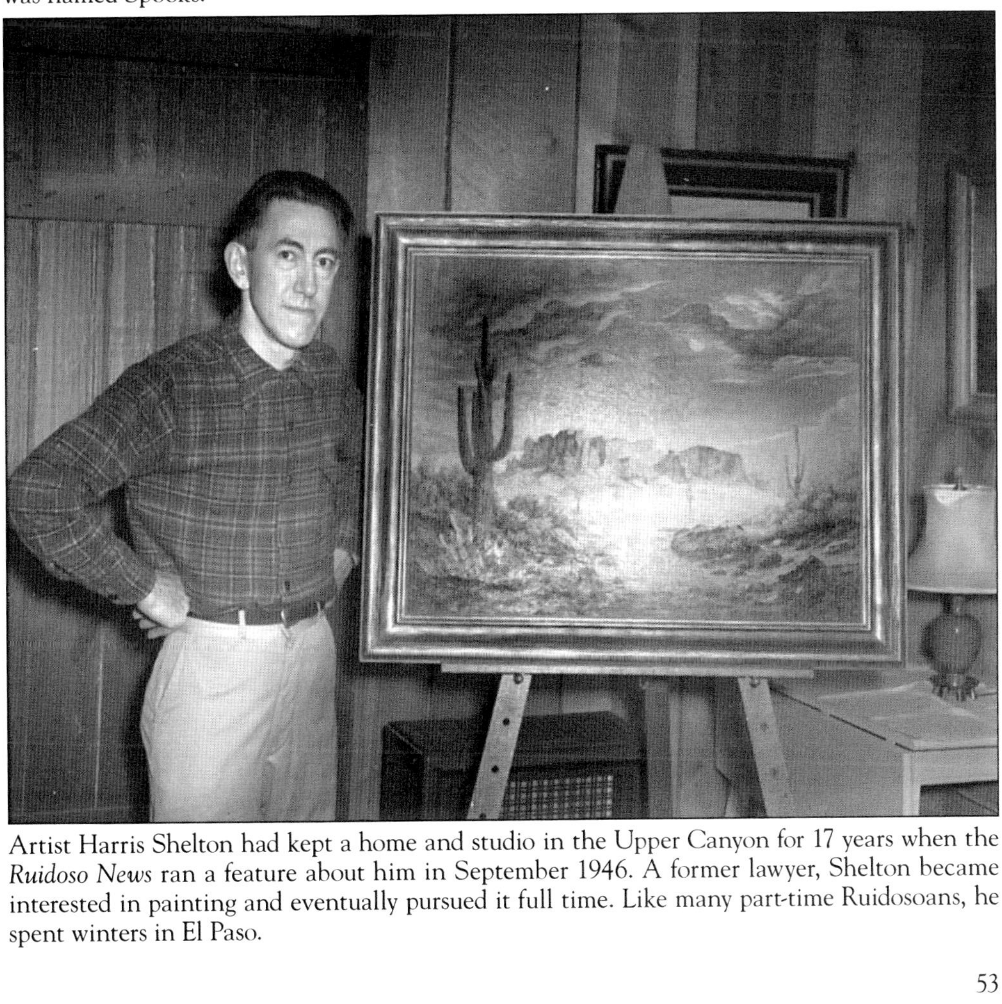

Artist Harris Shelton had kept a home and studio in the Upper Canyon for 17 years when the *Ruidoso News* ran a feature about him in September 1946. A former lawyer, Shelton became interested in painting and eventually pursued it full time. Like many part-time Ruidosoans, he spent winters in El Paso.

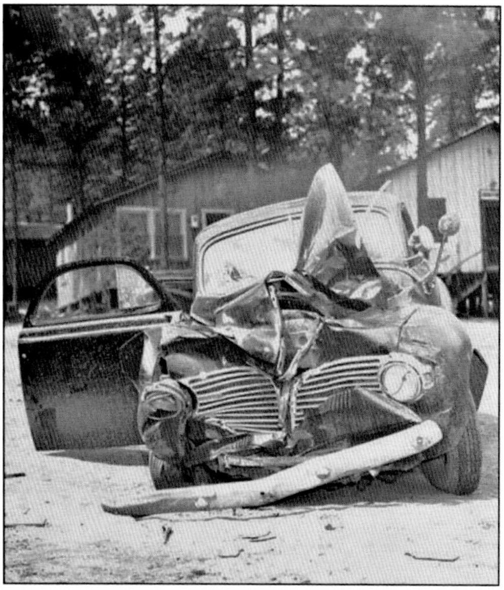

Car wrecks were a frequent occurrence, given the narrow mountain roads and drivers who were inexperienced in navigating the terrain.

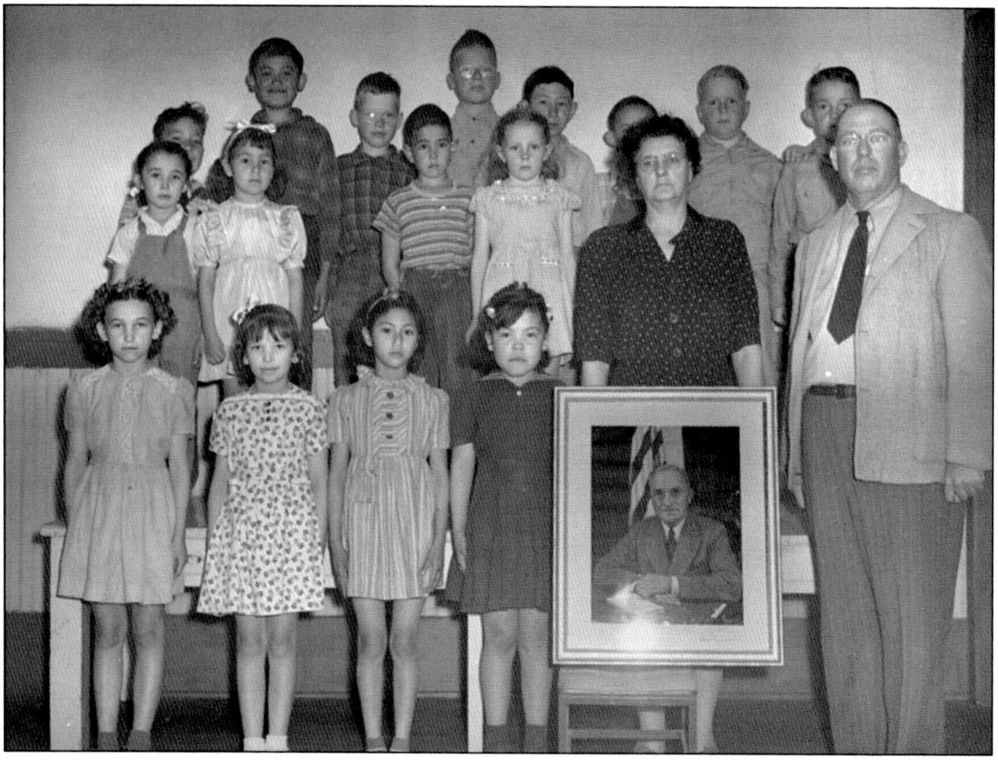

In an effort to increase circulation, in 1947, the *Ruidoso News* launched a campaign to gather news from the surrounding area and to sell subscriptions. Students of Tinnie, a small town in the Hondo Valley, won the subscription-drive contest. The prize was a framed portrait of Pres. Harry Truman. From left to right are (first row) Liria Trujillo, Viola Trujillo, Helen Maes, Cecilia Frequez, Mrs. Bert Smith, and Lloyd Bloodworth; (second row) Pita Salas, Helen Chavez, Joe Alvarez, and Joy Mason; (third row) Bill Romero, Jake Fresquez, Jack Casey, Robert Casey, Modesto Chavez, Carson Salas, Burt Purcella, and Don Mason.

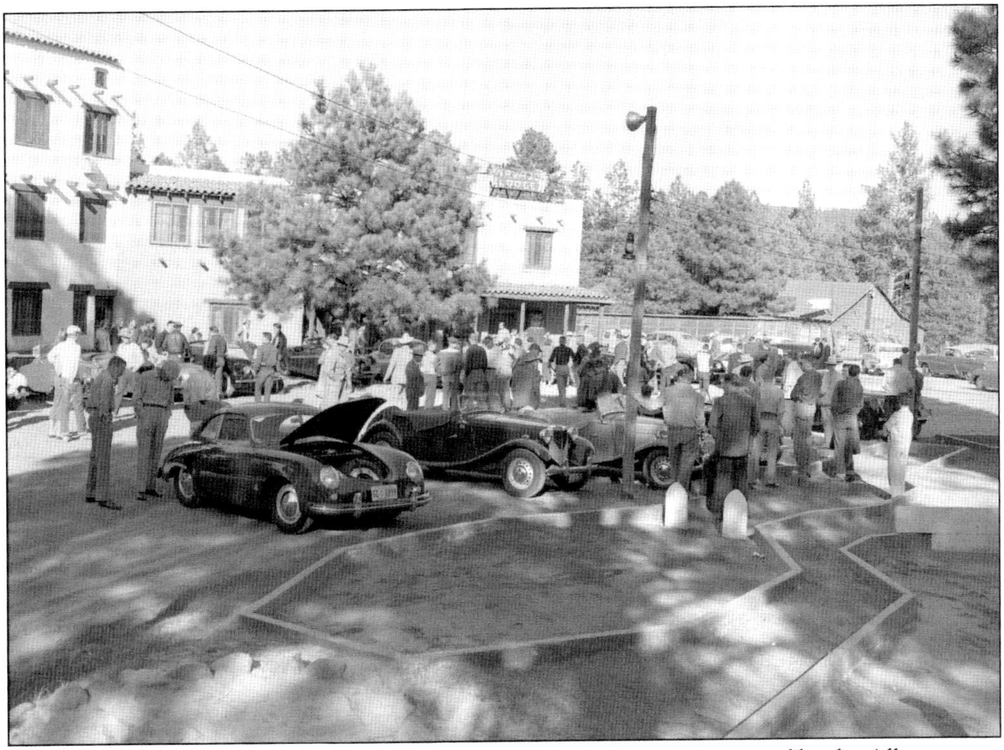

Held on February 20, 1954, Washington's Birthday Road Rally was organized by the Albuquerque Sports Car Club Association, the Southwest Sports Car Club of El Paso, and the Ruidoso Chamber of Commerce. Some 60 participants competed in two 25-mile races on a dirt track north of town, near Cree Meadows Golf and Country Club. The New Mexico Amateur Radio Operators heard about the event and decided to meet in Ruidoso on the same weekend. In the photograph above, some of the participants display their vehicles outside the Navajo Lodge. The lodge's miniature golf course is seen in the foreground.

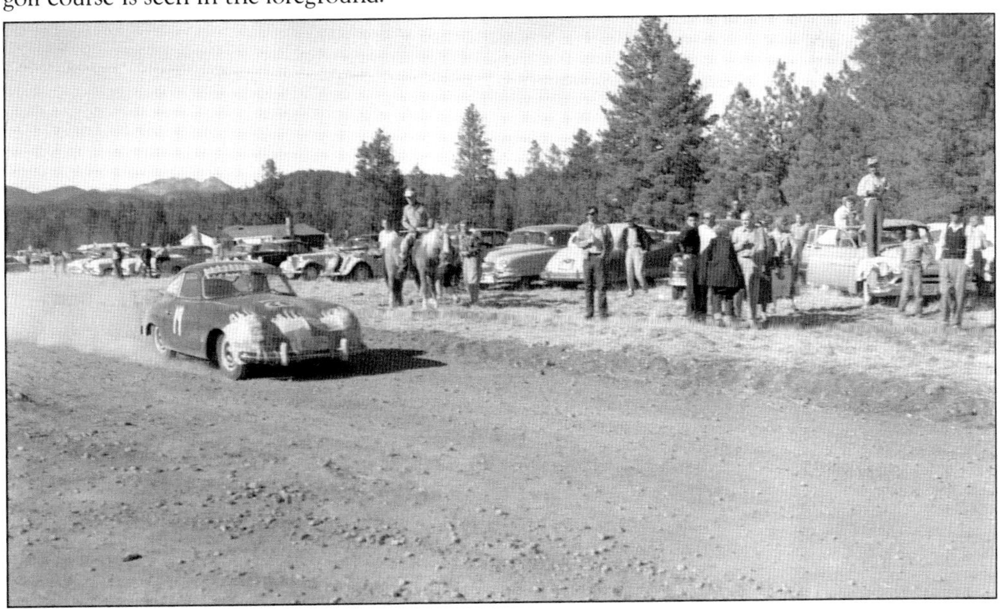

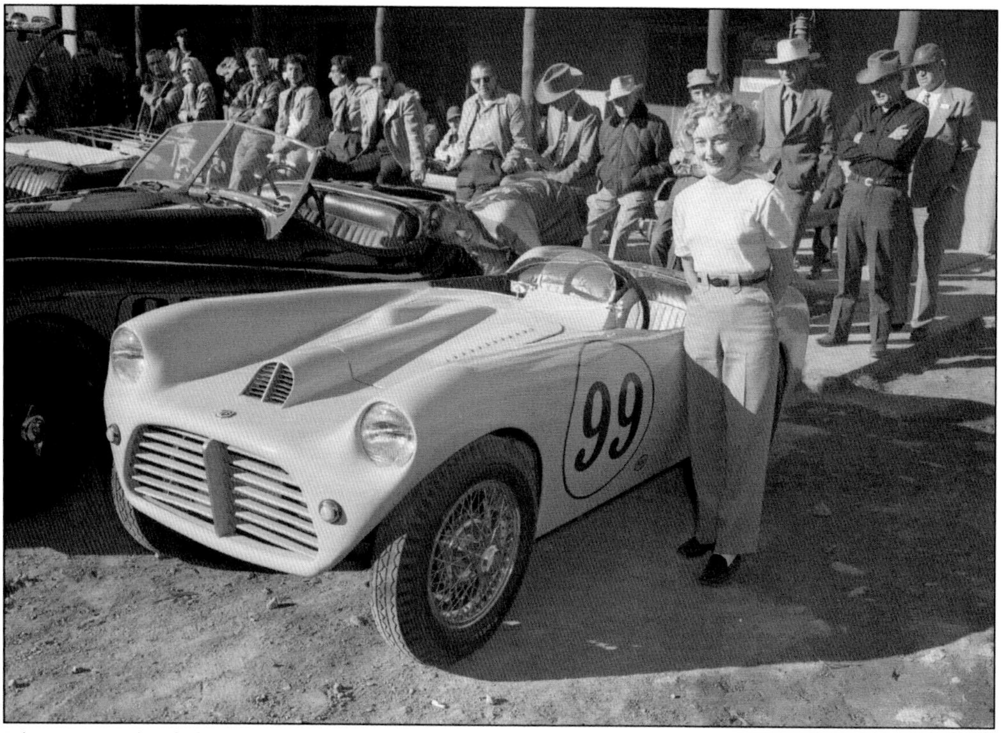

There were also field events held at Palmer Gateway, in which drivers had to carry eggs in spoons, break balloons, and otherwise display their driving skills. Pictured above is Sally Trussell of El Paso, the third-place winner in the women's division of the field trials. The car was a custom design, with a "fibre glass body and MG motor," according to a *Ruidoso News* article on March 5, 1954.

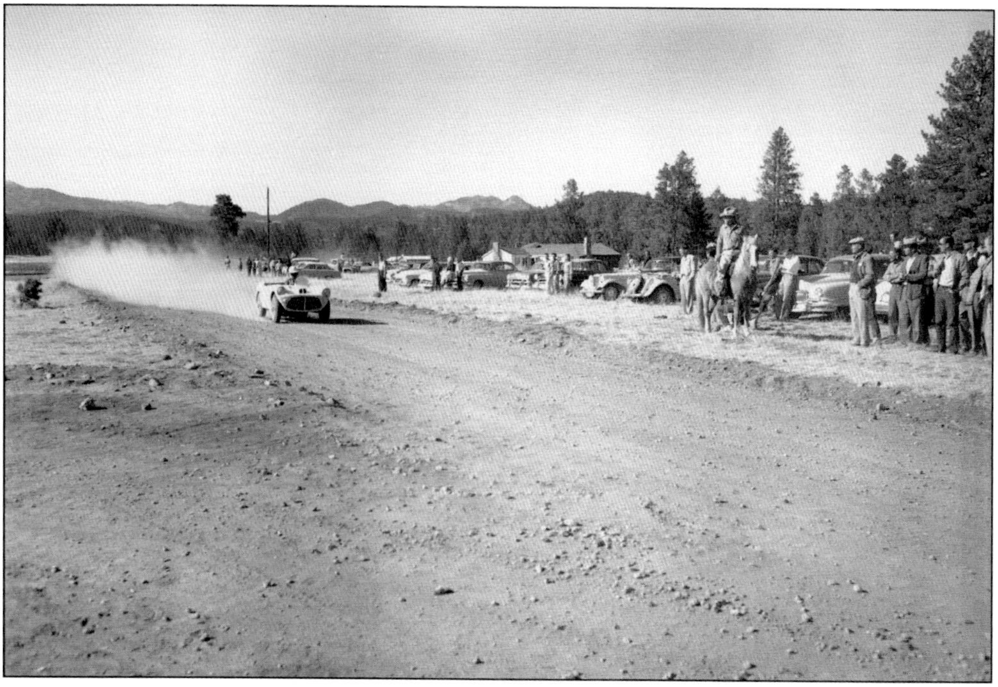

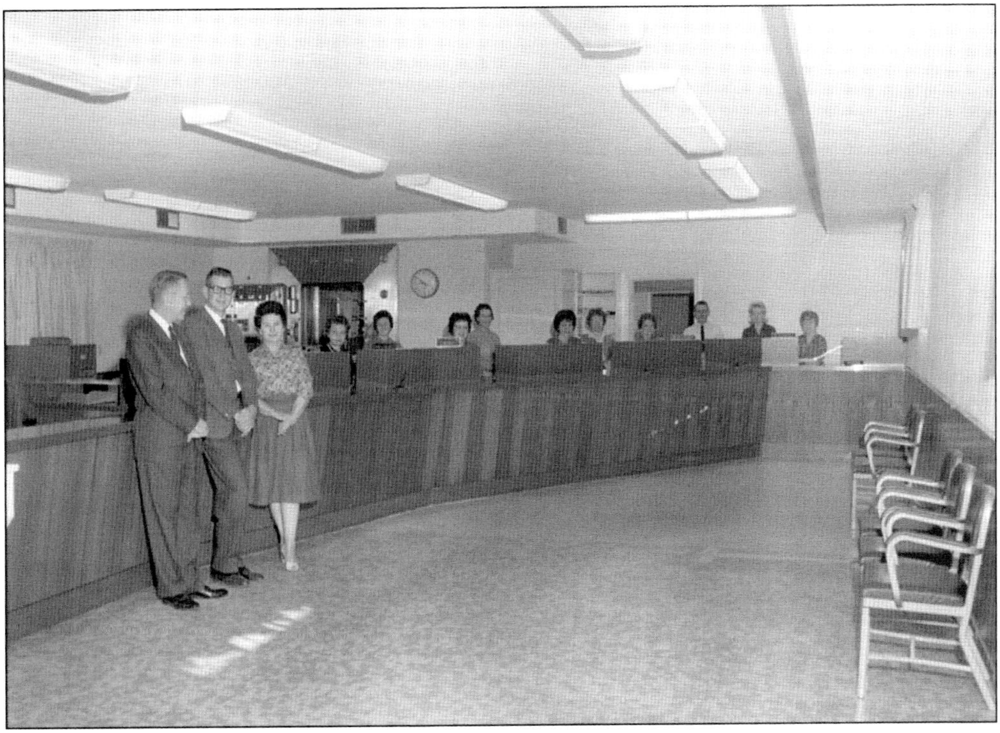

The town had no bank until the Ruidoso State Bank opened in 1954. Merchants were obliged to drive to Alamogordo or Roswell to do their banking. Weighed down by coins from the slot machines, Bill McCarty would make this trek to deliver sacks of money to the bank in Alamogordo for his uncle, who owned several bars. Posing in this 1963 photograph are, from left to right, executive vice president T.B. Hood and cashiers Ed Wimberly and Ethel Carroll.

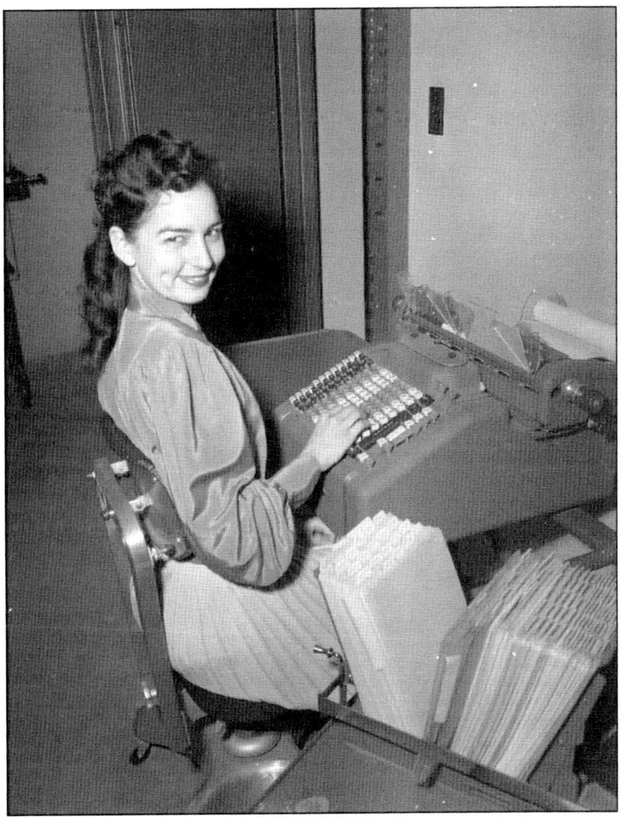

In April 1954, Betty Cleaver, bookkeeper and secretary, posed with an impressive adding machine in the newly opened Ruidoso State Bank.

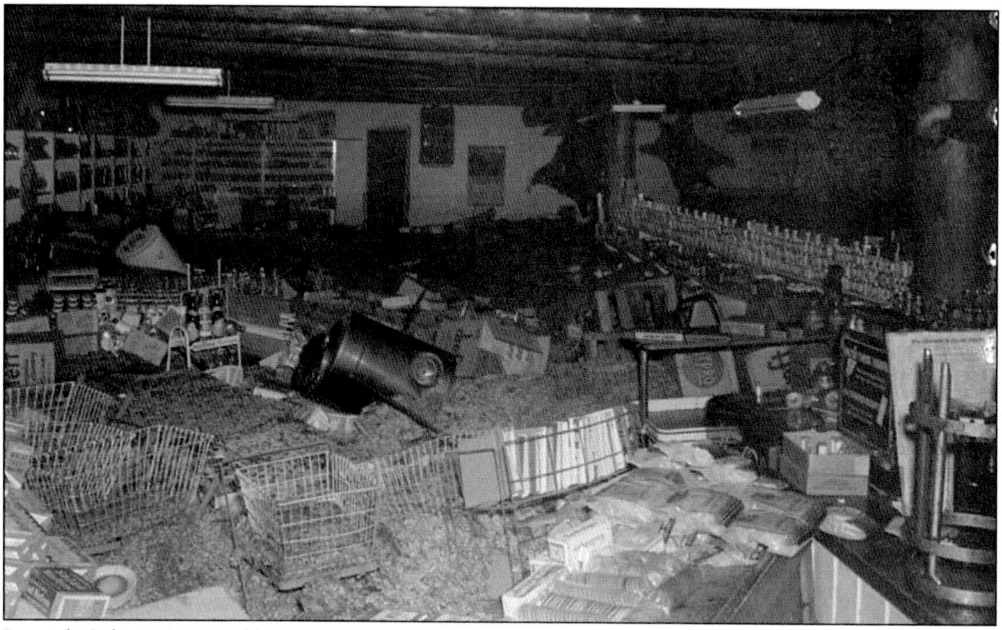

In early July 1946, a sudden storm, common during monsoon season in the mountains, brought 2.8 inches of rain in 50 minutes. The temperature dropped from 84 to 42 degrees, and hail flooded McElhaney's grocery store, located at the corner of Main Road (now Sudderth Drive) and Center Street. The July 5, 1946, issue of the *Ruidoso News* reported, "The center of the storm hit the Self-Serve Grocery, owned by O.W. McElhaney, mayor of the village of Ruidoso. Hail piled into the store from under the windows, up through the sewer and in through the door." Apparently, storm drains were clogged with debris, which added to the problem.

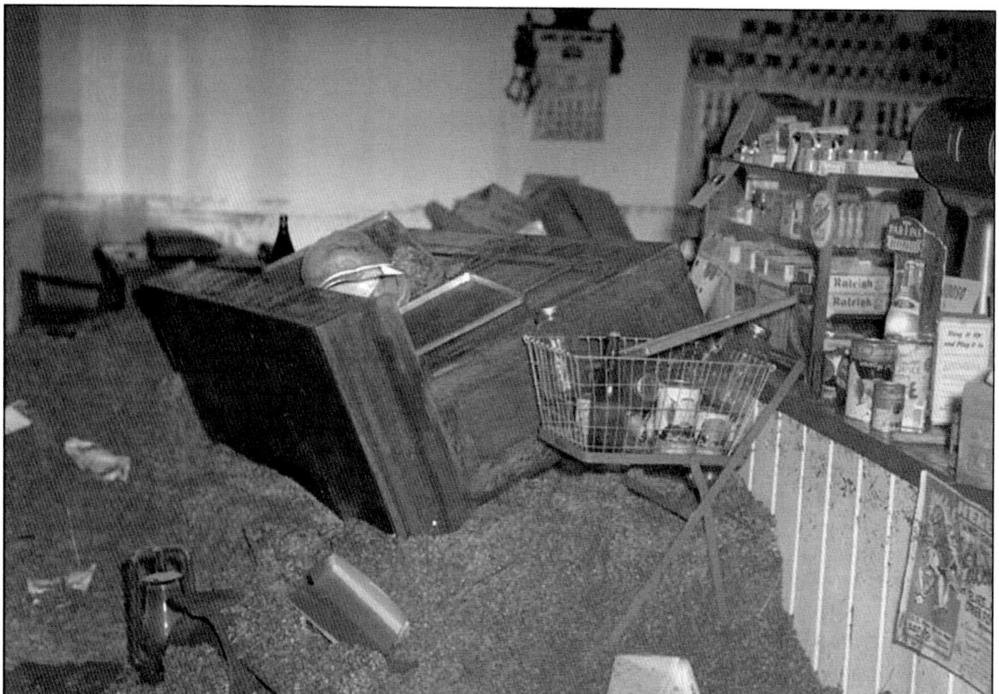

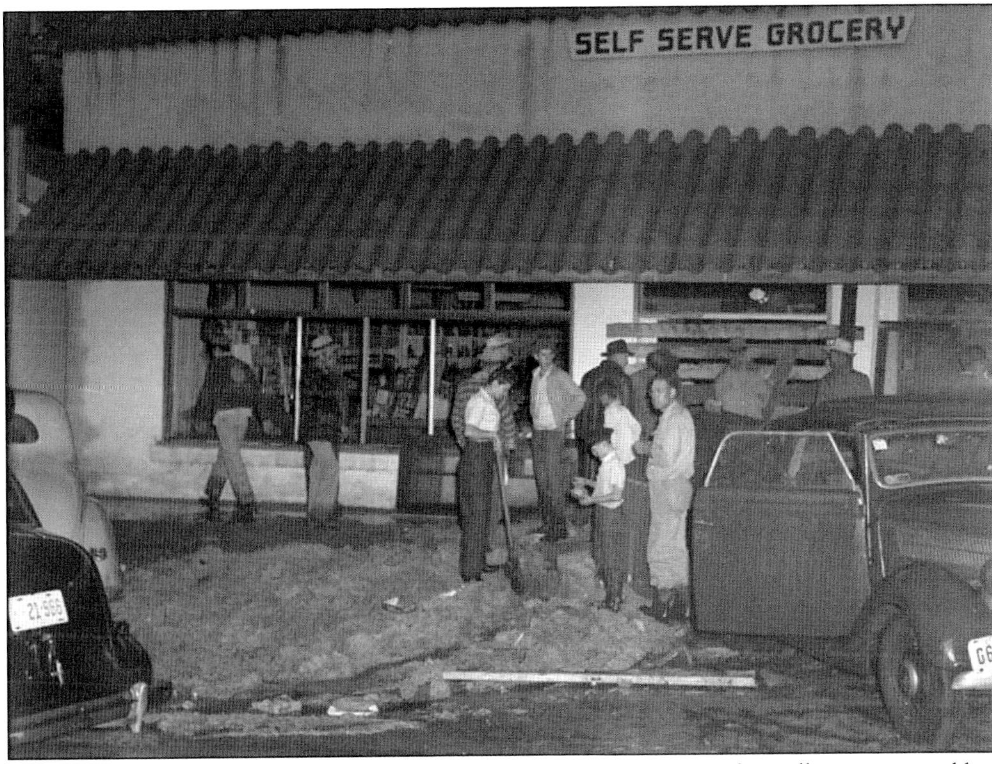

In the July 12 issue of the *Ruidoso News*, the editorial said, "Businessmen from all over town grabbed shovels and began to help clean out the mess." Dave Parks, who worked with Wade Hedgecoke for two days to clean out the store, recalled that 50 or 60 people showed up at various times to help, with local children gathering canned goods that had washed down to the river.

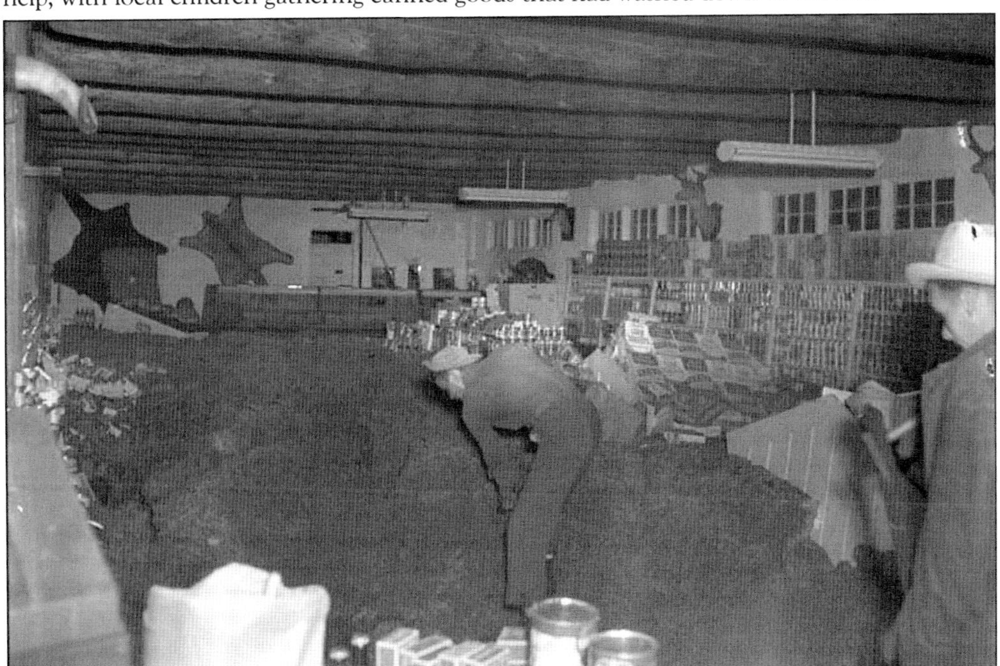

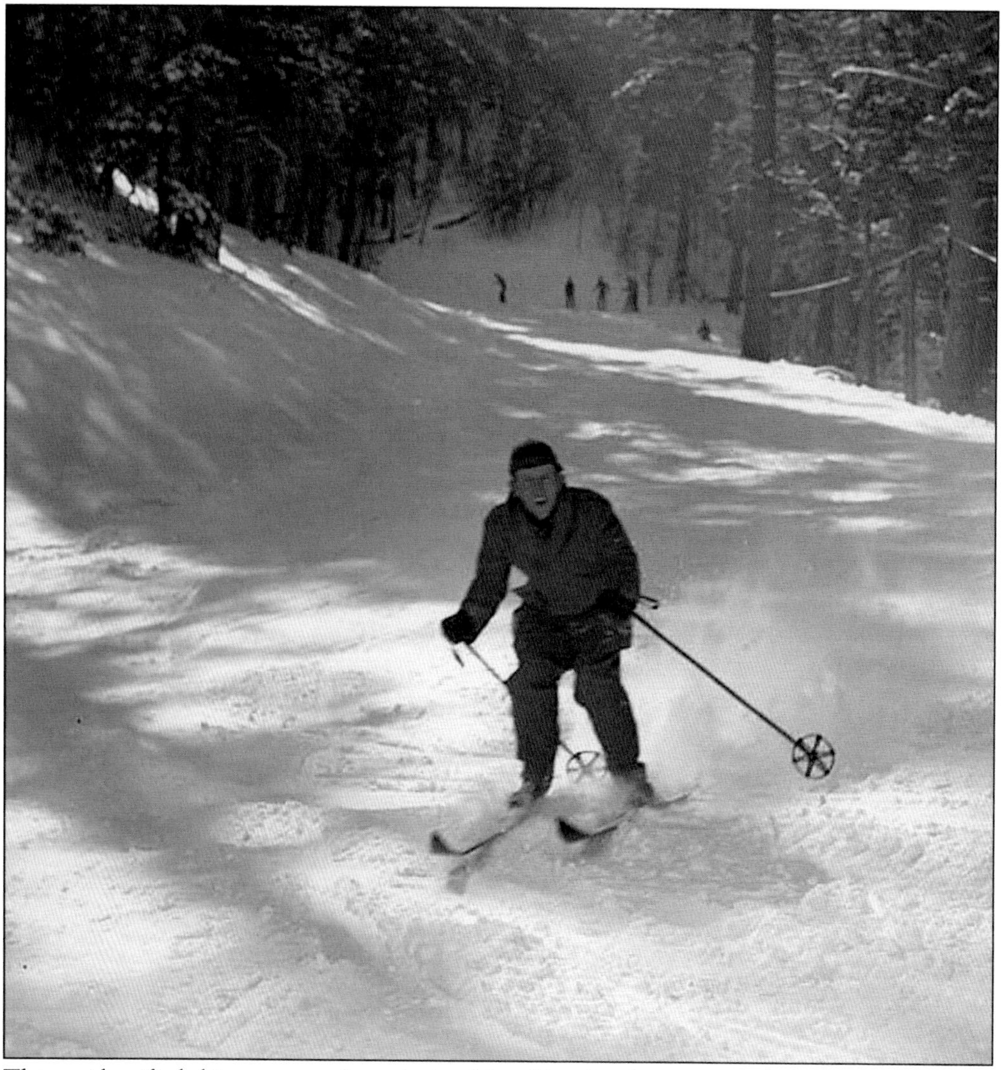

This unidentified skier seems to be enjoying himself at the ski are in Cedar Creek. The higher elevation and shade provided by the Ponderosa pines helped create good conditions. Snowfall amounts were considerably greater at that time than in the 1980s and 1990s.

Five

Winter Fun

Early visitors came to Ruidoso for the summer and retreated from their simple, uninsulated cabins as soon as temperatures dropped. After World War II, village leaders began to focus on ways to make the town more attractive during the winter. In 1946, the *Ruidoso News* proclaimed, "The village is no longer limited to the three-months-out-of-the-year 'season' during which everybody made all the money he could in order to hibernate the remaining nine months of the year."

The town's first ski area opened in 1938 at the end of the road along Cedar Creek. Workers with the Civilian Conservation Corps cleared trees on a gentle slope and built a few log shelters. Skiers walked up the hill, carrying their skis. In 1941, an article in the *El Paso Times* noted that "Ruidoso had a toboggan slide a half mile long" and that "Ruidoso businessmen have put up $1000 to install a rope tow."

Heraled as "the biggest day for Winter Sports on the Ruidoso," New Year's Day 1950 saw incredible success at Cedar Creek. The *Ruidoso News* reported that at least 100 skiers had enjoyed the slopes, with twice as many people looking on and the rope tows operating for eight days straight. Cedar Creek's acclaimed popularity provided a platform for the future development of other ski areas, with the *Ruidoso News* claiming that this success "should wake up the local people to continue to push and push again the plans of the White Mountain Sports Association to get in their proposed ski run in White Mountain Park."

"Doc Horton, Bill Hart and I worked at the Cedar Creek ski area," Phillips remembered. "Friday nights we would meet at Bill Hart's grocery store and make up a bunch of sandwiches. Saturday mornings we'd get up early and haul everything up Cedar Creek, set up the two rope tows with gasoline engines and get everything ready. We mostly wanted to get people's signatures on a petition to have White Mountain Park removed from its wilderness classification so we could have a ski area." (White Mountain Park was the name of the open area where the lodges of Ski Apache were located in 2014.)

In 1960, the US Forest Service granted permission for the construction of a ski area on Sierra Blanca, a project financed by oilman and rancher R.O. Anderson. The Sierra Blanca Ski Resort opened in 1961 and, in December, set a state record for the number of visitors in a single day. In 1963, Anderson sold the area to the Mescalero Apache tribe for $1.75 million. The area was renamed Ski Apache in 1985.

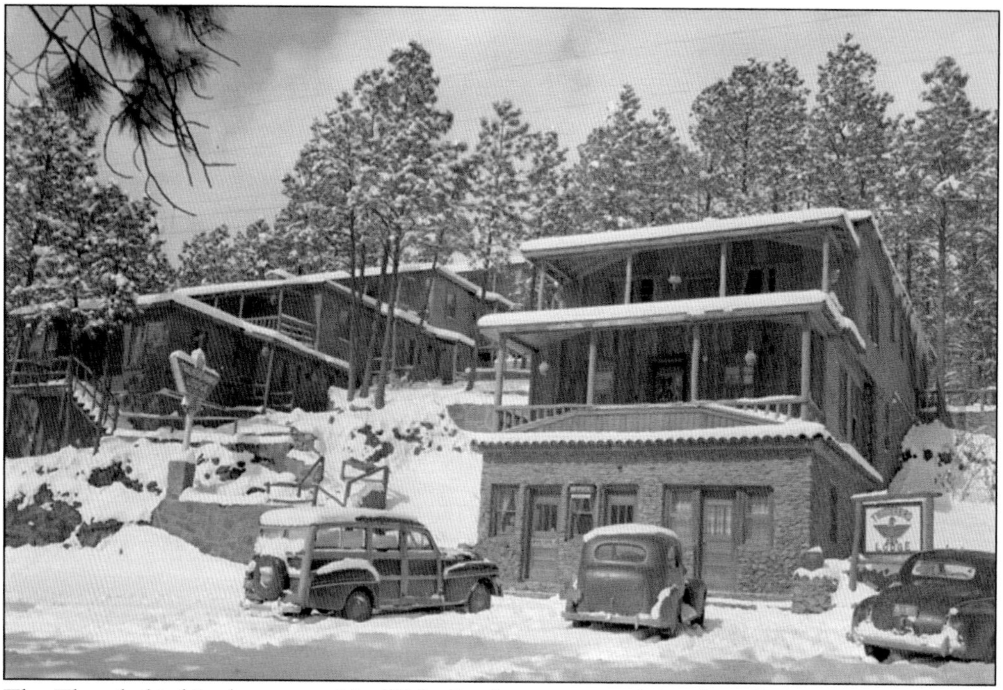

The Thunderbird Lodge, opened by Walt Crosby, was one of the closer lodging establishments to the Cedar Creek ski area. Potential winter visitors needed assurance that they would have comfortable accommodations, including heat and running water.

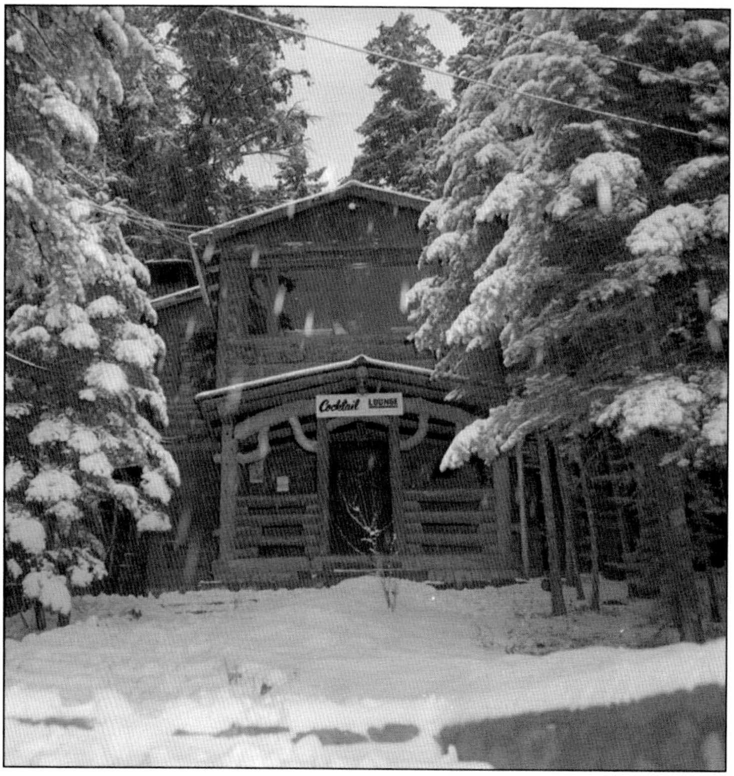

The Noisy Water Lodge, near the end of Upper Canyon, was built by Morris Baretz of El Paso. Catering to a wealthier clientele, a 1946 advertisement in the *Ruidoso News* offered lodging and meals for $8.50 per day, per person. Carmon Phillips and his group, the Mellotones, played in the dance hall. A large horse-drawn sleigh took guests for rides through Upper Canyon. As of 2014, the lodge is still in operation.

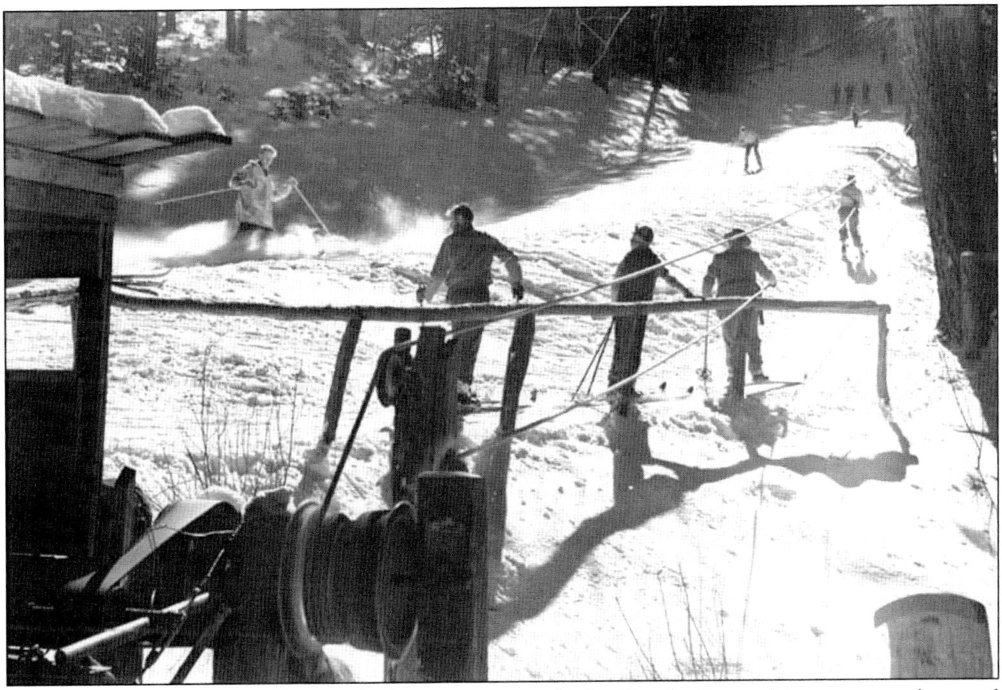

In this 1946 photograph, skiers ride the rope tow in Cedar Creek. Some skiers apparently opted to walk up instead. The hill is not particularly steep, but the heavier wooden skis made it more difficult to make turns and to control speed.

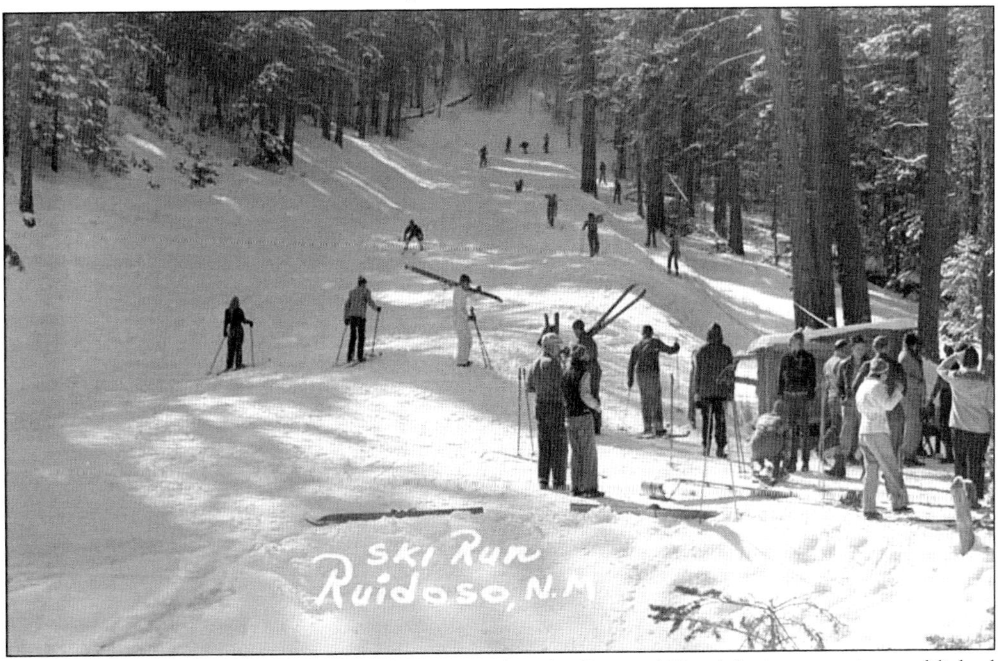

In 1952, several of Phillips's photographs appeared in the *Pictorial New Mexico* magazine, published in Albuquerque. The article noted, "Ruidoso is drawing hundreds of persons seeking winter fun on snow-covered slopes, where the waxed runner of the skis and the slick-bottomed toboggan slash along specially prepared runs."

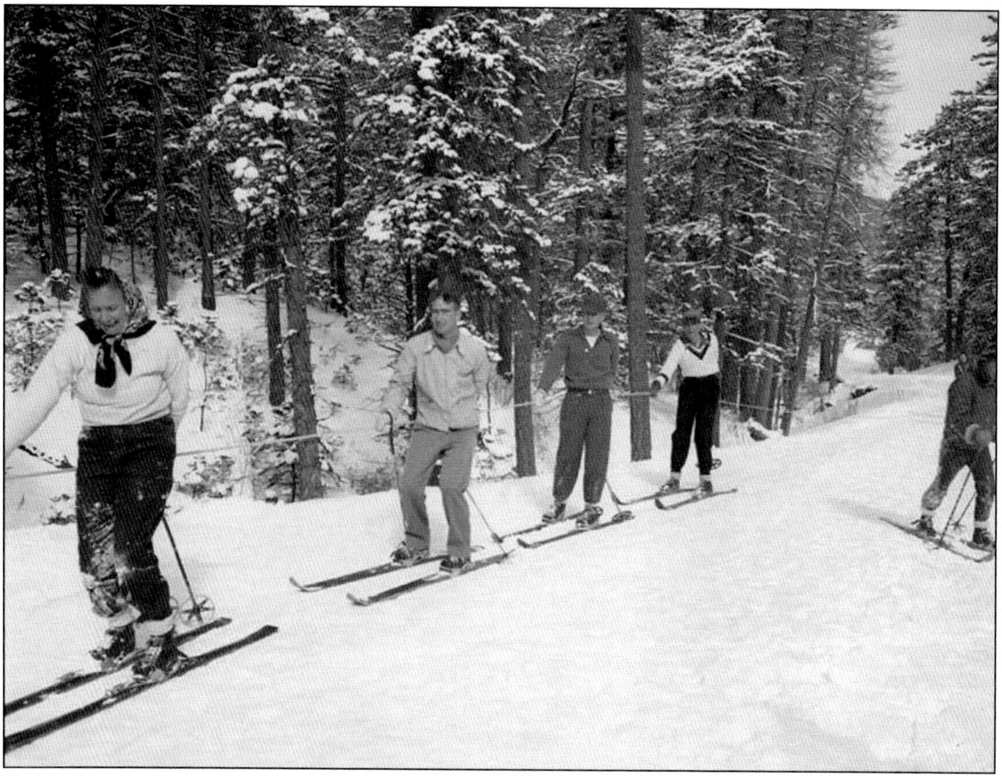

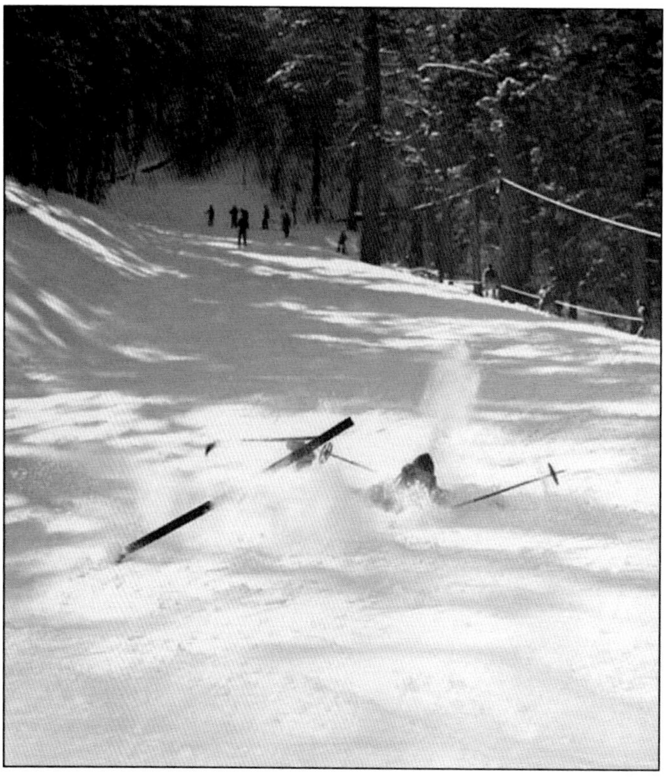

In March 1952, *El Paso Herald-Post* reporter Bill Broom came to Ruidoso to try skiing. He wrote, "Most ski runs have a tow, an evil-looking piece of rope that slithers through the snow. On one end of the tow is a wheezing motor. On the other is a pulley. In the middle are slothful skiers, too lazy to walk up." Broom also noted, "There is no use in skiing for a fanny except to fall on."

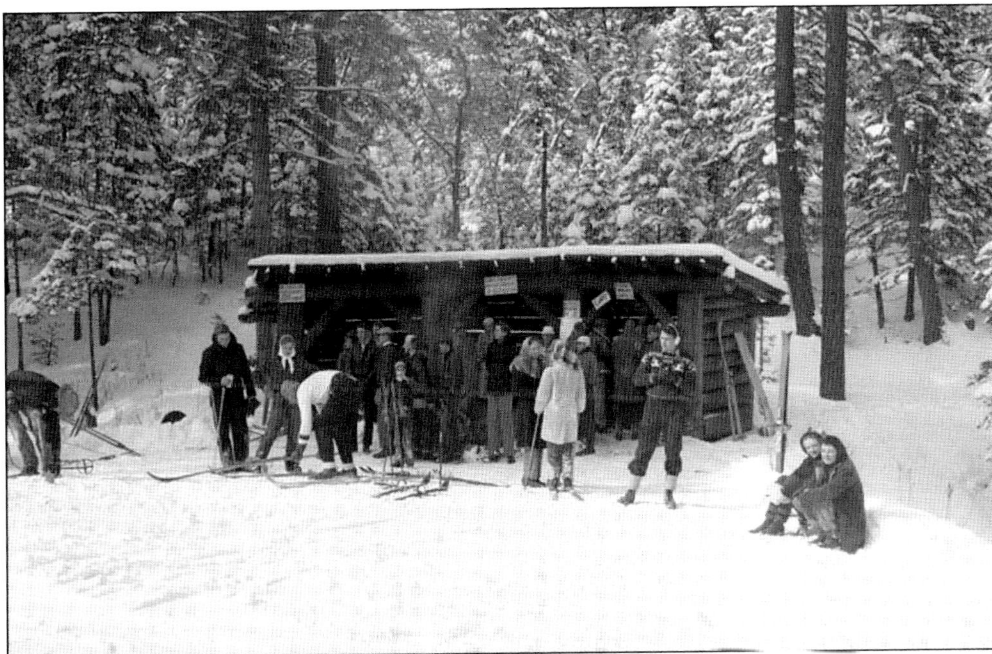

The small log shelter, built by the Civilian Conservation Corps in the 1930s, offered a bit of protection from the weather , as well as serving as a refreshment stand. The people with their toboggan below are perhaps enjoying the antics of the skiers on the hill. From left to right are unidentified, Mary Ellen Wells, unidentified, and Dickie Lansdown.

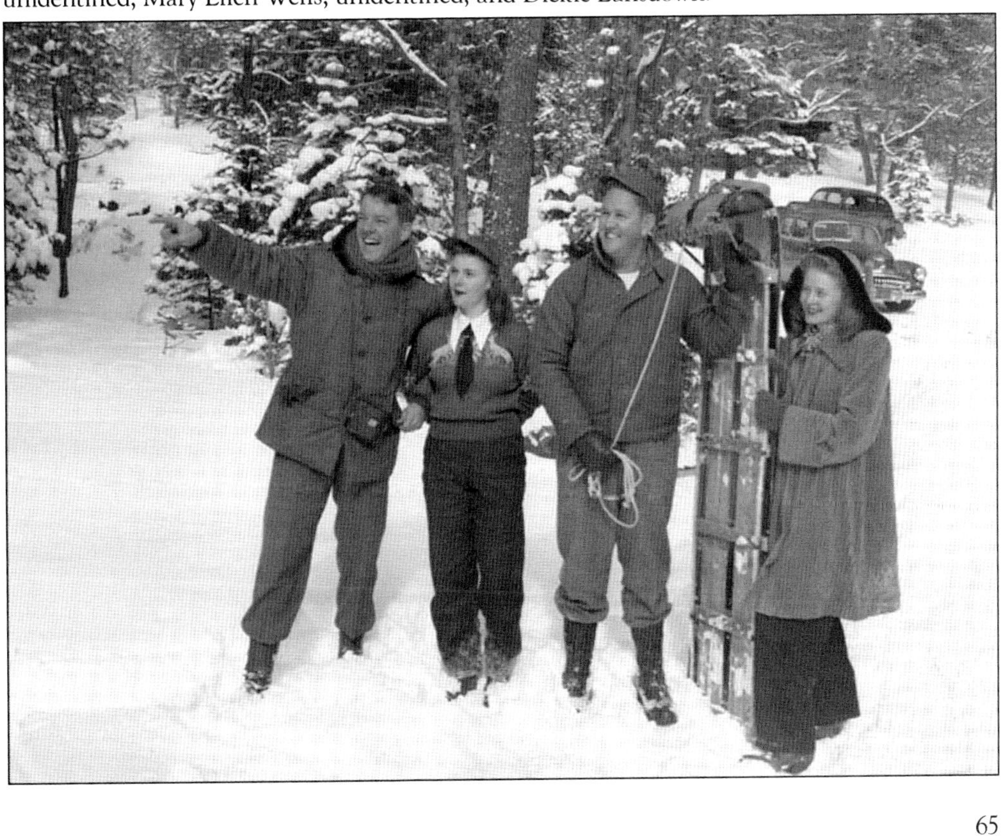

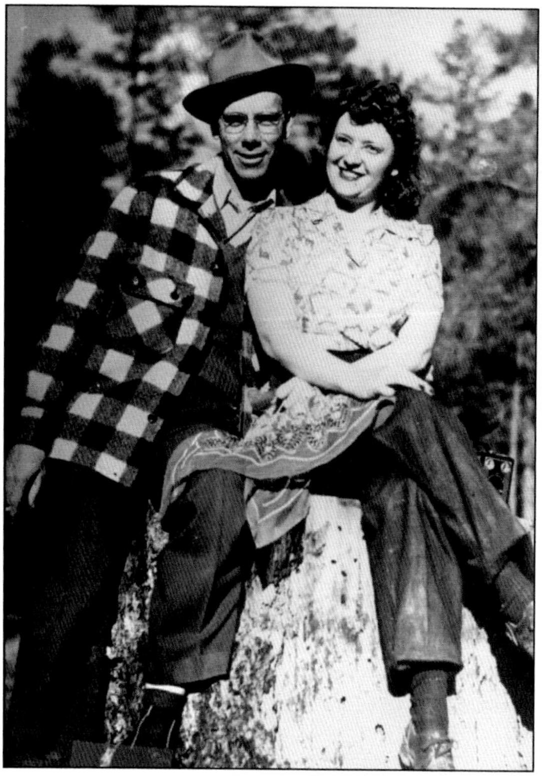

Although skiing in Cedar Creek was pleasant, the real skiing aficionados had their eyes on the heights of Sierra Blanca. In January 1950, Carmon Phillips and Ralph Brown flew to Colorado to learn more about the operation of several ski areas. In 1954, the New Mexico State Tourism Bureau sent a representative to "study the feasibility of erecting a ski-tow from Cedar Creek to White Mountain Park." Bill Hart provided jeeps and horses for the tour.

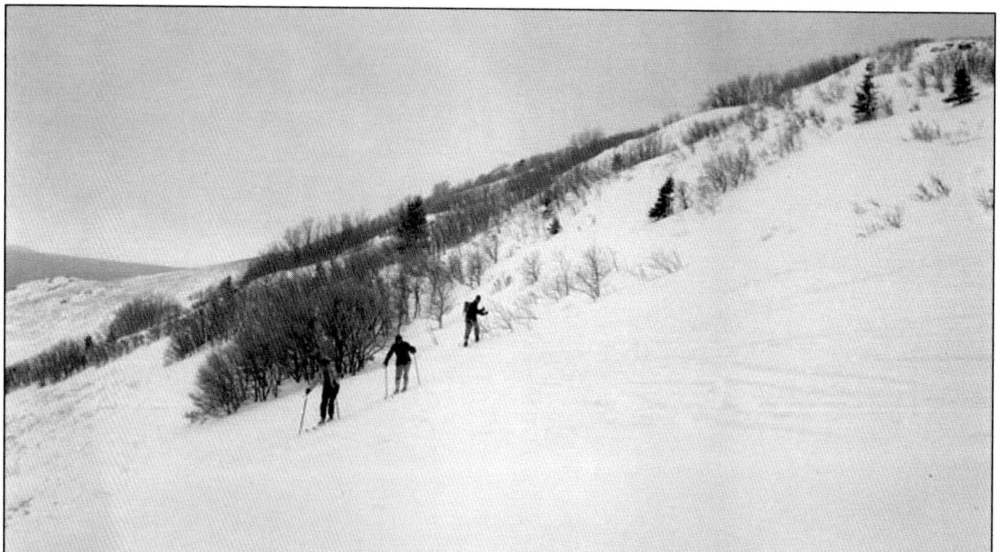

Skiers who wanted more of a challenge than Cedar Creek could provide traveled by jeep or horseback to higher slopes and skied down. Carmon Phillips remembered a horseback and skiing trip with Bill Hart: "Bill and I were up there [at the site of the current Ski Apache] having a wonderful time skiing. When we started coming out we got caught in the dark. We skied down real slow, poles out in front to keep from running into trees. When we felt something in our path we'd just drop down in the snow. Finally the moon came out the later quarter of the distance and made it easier. I never want that to happen to me again."

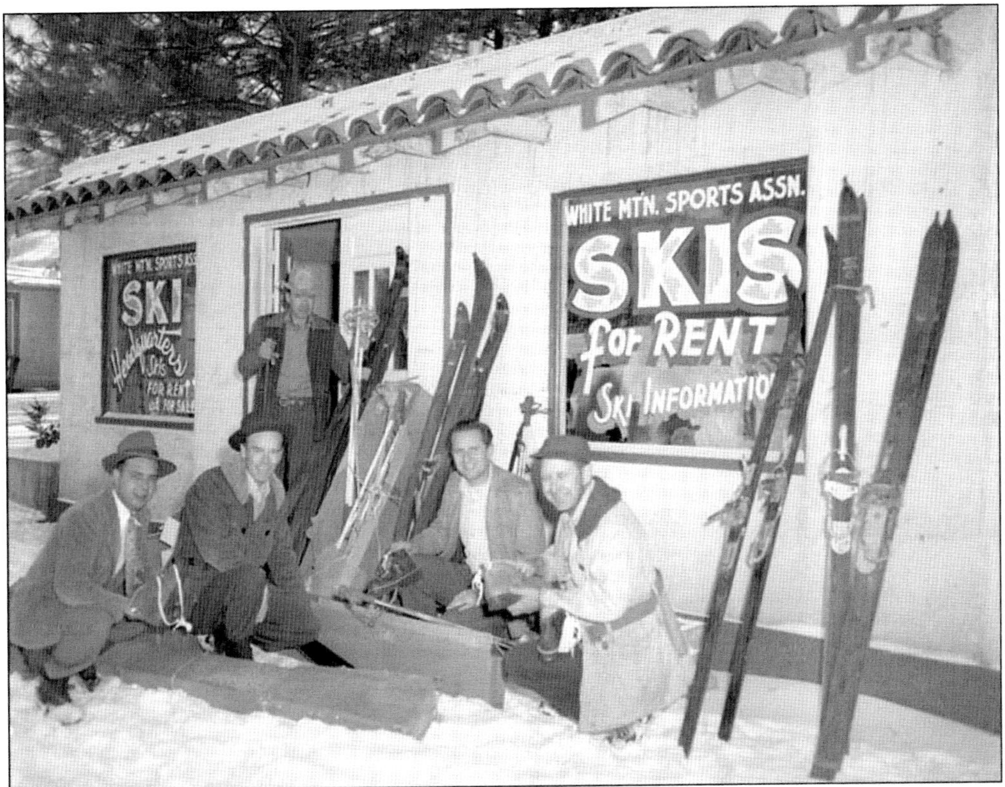

Carmon Phillips was head of the White Mountain Sports Association from its founding in 1948 to 1952. Several members pose in front of their headquarters in 1949. They are, from left to right, Willie Horton, Carmon Phillips, unidentified man in the doorway, unidentified, and Bill Hart. The people in the convertible, perhaps preparing for a parade, are also unidentified.

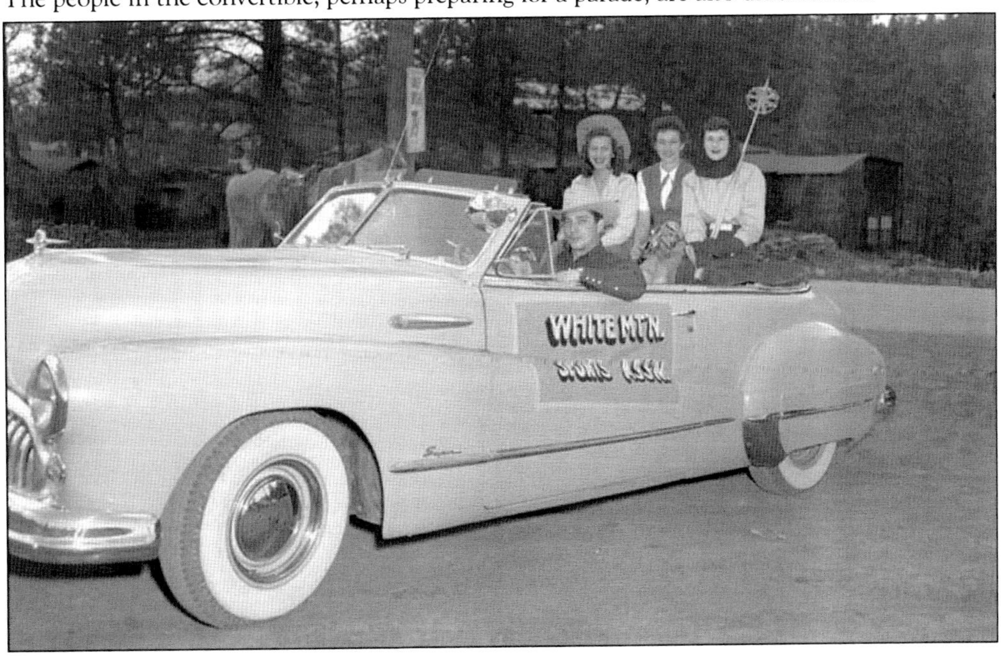

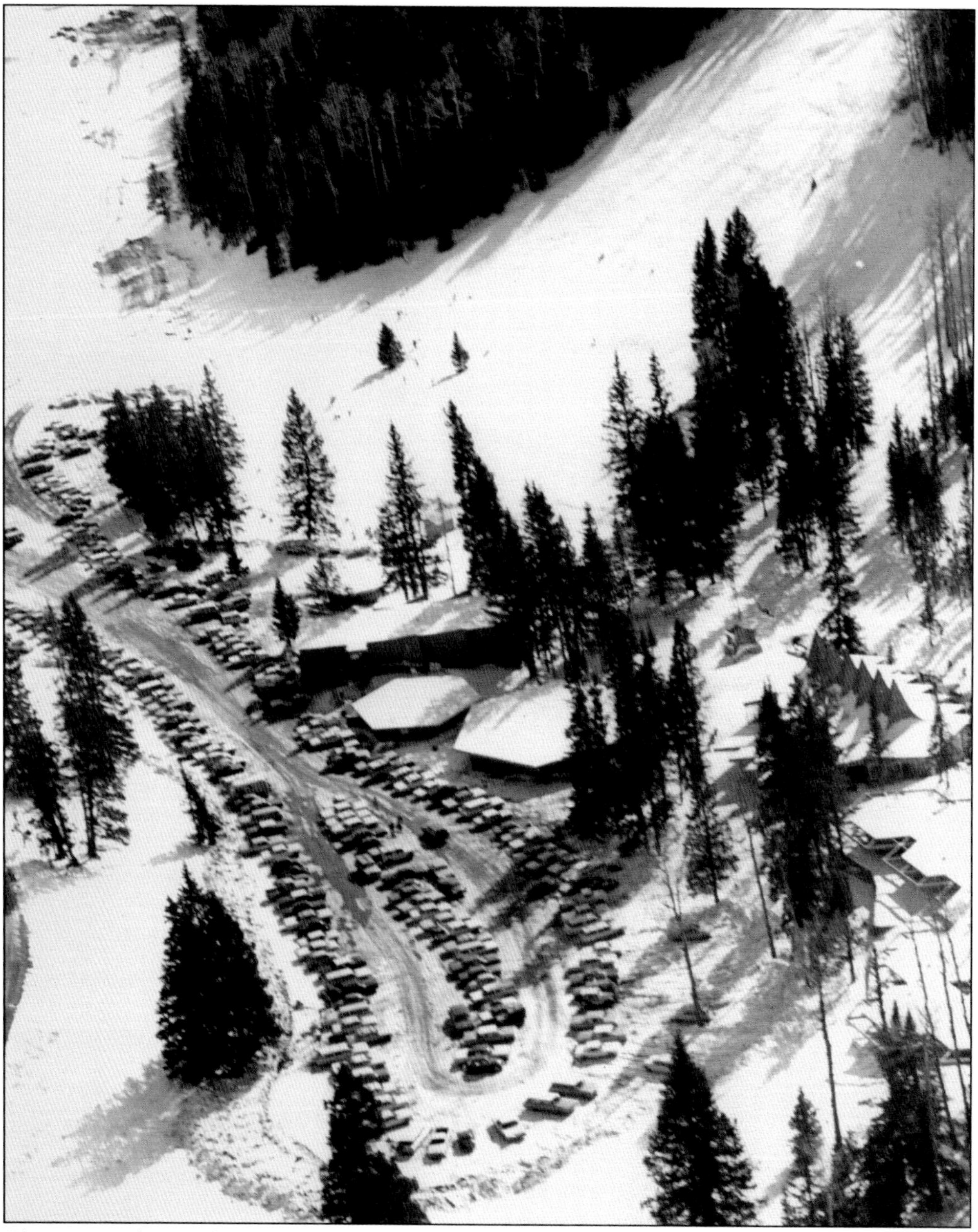

The Sierra Blanca Ski Resort was established in 1961, its opening delayed by heavy snowfall. The hexagonal buildings, designed to look like snowflakes, were first used for lodging and later housed the children's ski school.

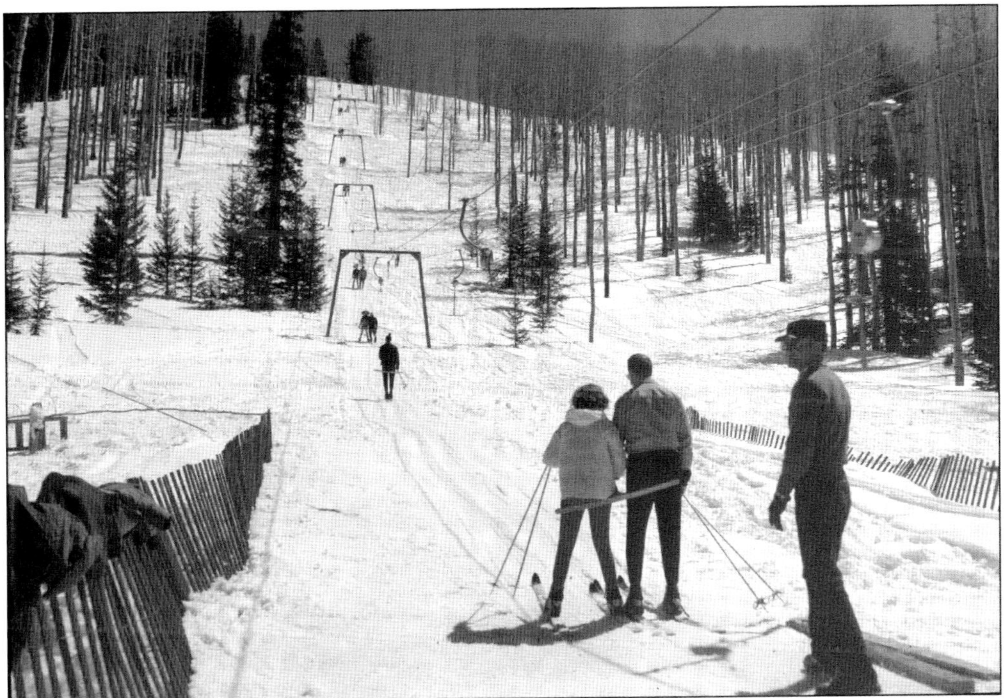

Skiers ride one of the three early T-bars at the Sierra Blanca Ski Area. An article in the *El Paso Herald-Post* in November 1965 noted the creation of new trails, including the Incredible, and the installation of a new double chairlift.

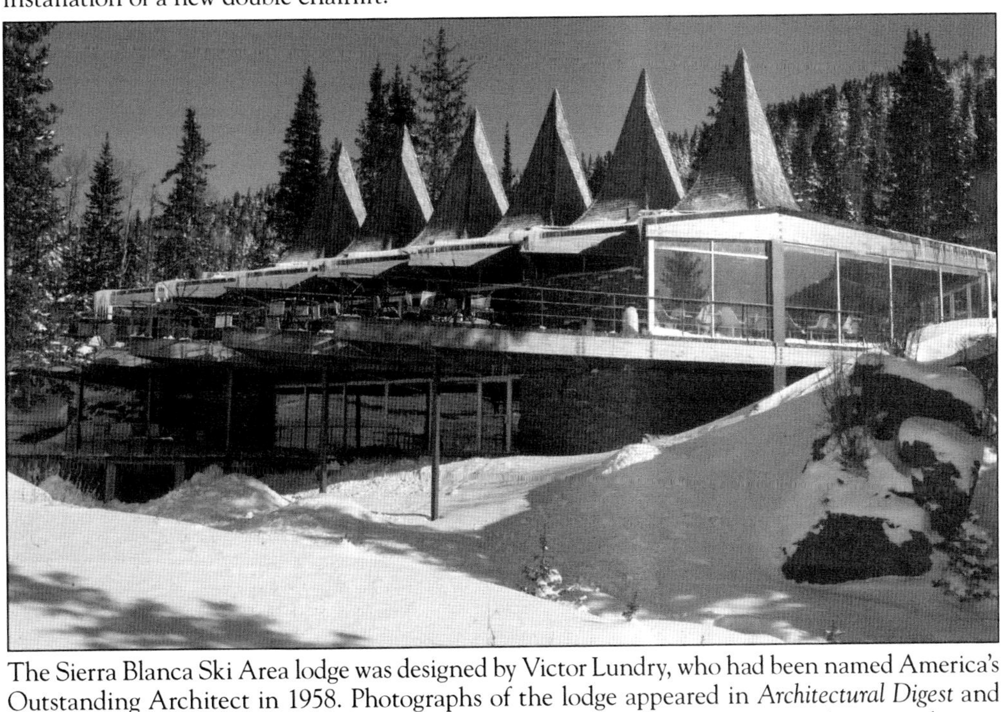

The Sierra Blanca Ski Area lodge was designed by Victor Lundry, who had been named America's Outstanding Architect in 1958. Photographs of the lodge appeared in *Architectural Digest* and *Sports Illustrated* in 1963. Lundry was known for his unusual roof treatments. The pointed cones on the lodge's roof suggest mountain peaks.

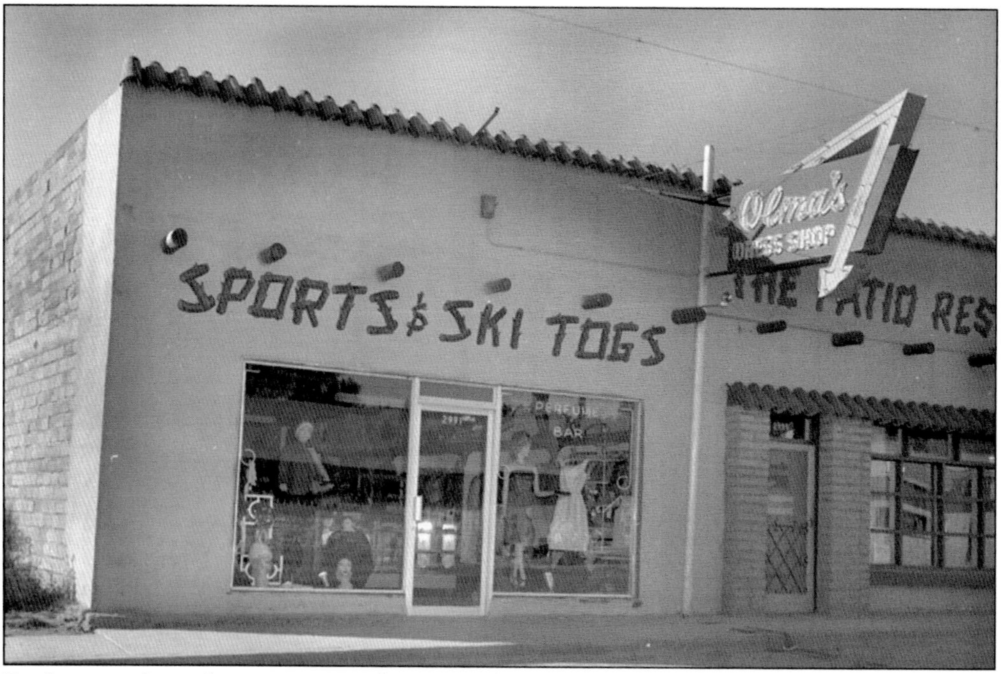

Ruidoso merchants lost no time in adapting to their new skier clientele. Jackets, boots, and poles were often squeezed in with Indian pottery and jewelry. Olma's Dress Shop, offering sports and ski togs, was located east of the intersection of Sudderth Drive and Center Street. These photographs date from the early 1960s.

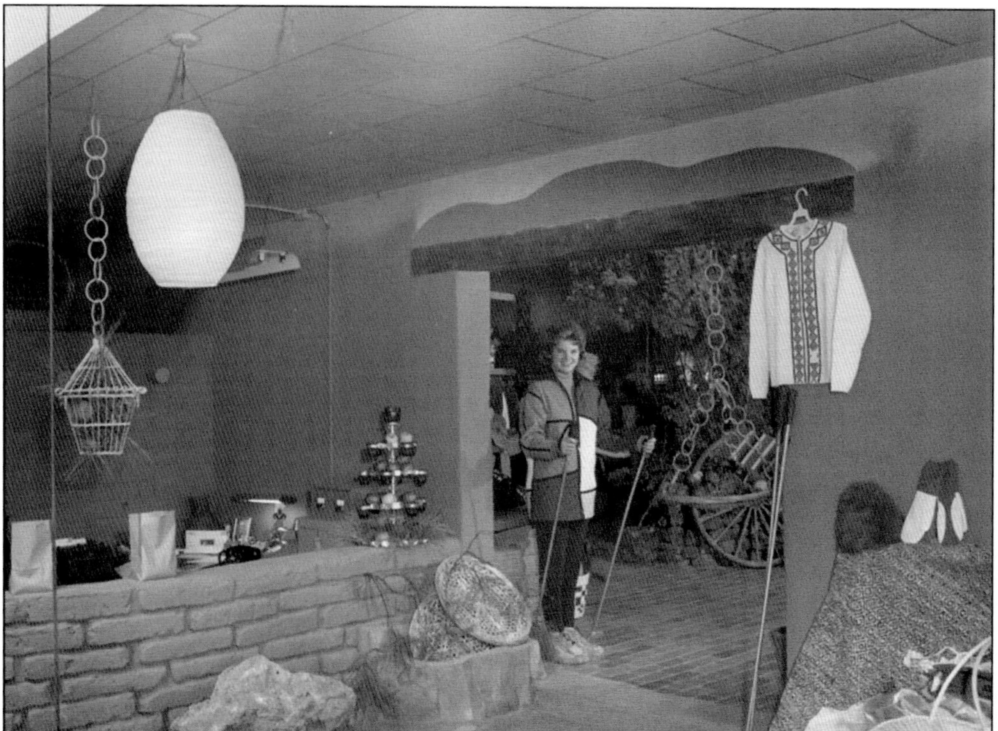

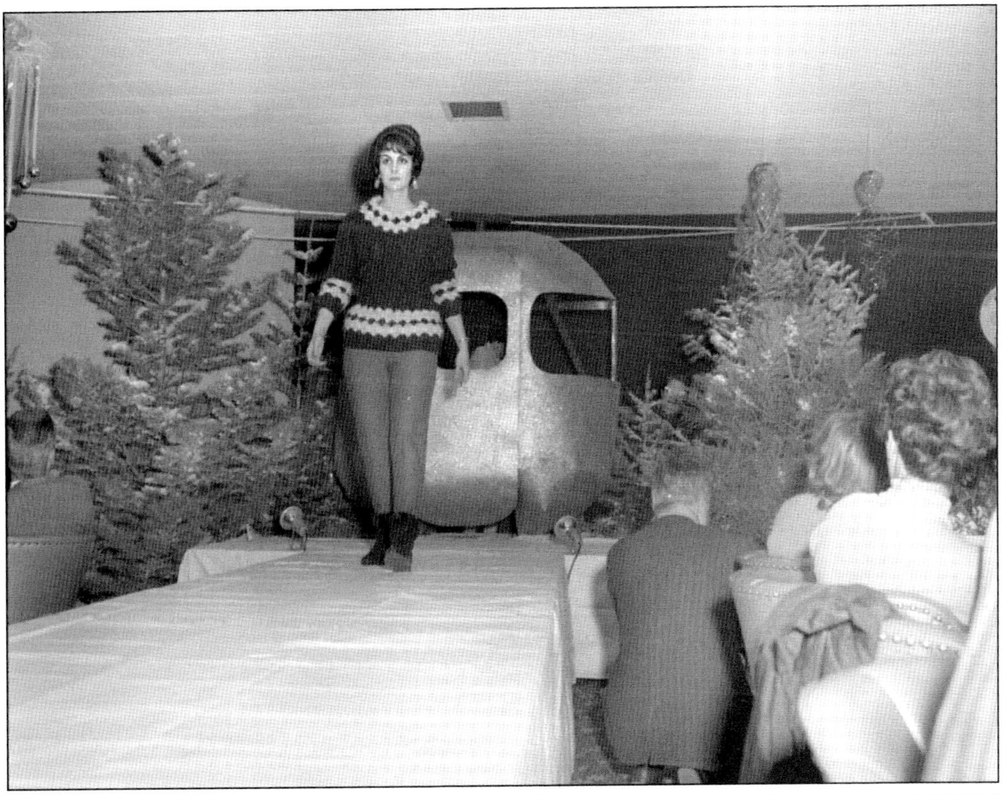

Of course, a new ski area meant creating a new event. The Ski-O-Doso Pageant was held in late November for several years, usually featuring a fashion show, beauty pageant, banquet, and dance. This modest gathering took place in 1962. The papier-mâché gondola car celebrated the installation of the Swiss-made gondola at the ski area that year.

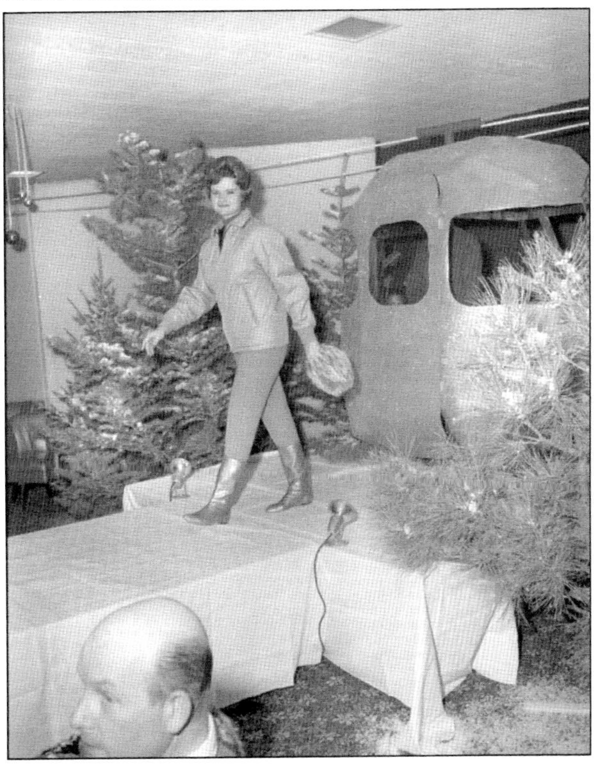

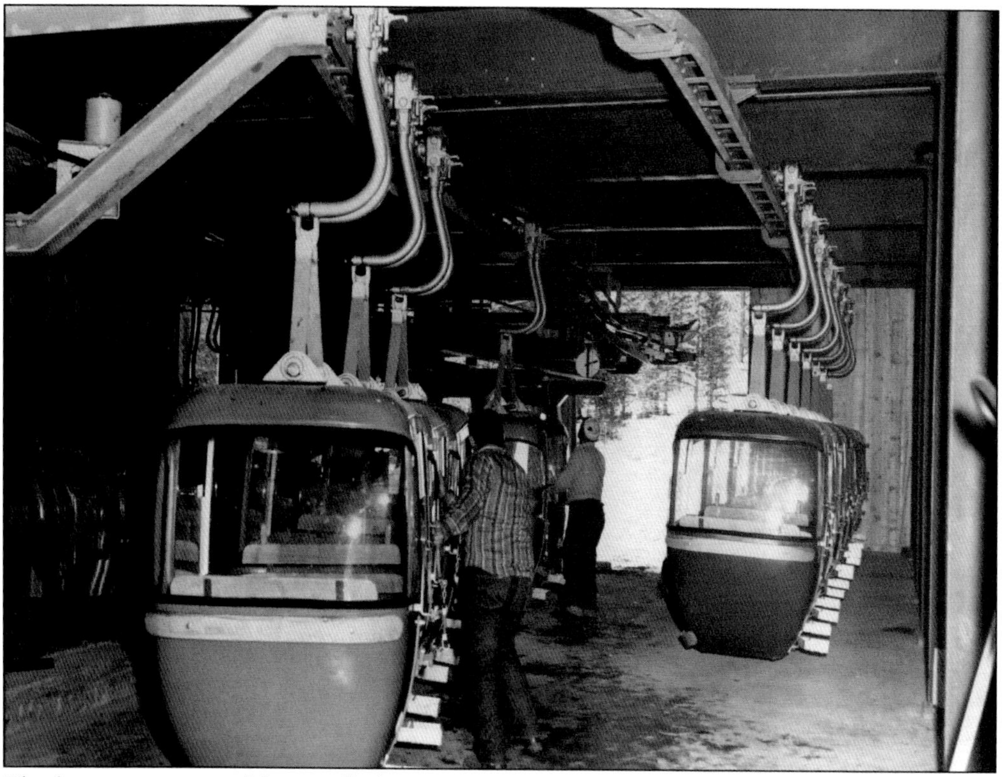

The four-passenger gondola, installed in 1962, was such a novelty that hundreds of people came to ride it in the summer, as well as for special moonlight rides in the winter. In 2012, it was damaged during the Little Bear Fire and replaced by an eight-passenger Apache Arrow gondola, made by the Austrian company Doppelmayr. As of 2014, it was still the only gondola in New Mexico.

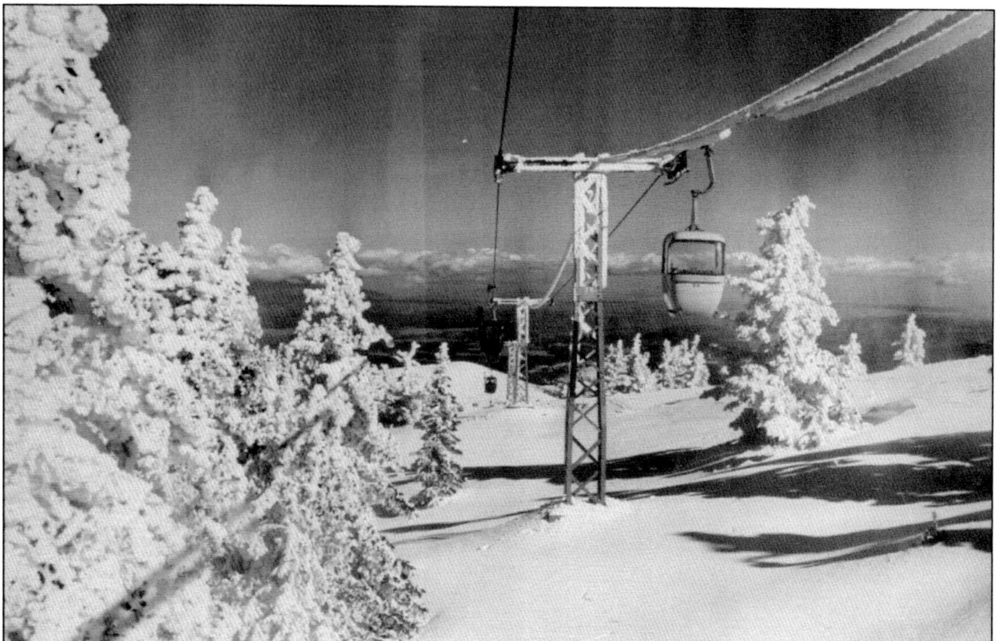

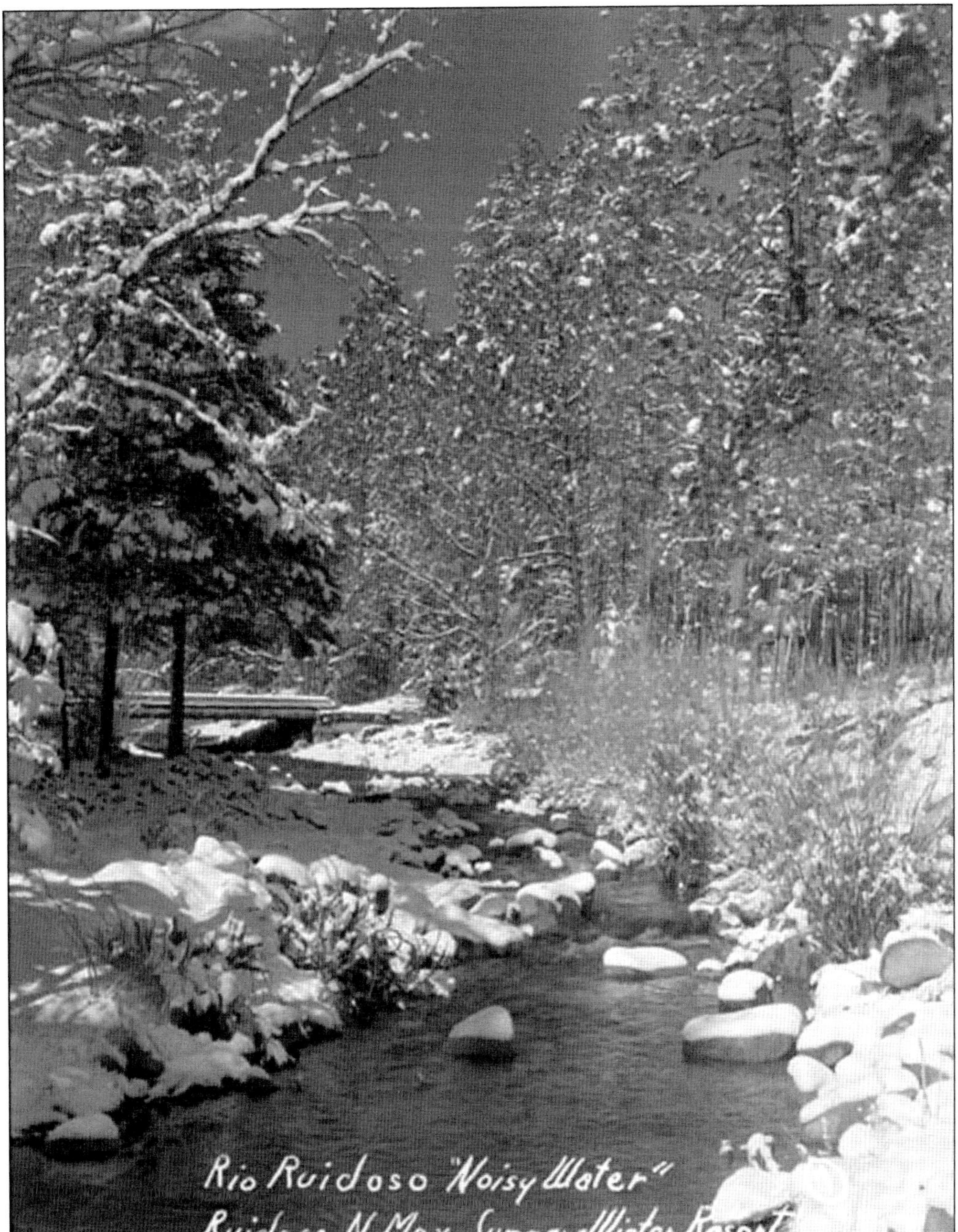

For those seeking less strenuous pleasures, Ruidoso offers beautiful mountain scenery in any season. Carmon Phillips made it his life's work to capture the beauty of the river and mountains.

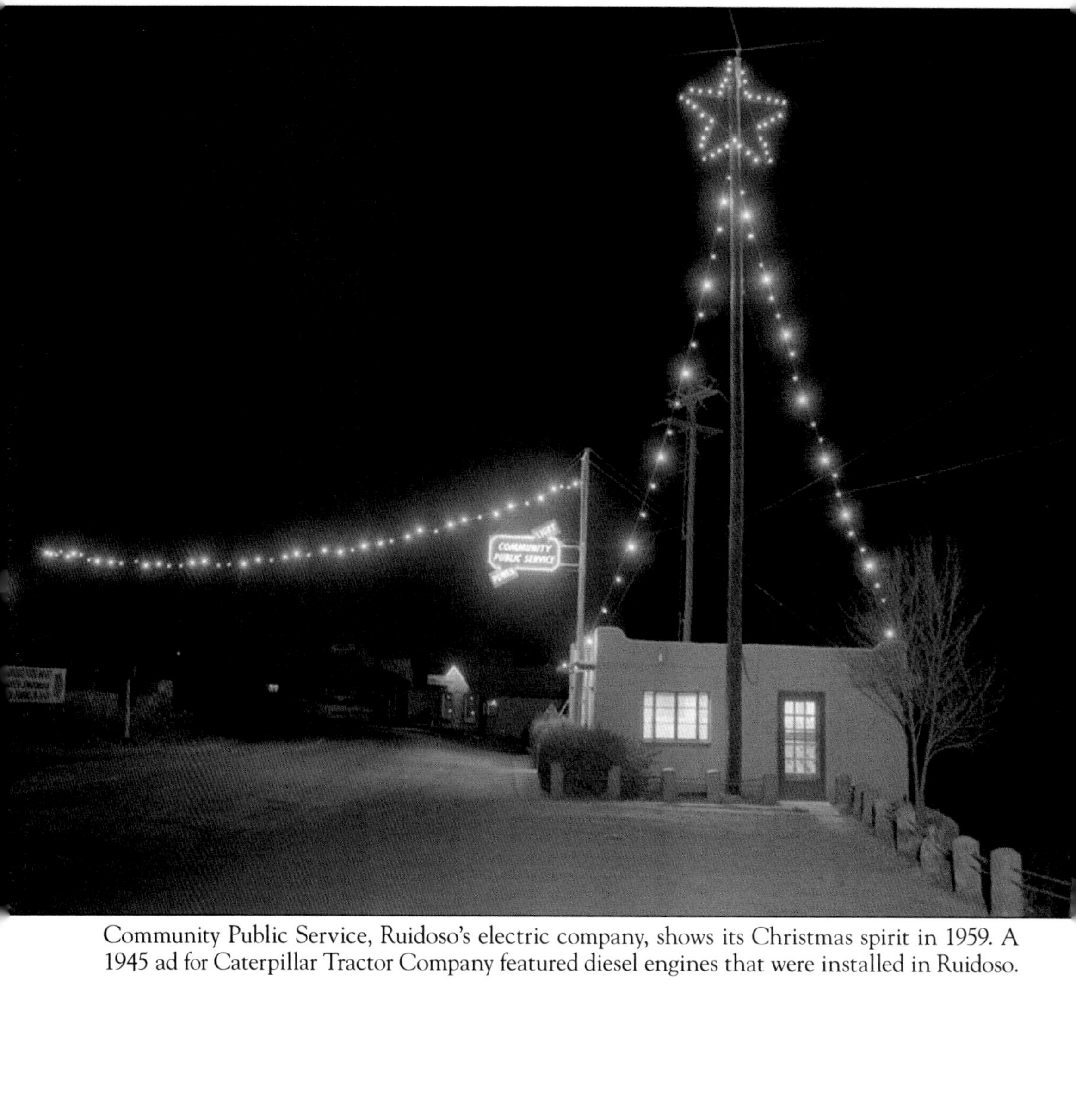

Community Public Service, Ruidoso's electric company, shows its Christmas spirit in 1959. A 1945 ad for Caterpillar Tractor Company featured diesel engines that were installed in Ruidoso.

Six

A Little Mountain Community

Having a good time has always been Ruidoso's reason for existence. While coping—often in unusual ways—with the problems that every town or city faces, Ruidoso residents have prided themselves in their ability to solve problems.

A headline in the *Ruidoso News* in January 1947 asked, "Have You Done Your Part?" to elicit support for the completion of the Ruidoso school gymnasium. Residents donated "a day's work, money or materials" to complete the project, which had been started by the Civilian Conservation Corps. According to Dave Parks, work stopped when the program was disbanded after Pearl Harbor. "The toilets and showers were all installed, but there was no plumbing or septic tanks," he said. "Before we could use the building to play basketball, the team went out with shovels and dug holes for the septic tanks. People would see us, grab shovels, and start digging, too." The article went on to encourage the sale of tickets to the minstrel show, performed by the Lubbock Lions, the proceeds of which would cover the cost of stage curtains and chairs. That summer, Jack Hull donated the receipts from the Snack Shop's opening day to the gymnasium.

From its opening in 1950, the Ruidoso-Hondo Valley Hospital, built on land donated by the White Mountain Development Company, seemed to experience widespread financial difficulty. Requests for funds and donations of items like baby clothes and bedspreads went out periodically during its initial years of operation. Throughout the busy summer, Dan Dee Cabins loaned its cots to the hospital, and a Roswell funeral home provided a hearse for use as an ambulance. In 1952, a group of summer residents donated $1,800 to the hospital and challenged locals to match it, which, after several months, they managed to do. In 1955, the Hollywood Park racetrack (later, the Ruidoso Downs racetrack) donated a day's receipts to the hospital.

In 1954, the village admonished residents: "Due to a shortage of manpower, we will be unable to collect delinquent water bills from house to house as in the past."

The chamber of commerce sponsored fly-ins to encourage owners of private planes to visit the area. In 1950, the airport's dirt runway was paved, and Alto Road (later, Mechem Drive) was paved from the intersection of what is now Sudderth Drive to the airport. Carmon Phillips later referred to the festivities that accompanied this achievement as "the biggest celebration for the smallest amount of pavement ever laid," which was not quite two miles.

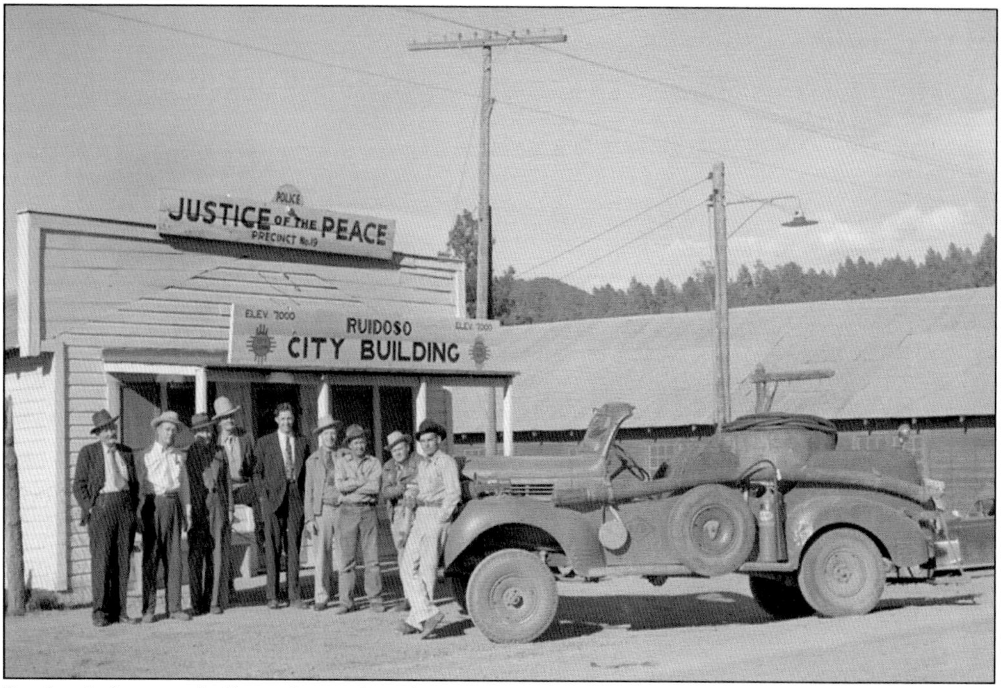

Ruidoso's first city hall was located at the corner of what is now Eagle and Sudderth Drives, in a building that had once been a grocery store. According to Betty Bennett, who grew up in the Ruidoso area, "This was the only fire truck." Second from left is George McCarty. Fourth from the left is "Pop" Ivey, the town marshal. Seen in the center is Mayor Dan D. Swearingin, wearing a tie and no hat, with Joe Dryden at his right. Joe Barajas is on the far right.

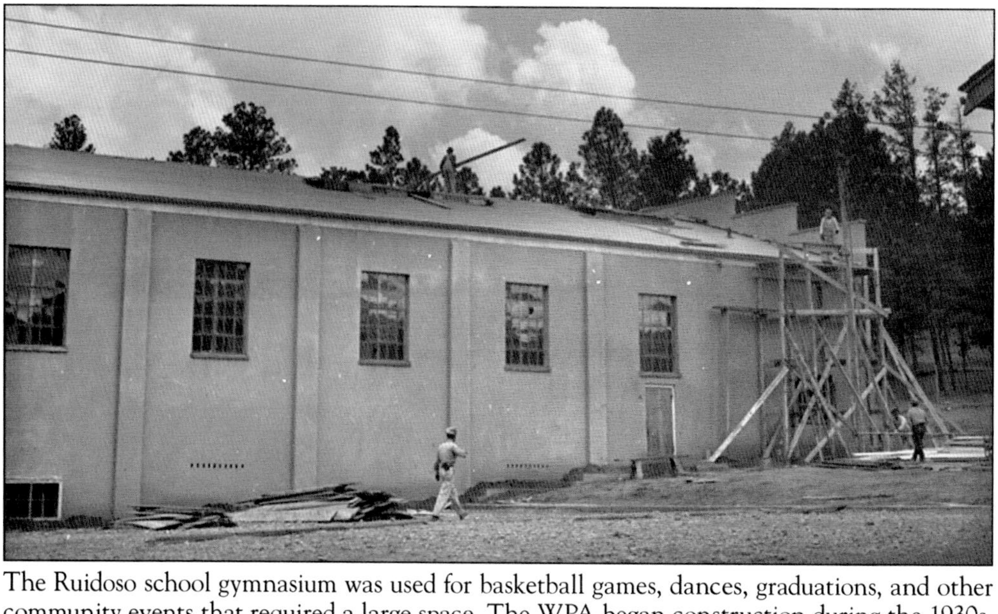

The Ruidoso school gymnasium was used for basketball games, dances, graduations, and other community events that required a large space. The WPA began construction during the 1930s, but the building was not completed until after World War II. The building was used for school and community functions until 1959, when a gymnasium was built next to the high school. The building was the Ruidoso Athletic Club in 2014.

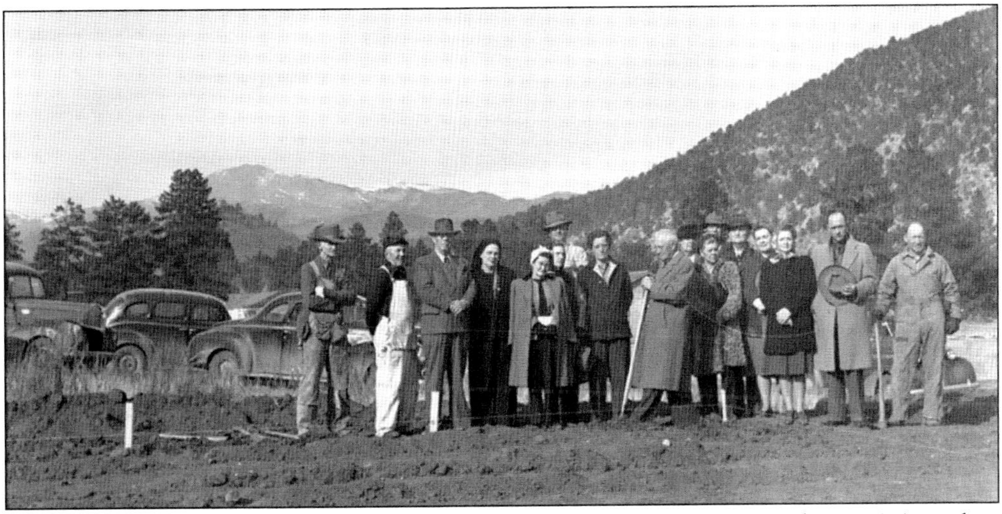

Church members break ground for the Community Methodist Church in December 1946. Attending the ceremony are, from left to right, F.H. Alexander, Harry Fairbanks, Lloyd P. Bloodworth, Ida Bloodworth, Mrs. Ike Kennedy, unidentified, Mrs. T.S. Barcus, W.D. Crosby, Mrs. Ike Wingfield, Dr. Thomas S. Barcus (with shovel), Mrs. Dan D. Swearingin, L.B. Autry, Mrs. Autry, Mrs. J.W. Bounds, Mrs. Joe Palmer, Mayor George McCarty, and Henry Verhaeghe. Until the new church was built, Methodists held services in the school.

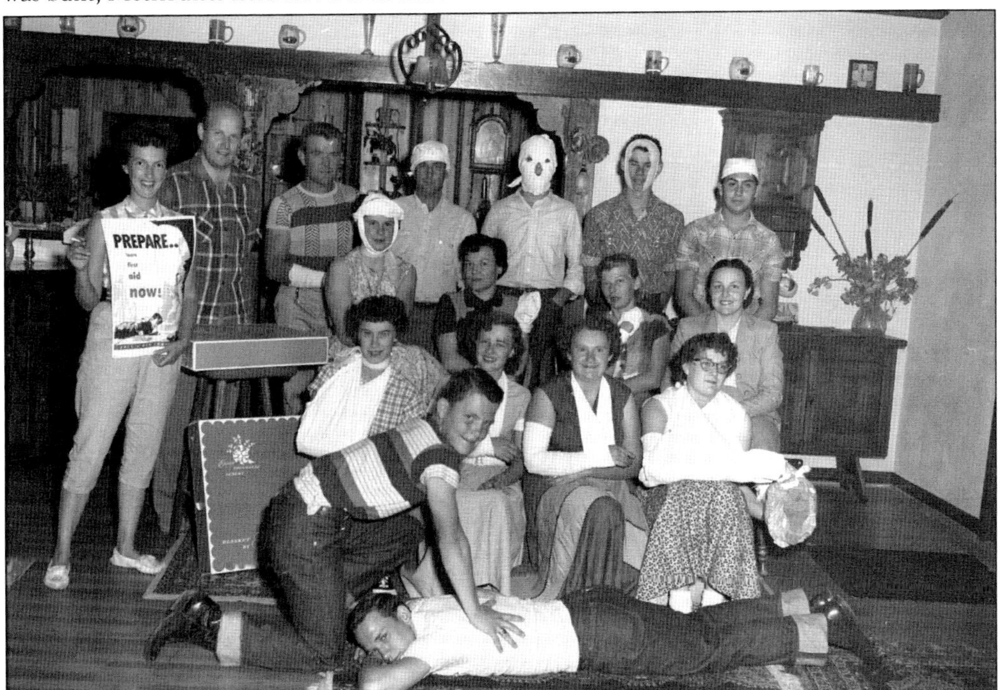

High school students participate in a first aid class around 1954. Max Jones kneels on the floor with an unidentified victim. From left to right are (first row) Linda Moore, Jo Betty Reese, Betty Bennett, and Mary Jo Hart; (second row) Mrs. Lucy Vanderstok, Dr. Bram Vanderstok, three unidentified, Billy Russell, and Bingo Morales. Vanderstok was a Dutch fighter pilot who escaped the Nazi prison, Stalag Luft III. The story was later told in the movie *The Great Escape*.

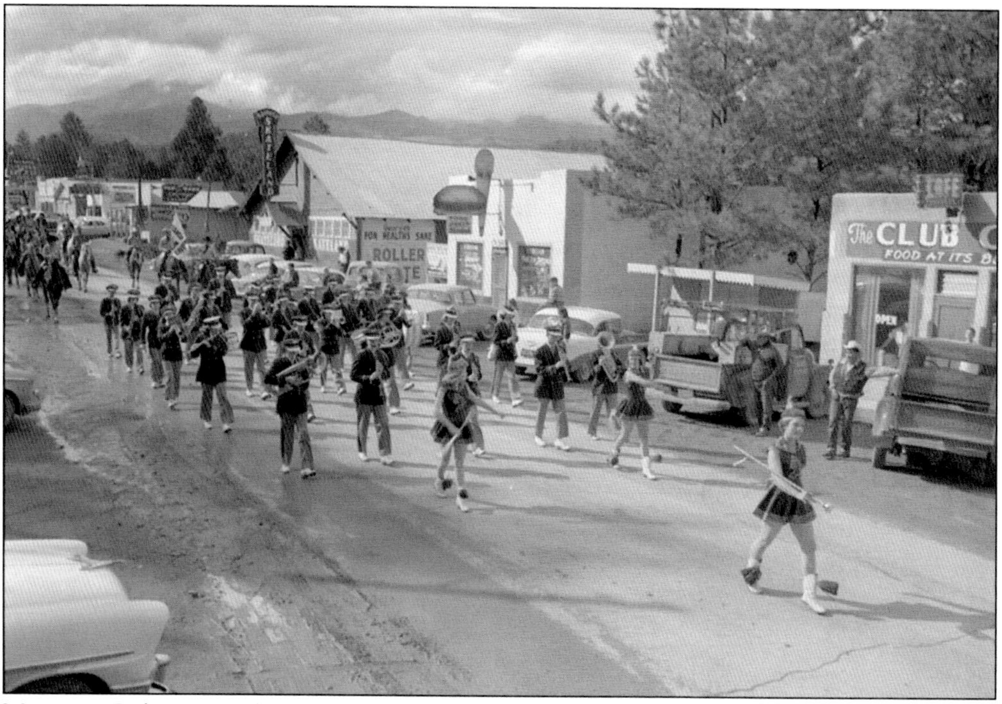

Majorette Judy Barajas leads the Ruidoso High School band in the 1958 Aspencade Parade. Aspencade began in 1947 as a horseback ride in the mountains to enjoy the fall foliage, especially the golden aspens. Over the years, the event has evolved into a local celebration marking the end of the busy summer season and the start of a new school year. Aspencade was ongoing as of 2014.

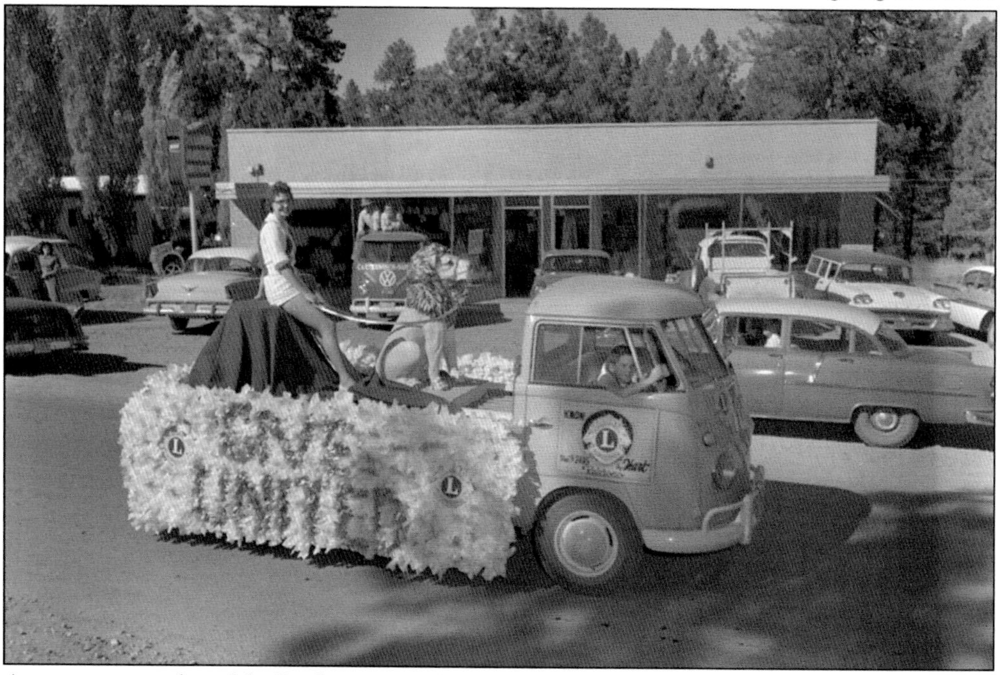

As an active member of the Ruidoso Lions Club, Carmon Phillips might have loaned his Volkswagen for the float on which Joanell Nosker is seen riding in the 1958 Aspencade Parade.

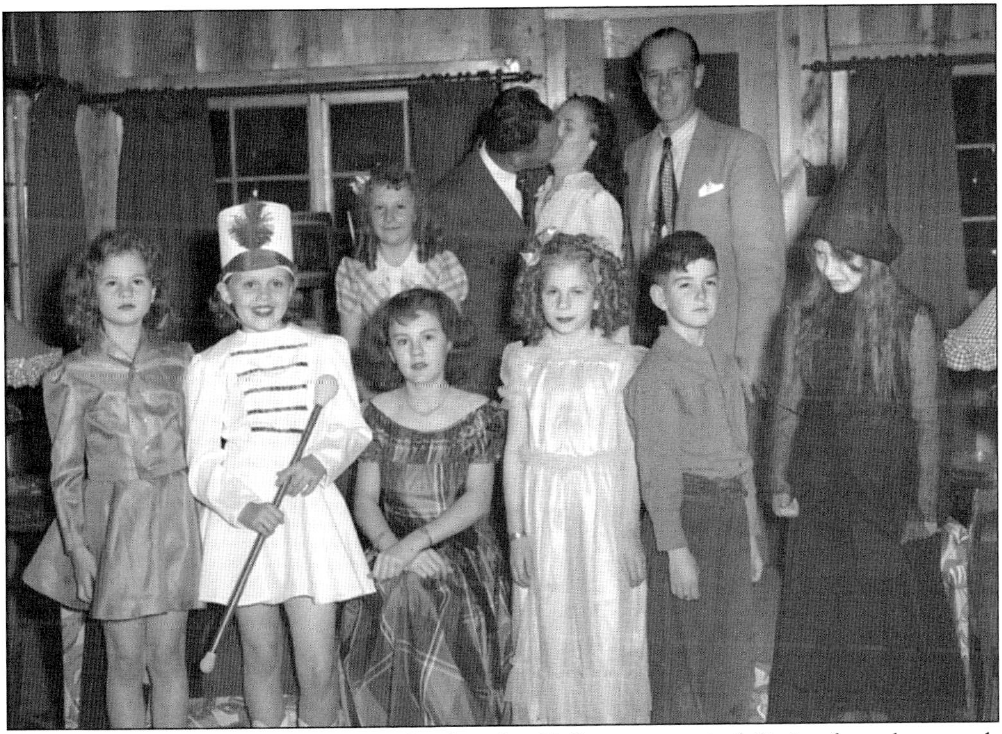

The PTA often raised money for the schools with a Halloween carnival. Posing for a photograph in 1947 are, from left to right, (first row) unidentified, Darlene Jones, two unidentified, Cecil Clark, and unidentified; (second row) Betty Bennett, an unidentified couple, and Carmon Phillips.

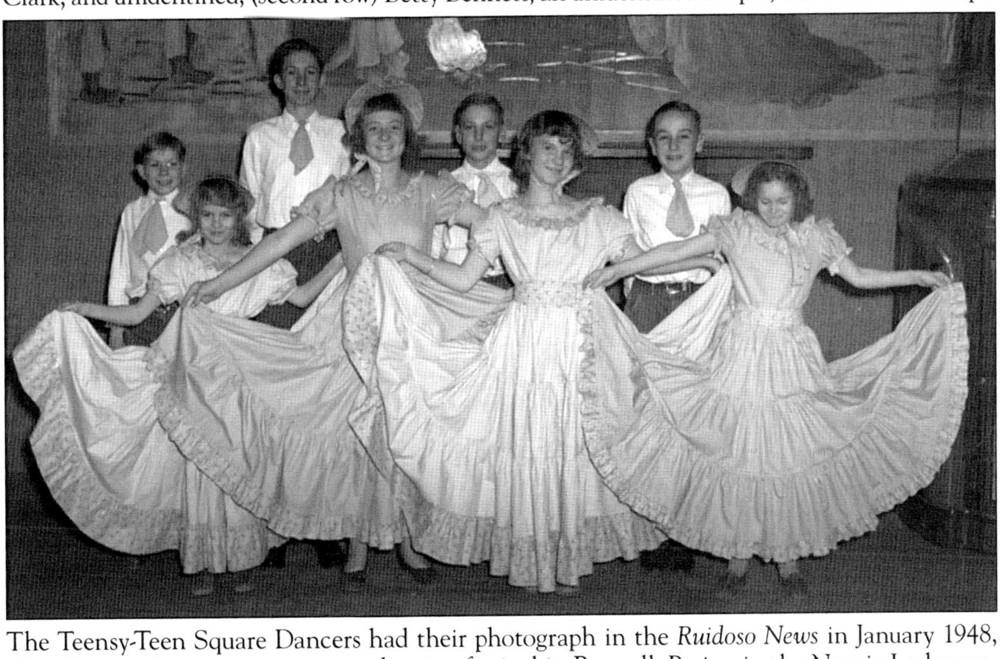

The Teensy-Teen Square Dancers had their photograph in the *Ruidoso News* in January 1948, after their performance at a square dancing festival in Roswell. Posing in the Navajo Lodge are, from left to right, (first row) Nancy Yates, Betty Boyce, Alice Yates, and Glenda Parsons; (second row) Harold Parsons, Don Parsons, Jackie Stanley, and Paul Stanley.

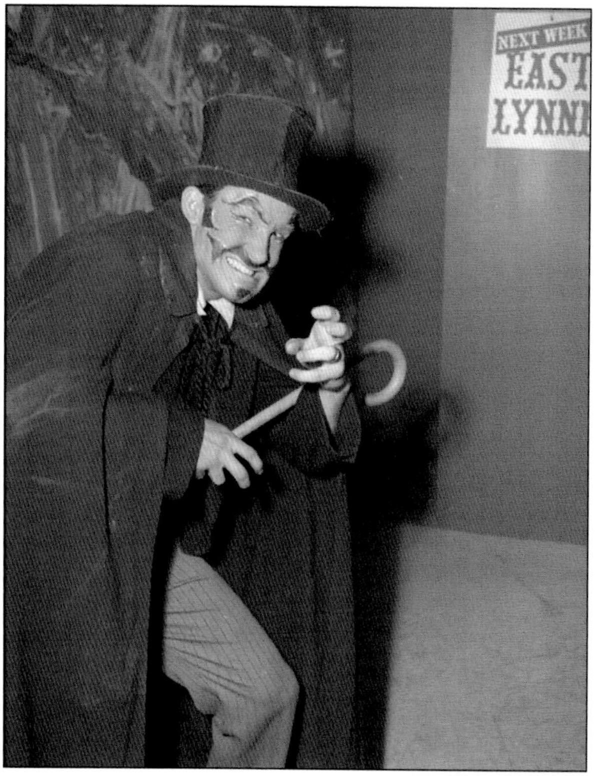

Amateur theatrical performances have always been popular in Ruidoso. Here, a group of unidentified actors perform a melodrama at the Navajo Lodge.

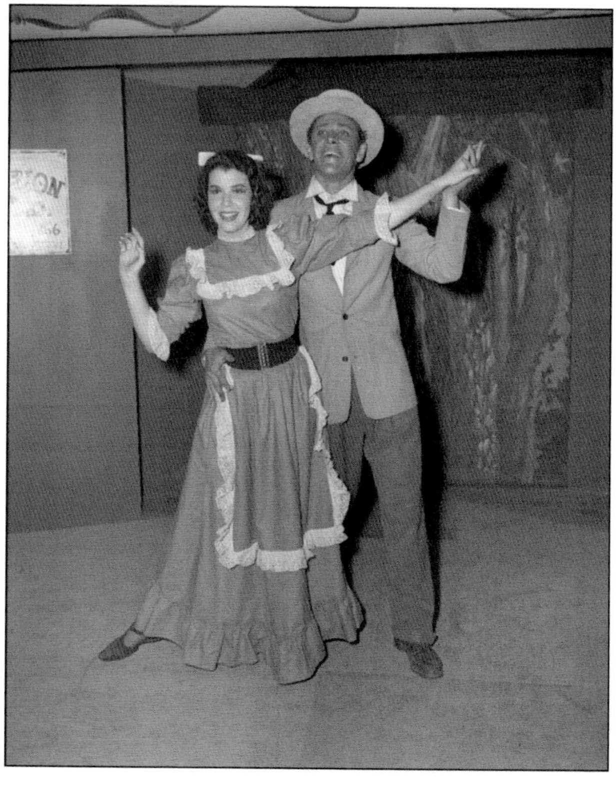

According to an article in the *Ruidoso News* in January 1946, "Mr. Henry Evans is 85 years old and bowls an outstanding game, often over 200 pins He is taking an active part in the newly organized bowling league and will be a team captain."

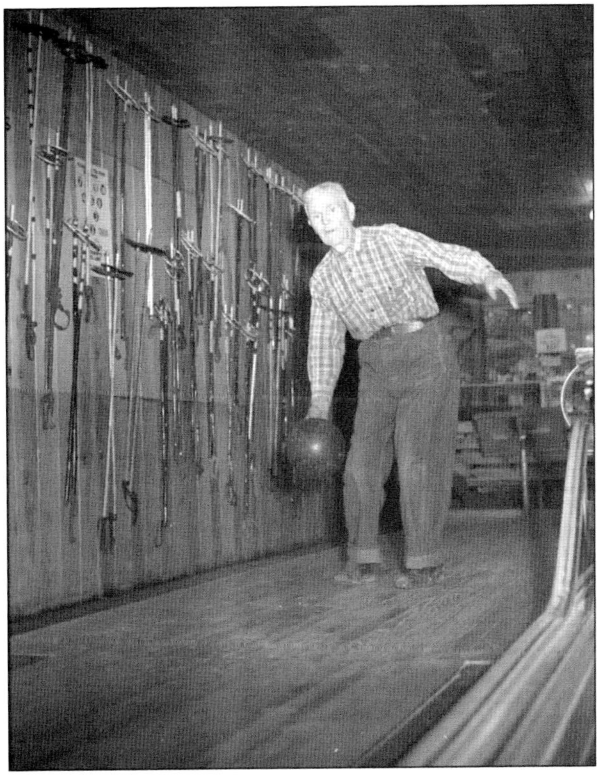

The bowling alley was located in the Ruidoso Clubhouse and Café, which also rented skis and toboggans in the winter. Built by the Hull family, it stood at the northeast corner of Main and Alto Roads (now Sudderth and Mechem Drives).

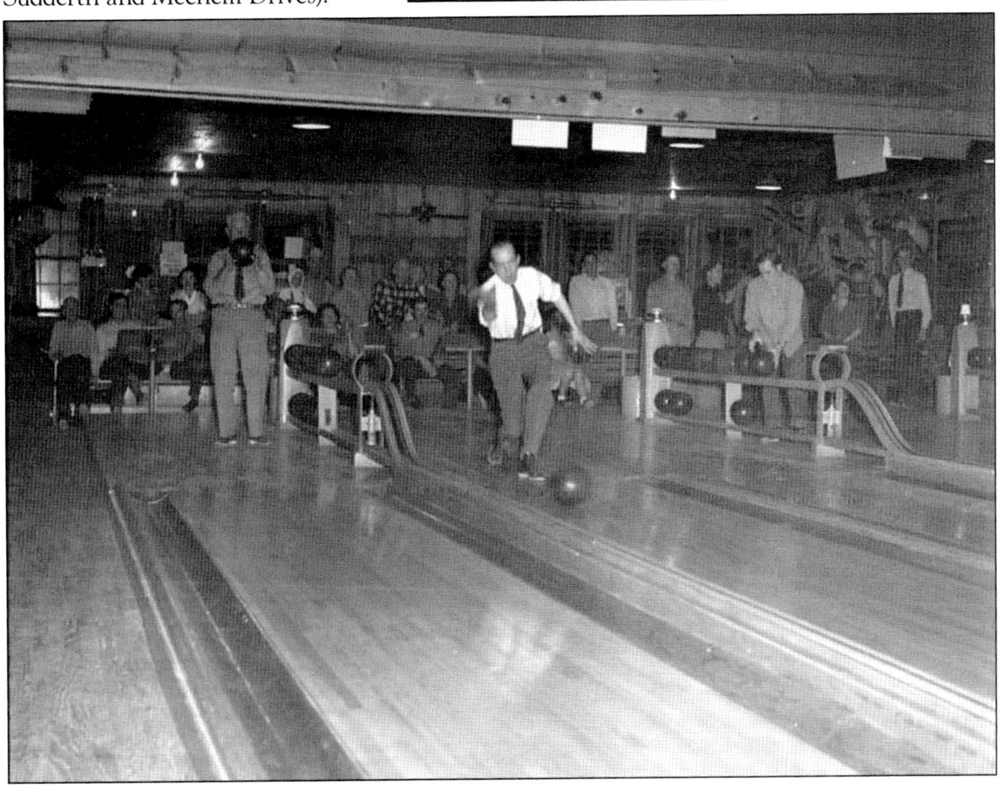

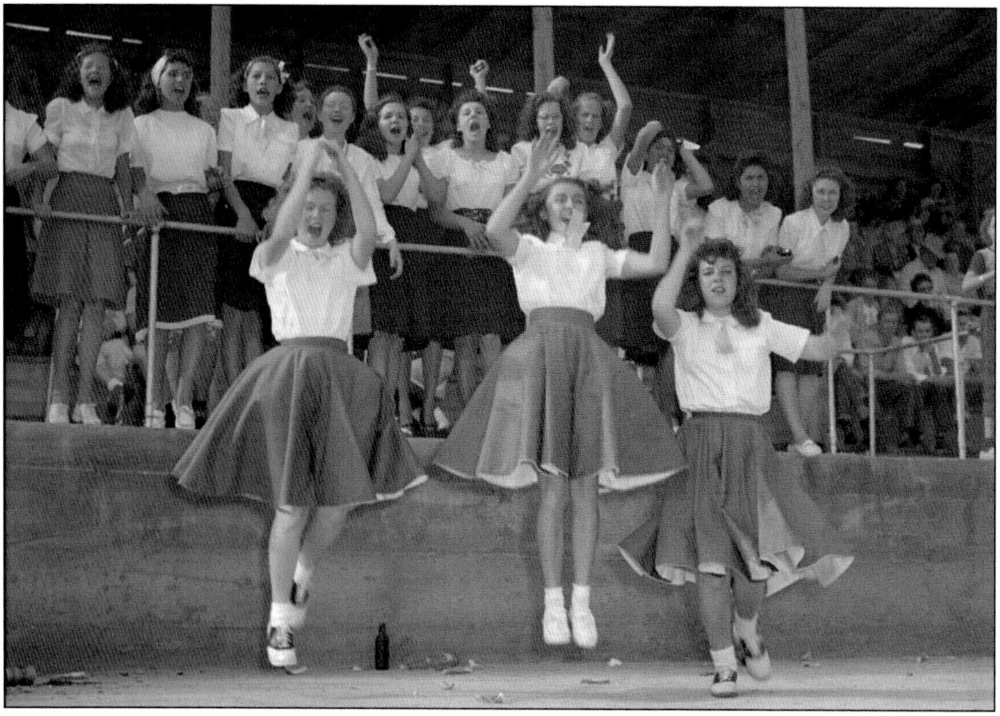

Cheerleaders rally the crowd for the Ruidoso Warriors. The only identified cheerleader is Mary Glenda Shook (center). Football games were played on the infield of the racetrack in 1947 and 1948. With the exception of summer, the field was also used as a pasture. As a member of the Ruidoso High School football team, Dave Parks would clean cow patties and rocks off the field with his teammates every Thursday afternoon before a game. Since there were no lights, games were played on Friday afternoons.

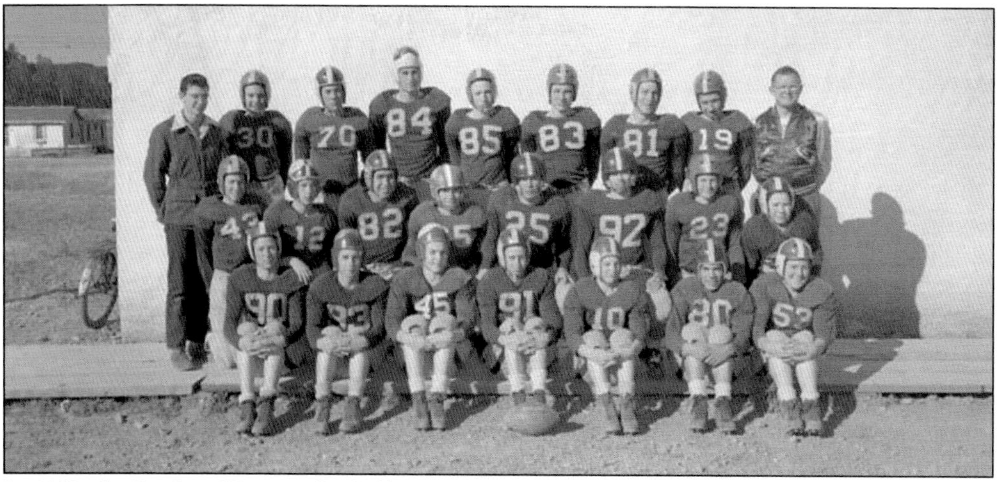

In 1950, the Ruidoso Warriors football team won its first state championship, with seven victories and one loss. The team consisted of, from left to right, (first row) Johnny Barajas, Bob Branson, Gene Nelson, Merle Riley, Buck Morrison, Miltone Sanchez, and Rex Whiteley; (second row) Dean Holman, J.W. Peterson, Joe Gallegos, Amon Ray Clarke, Wade Hedgecoke, Dave Parks, Scotty Haley, and Robert Rains; (third row) manager Bill Don Knox, George Perry, Herbert Carter, Jan McElhaney, Kirby Lewis, Marion Gayden, Wayne Lewis, Ronald Steward, and coach Cy Leland.

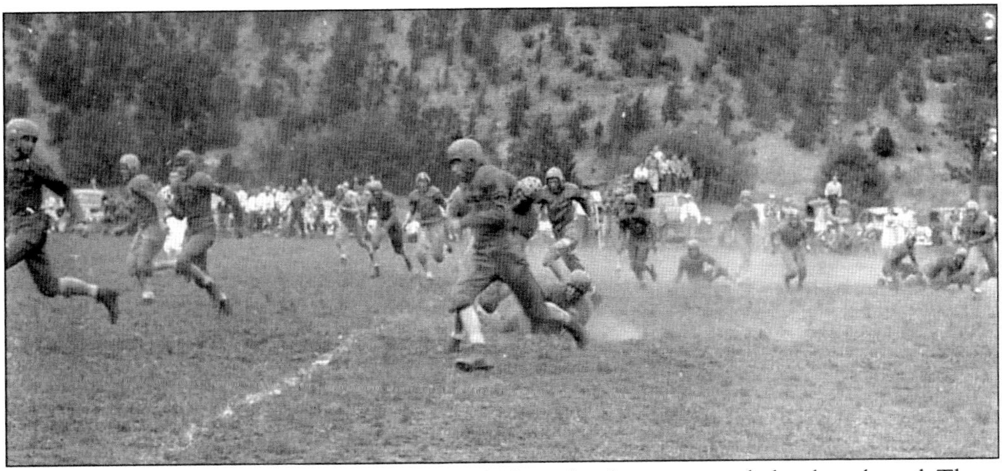

When the high school was about to open in 1946, a school mascot needed to be selected. There was a contest, at a penny a vote, for everyone in town to choose his or her favorite. Ida Bloodworth, wife of the newspaper publisher, thought the team should be called "the Snowballs." Dave Parks, who was a freshman in the new high school, recalled, "All the guys who were going to be on the football and basketball teams ran around town, working to collect votes for 'the Warriors'—anything but 'the Snowballs.' "

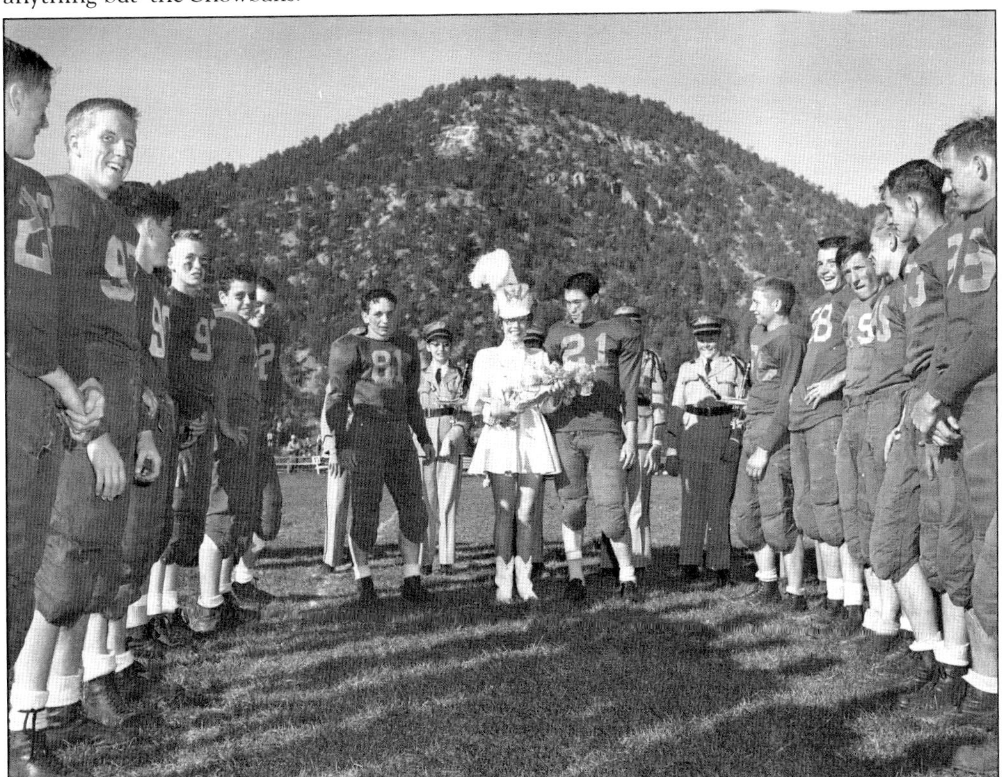

Drum majorette Shirley Holmes was crowned homecoming queen in September 1954. Posing with her are, Nyles Lackey (left, No. 81) and Glen Westfall (whom she later married, No. 21). Made of rocks and white paint, the letter "R" near the top of the mountain in the background would be repainted by high school students for the next 60 years.

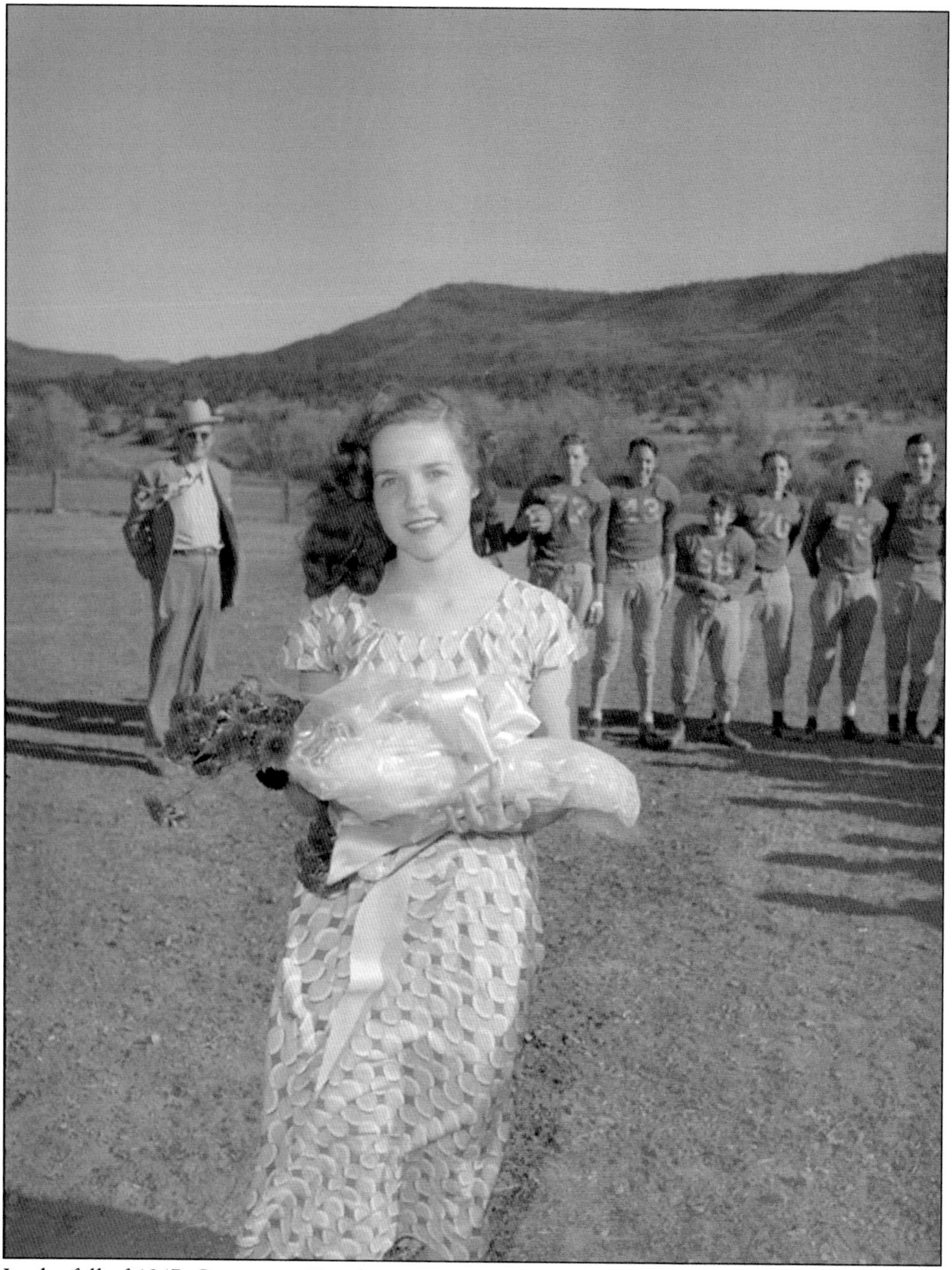

In the fall of 1947, Genevieve Hensley was crowned Ruidoso High School's first homecoming queen. Seen in the background at left, coach Cy Leland had been a halfback and quarterback at Texas Christian University as well as a member of the Southwest Conference Championship team in 1930. In 1952 and 1953, he was the announcer for the Texas Western College football games, broadcast by KEPO, El Paso.

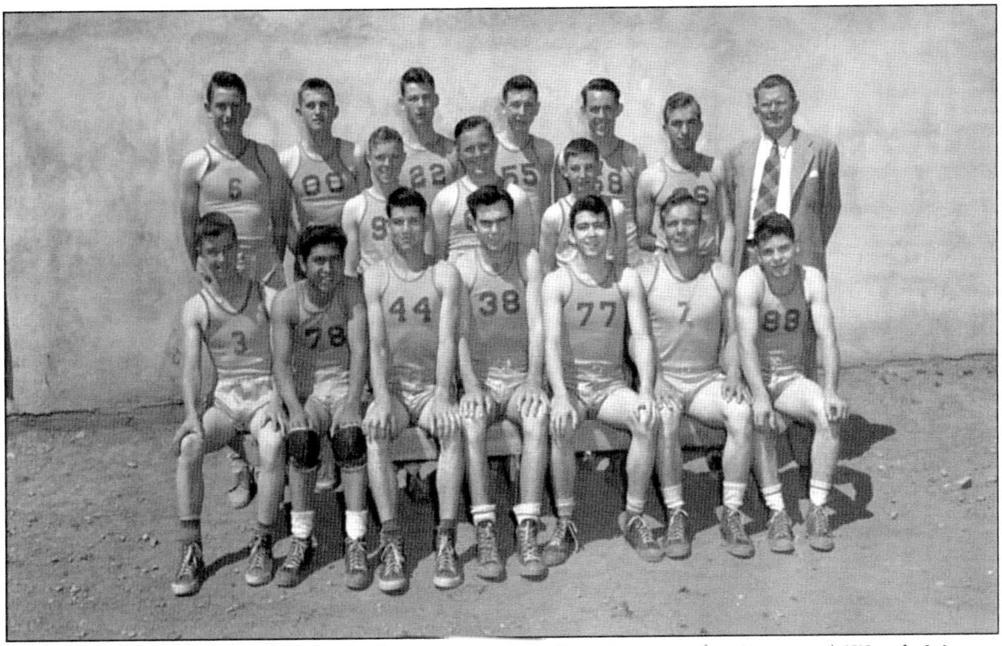

The Ruidoso High School basketball team included, from left to right, (first row) Woody Moore, Joe Gallegos, Jim Veater, Bob Langford, Dave Parks, Wade Hedgecoke, and Ray Clarke; (second row) Clayton Scott, Rex Whitely, and Buck Morrison; (third row) Harold Perry, Jan McElhaney, Jack Veater, Buzz Page, Wallace Whitely, George Neel, and coach Cy Leland.

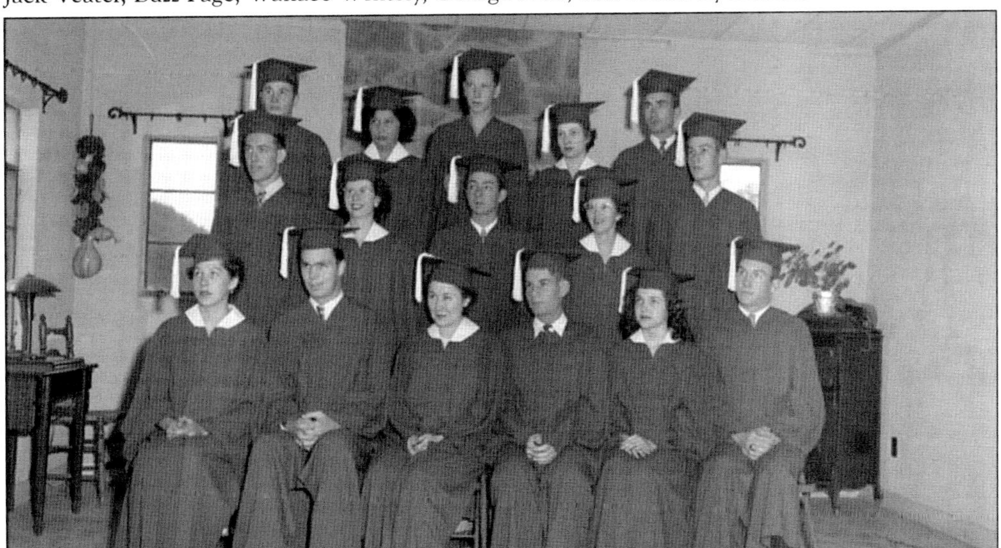

The Ruidoso High School class of 1950 poses in the home economics room. They are, from left to right, (first row) Rowena Coe, Bob Langford, Jimmie Ruth Gayden, Jim Veater, Genevieve Hensley, and Richard Ridgeway; (second row) Wallace Whiteley, Marilyn MacKay, Norman Whitman, Audrey Peterson, and Jack Veater; (third row) Don Alexander, Cleeta Hosetosavit, Buzz Page, Georgetta Akin, and George Neel.

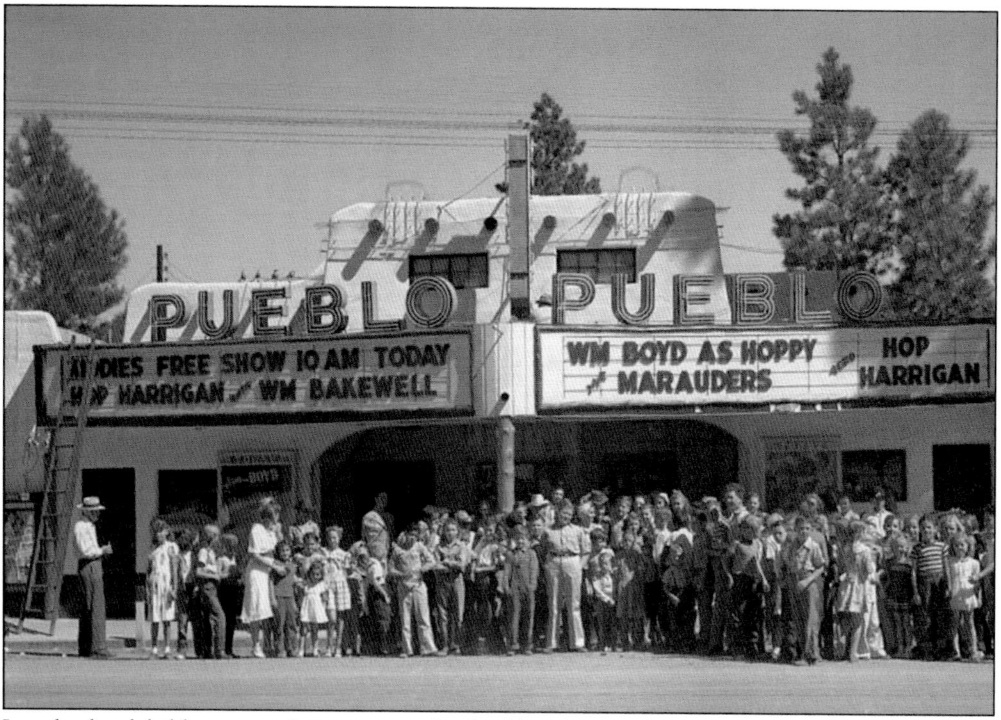

Local schoolchildren attend a movie at the Pueblo Theater, built by the Blaylocks. In 2014, it housed Books, Etc.

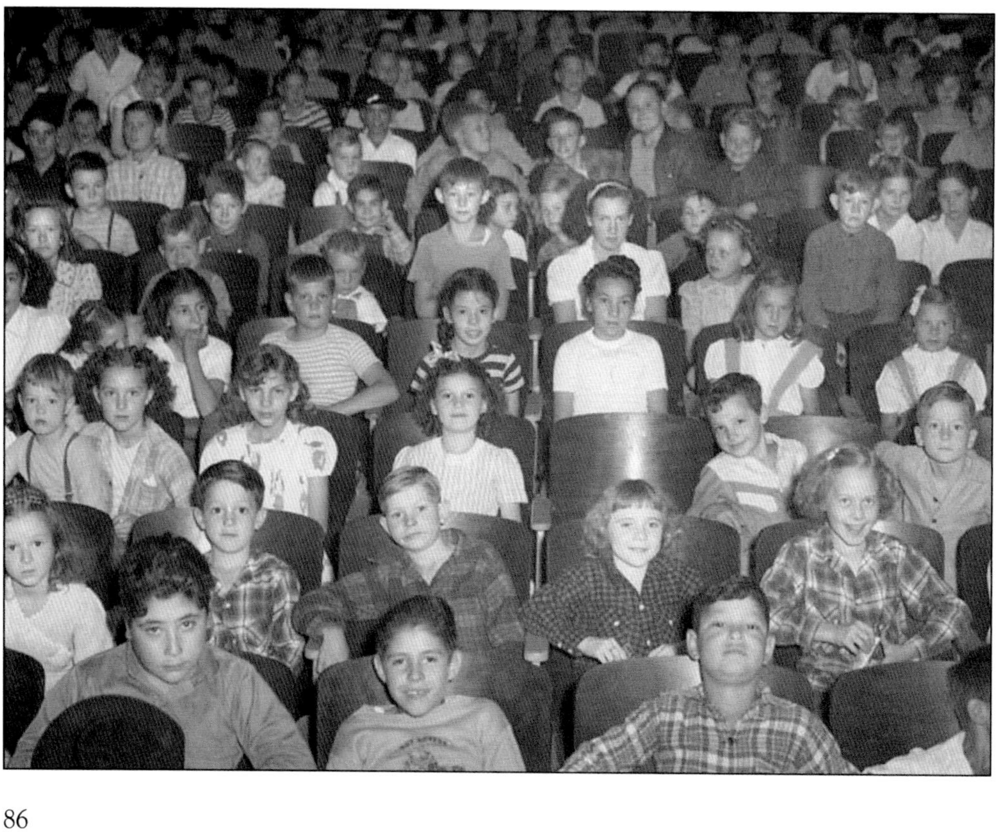

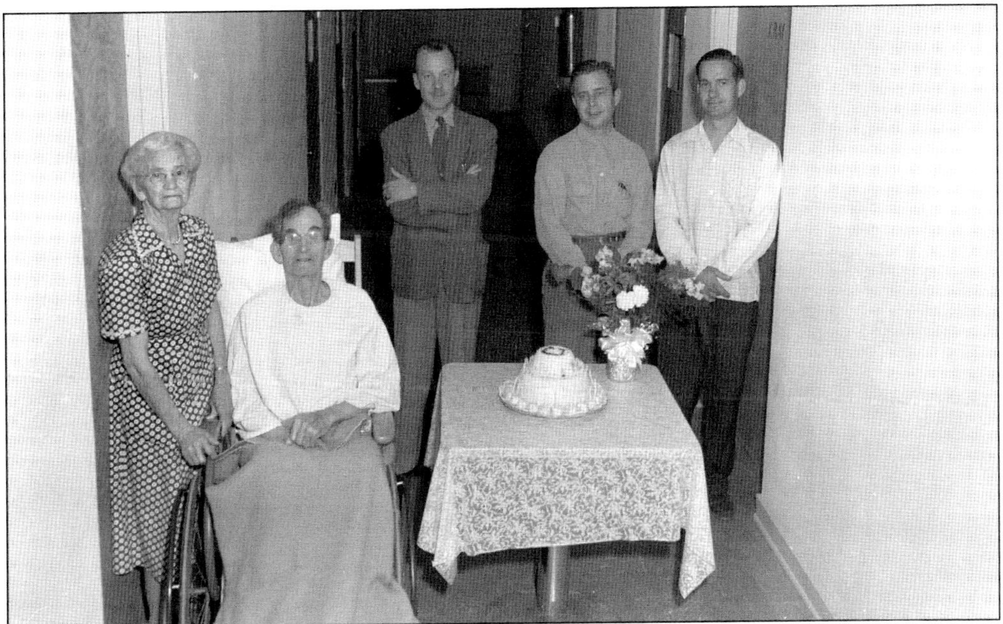

An unidentified patient and his visitor celebrate with, from left to right, Dr. Don Snyder, Dr. Willie B. Horton, and Dr. Larry Moore. As friends, Snyder and Horton moved to Ruidoso, together with their wives, in 1947. They all lived in a two-story building that also housed the doctors' office on the first floor. The village water system had not yet reached their neighborhood, so they hauled drinking water from a spring near the Thunderbird Lodge.

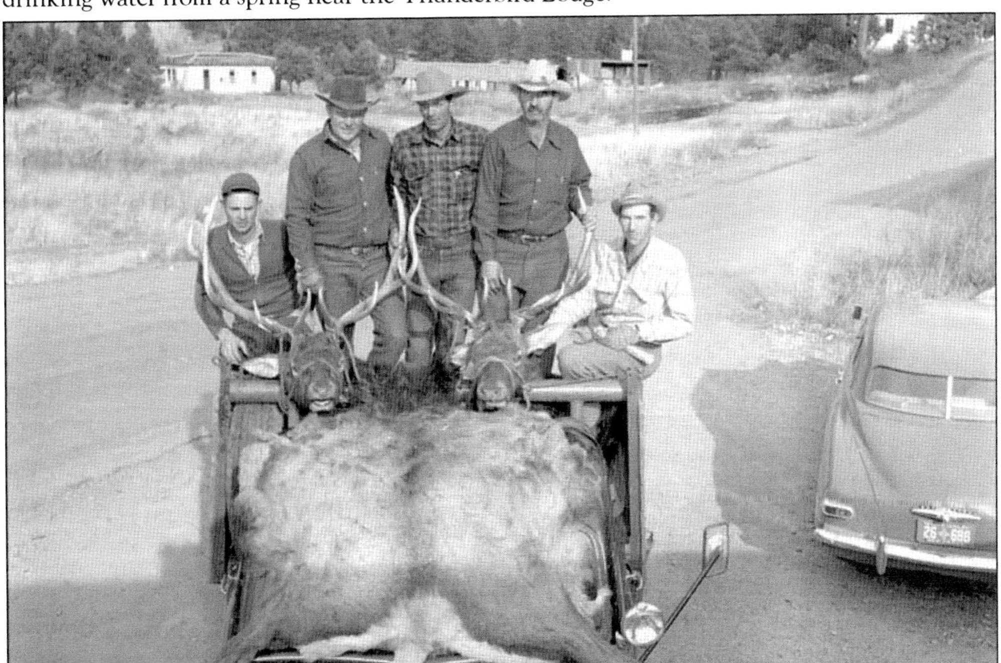

Men in a hunting party from the Hondo Valley display their elk. They are, from left to right, Roy Lamay, George Perry, Ralph Bonnell, Bert Pfingsten, and Fred "Peg" Pfingsten. The Sacramento Mountains are home to elk, deer, bears, and wild turkeys.

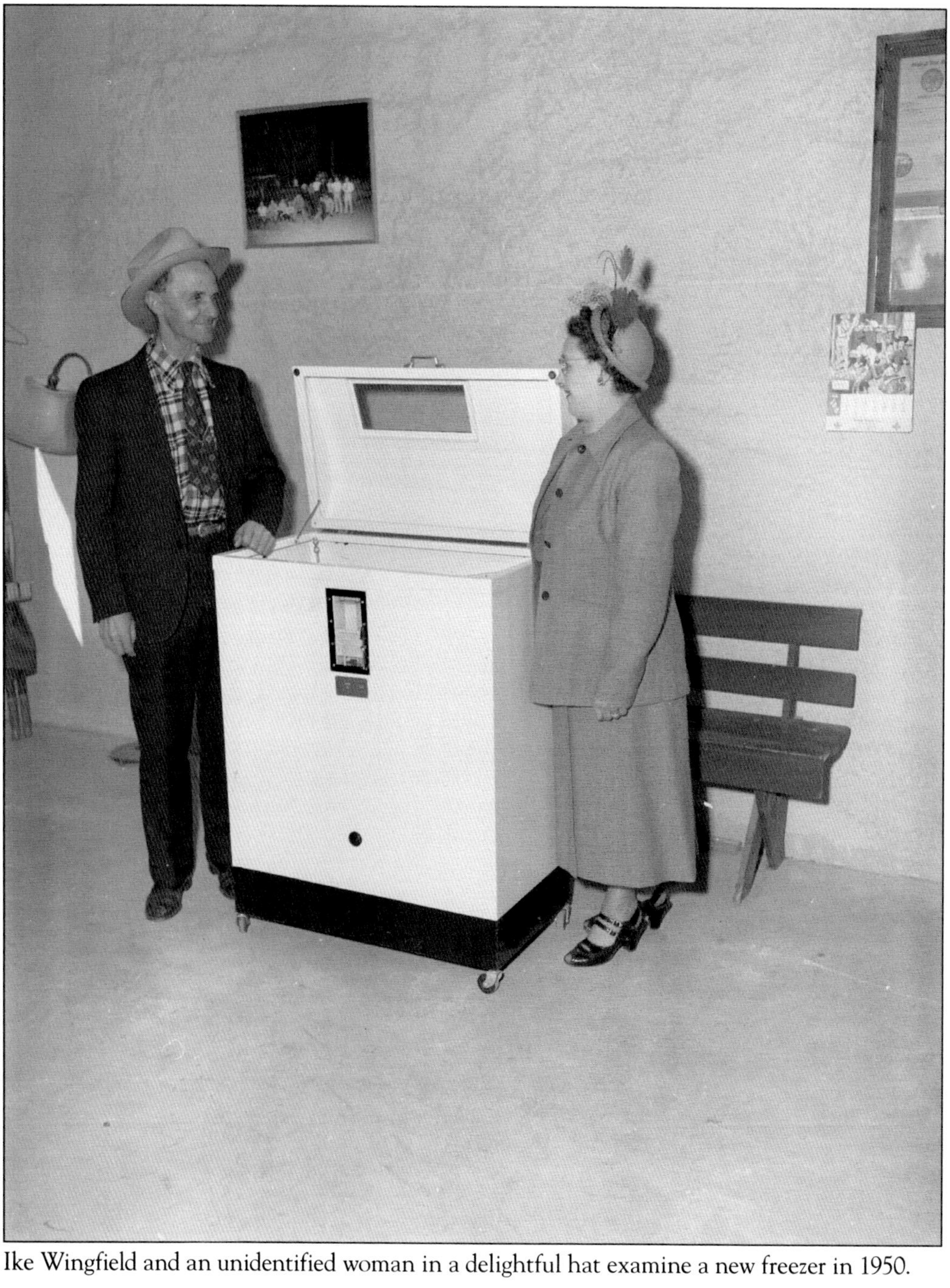

Ike Wingfield and an unidentified woman in a delightful hat examine a new freezer in 1950.

Seven

The Business of Business

Carmon Phillips was both a practical man and a businessman, dedicated to the idea of businesses working together to improve their community as well as their own business at the same time. As a photographer, he documented all types of establishments, giving the same attention to a laundry as an art gallery.

While working as a theater manager, he wrote a set of instructions for running a successful theater. One bit of advice was detailed as follows: "Take two or three hours off in the afternoon and visit with the various merchants in your town. Mind you—just visit—nothing else." His point was to understand the other person's point of view.

People remember Carmon Phillips as a quiet, thoughtful, and cheerful man. In giving his advice, he went on to say, "When you walk down the street, smile, even if it hurts, and speak to everyone you meet on the streets, whether you know them or not. Maybe business is bad—a frown on your face won't help."

Joan Bailey, executive director of the Ruidoso Valley Chamber of Commerce from 1970 to 2001, remembered visits from Phillips to her office. "I always made time for Carmon. He would just stop by for a brief visit, but he always had something interesting to talk about. And he always wore moccasins, so I could hear his soft footsteps coming down the hall. Carmon was always thinking of other people. He took time, busy as he was, to enjoy his life here. You were always a little happier after a conversation with him. He very quietly did very important things."

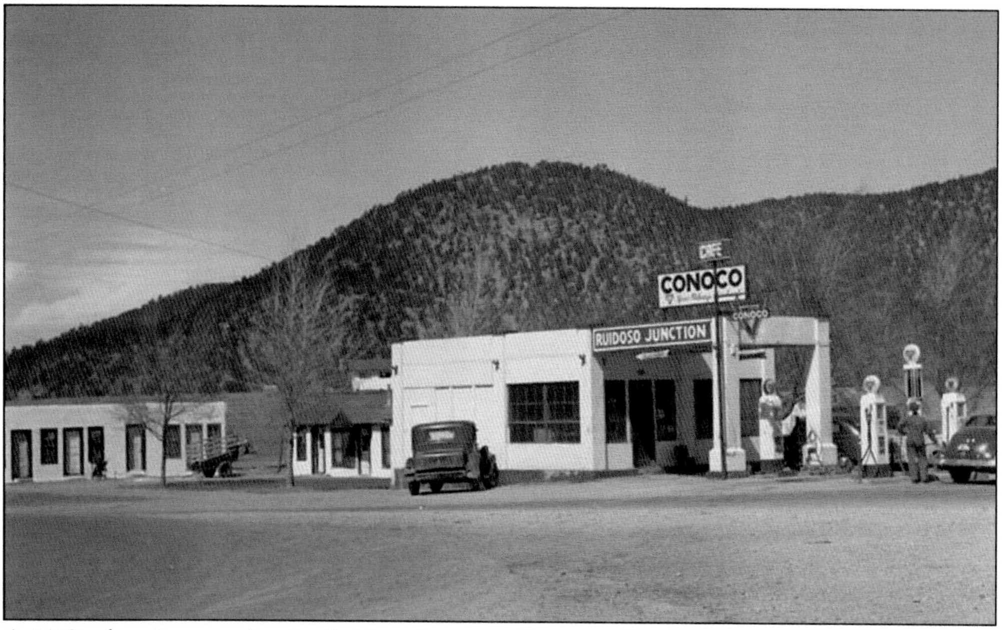

A 1947 advertisement for the Ruidoso Junction Station offered taxi service, tires, tubes, gas, oil, cabin rentals, café service, and Indian jewelry. The Ruidoso Junction was the bus stop and often the first bit of Ruidoso that travelers would encounter. It stood at the spot where Sierra Blanca Motors was in 2014. Junction Road was the first, and for many years the only, road from Highway 70 into Ruidoso.

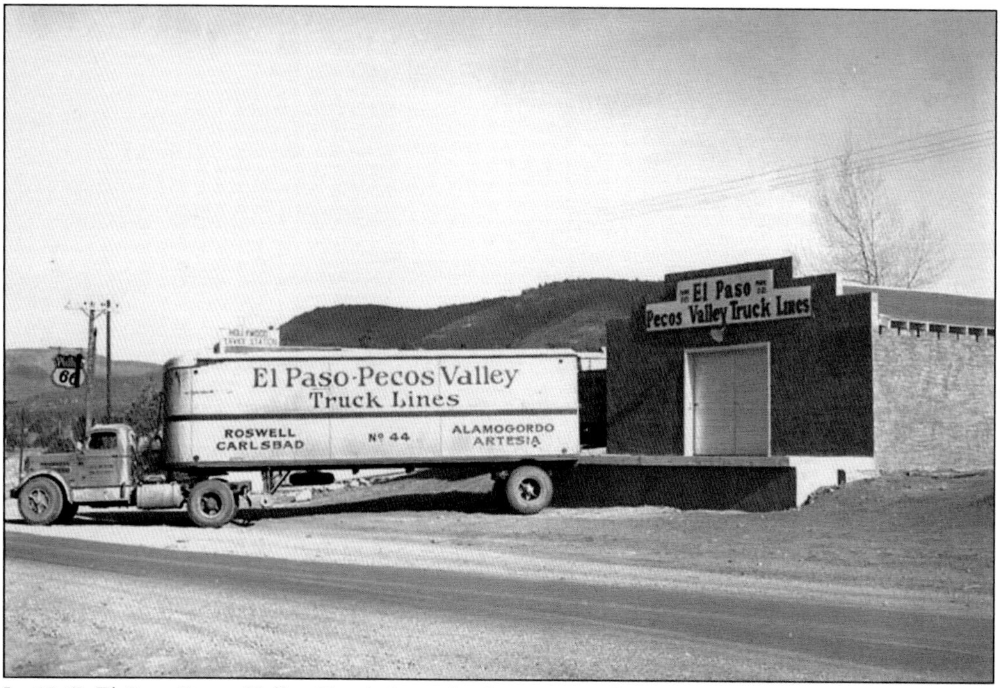

In 1947, El Paso-Pecos Valley Truck Lines built a terminal in Hollywood, a small community between Ruidoso and Ruidoso Downs. The company was started in 1923, when the only stores in town were Ike Wingfield's. By 1929, there was enough trade for the town to warrant its own agent.

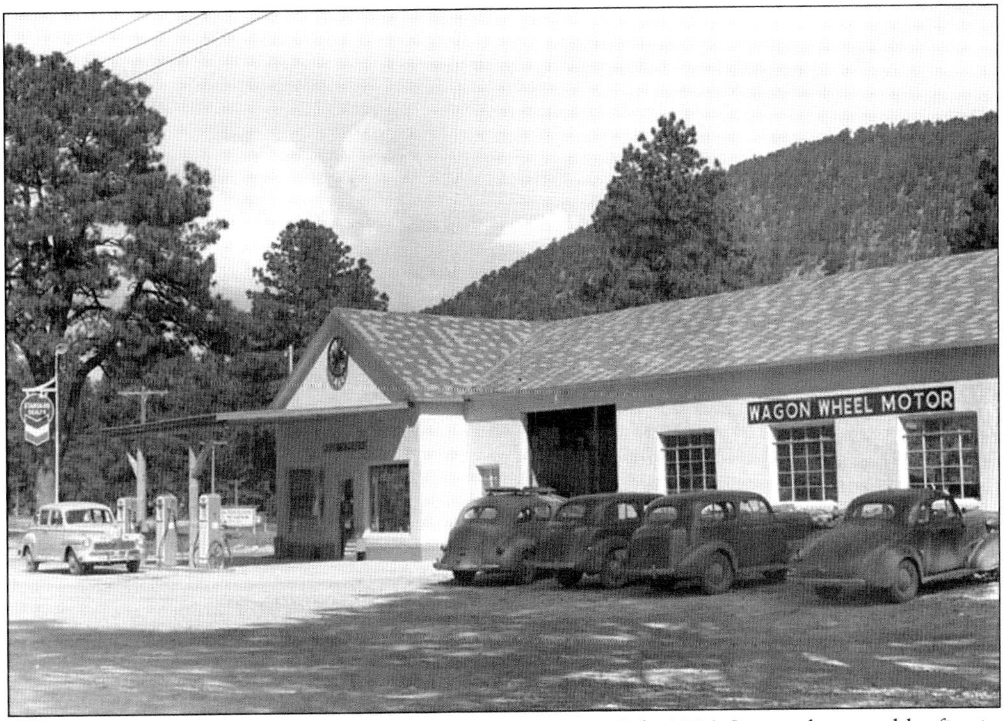

Wagon Wheel Motors was opened by J. Emmett Reese in July 1946. It was destroyed by fire in the early 1960s. The site was occupied by First National Bank in 2014.

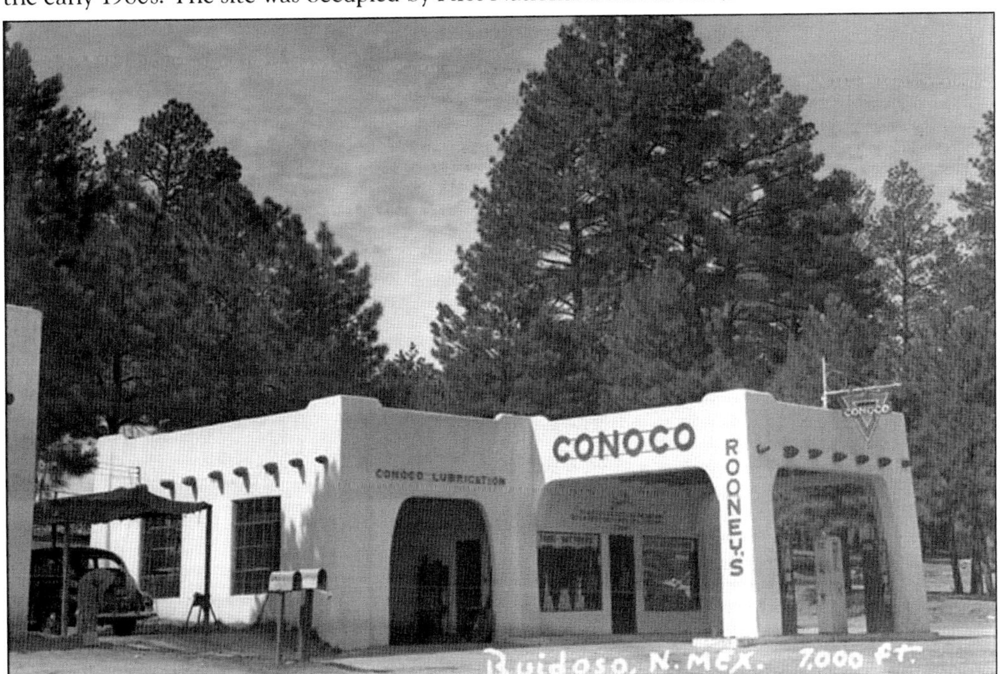

The Pueblo Revival–style Conoco station became Michelle's, a women's clothing store, in the late 1990s. During the renovation, some of the architectural elements were preserved, including the kiva fireplace.

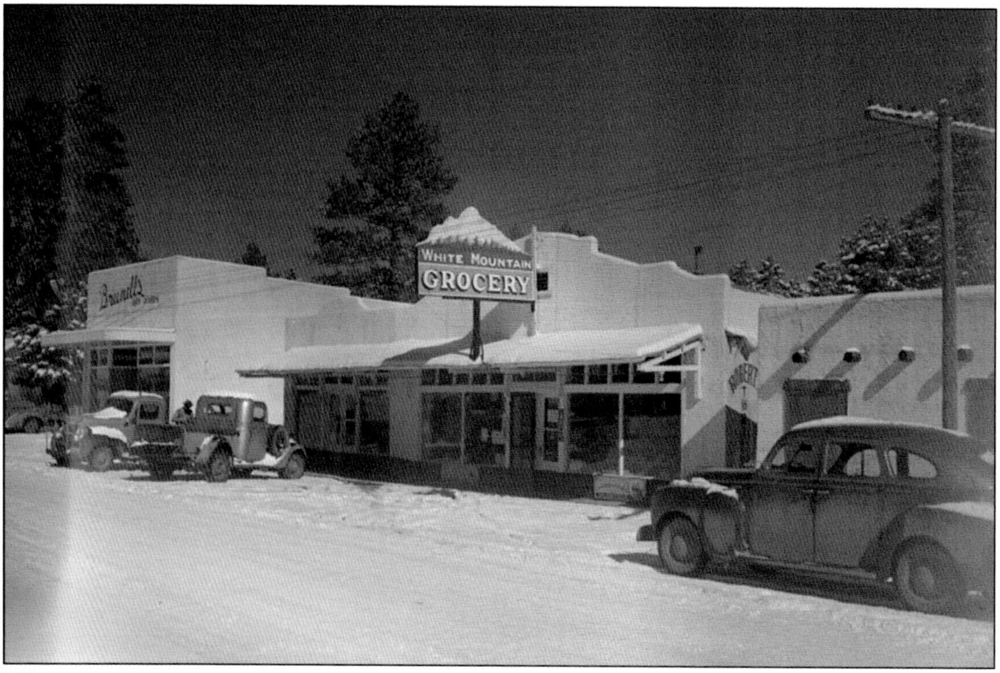

White Mountain Grocery was operated by Herbert Brunell Sr.'s in-laws, Samuel and Satie Stout. The building, which had been constructed in 1940, eventually became part of Brunell's Dry Goods.

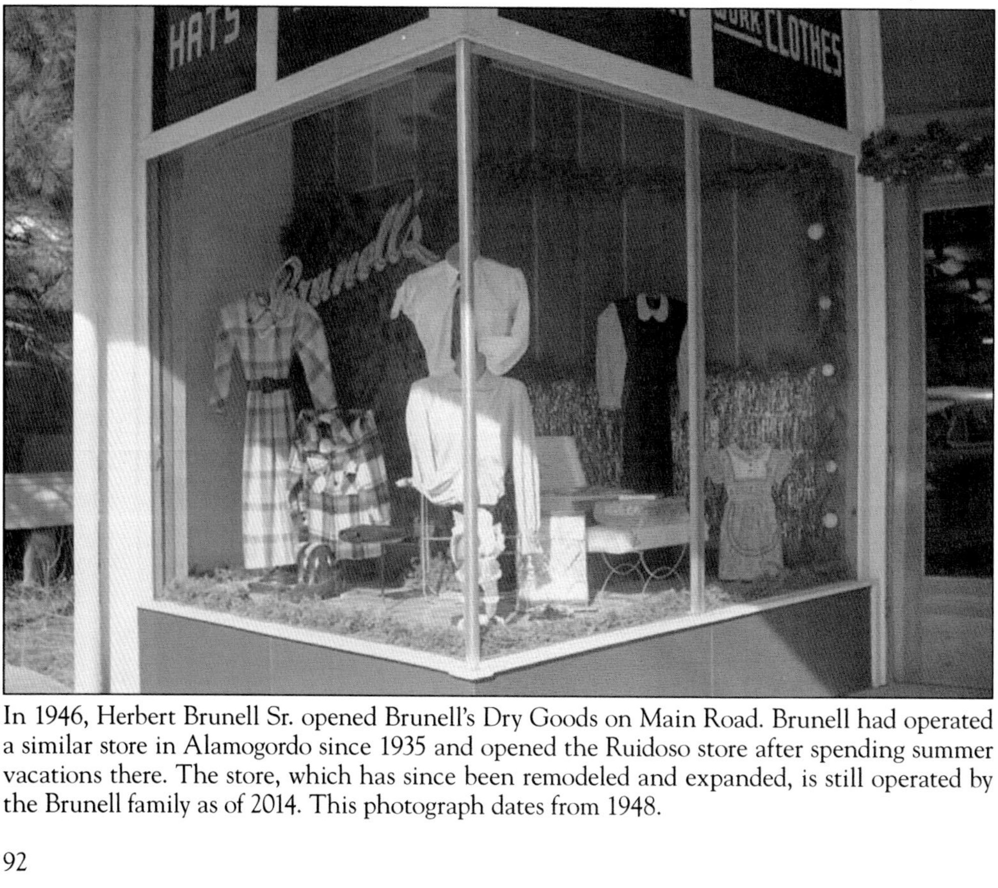

In 1946, Herbert Brunell Sr. opened Brunell's Dry Goods on Main Road. Brunell had operated a similar store in Alamogordo since 1935 and opened the Ruidoso store after spending summer vacations there. The store, which has since been remodeled and expanded, is still operated by the Brunell family as of 2014. This photograph dates from 1948.

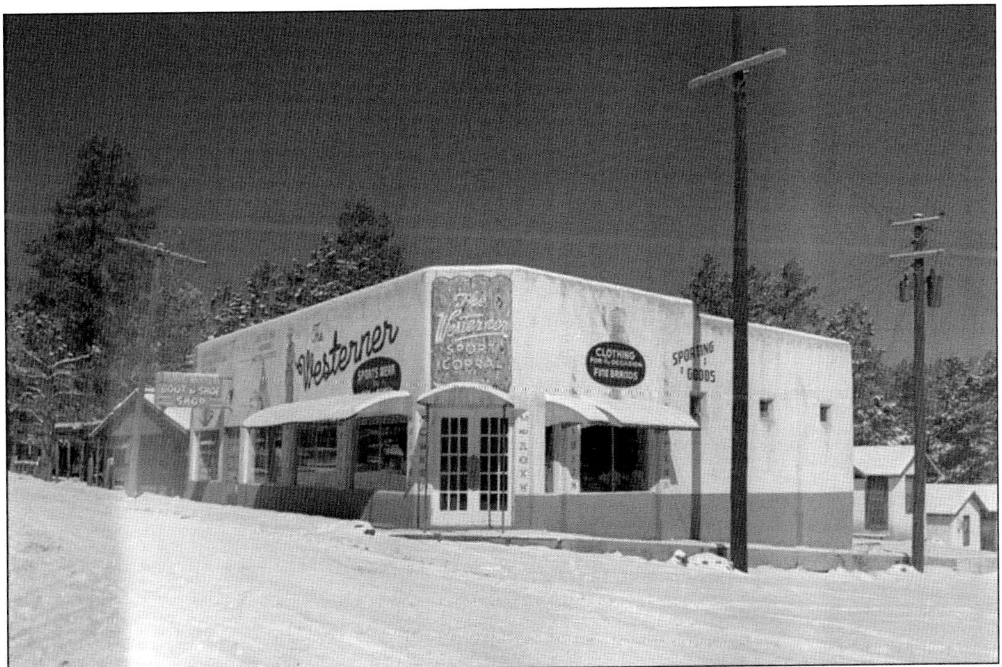

The Westerner stood at the corner of Main Road (now Sudderth Drive) and Center Street, from where it sold high-quality Western wear.

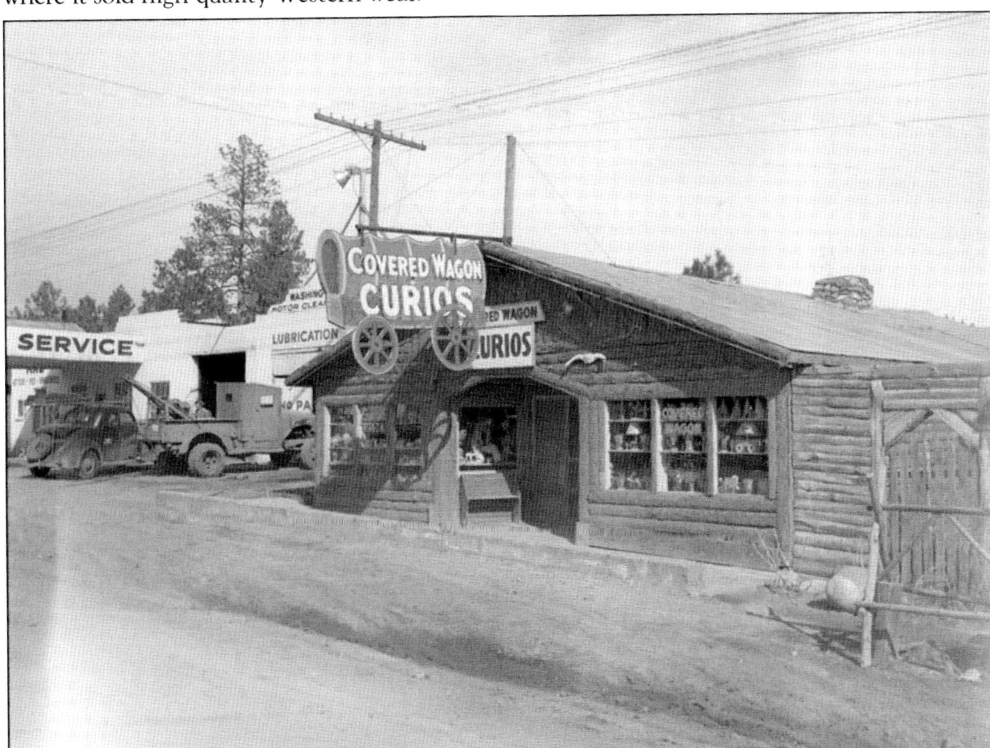

Although the exterior has been changed somewhat, Covered Wagon Curios, now known as the Wagon Wheel in 2014, has continued operation in the same location since the 1930s.

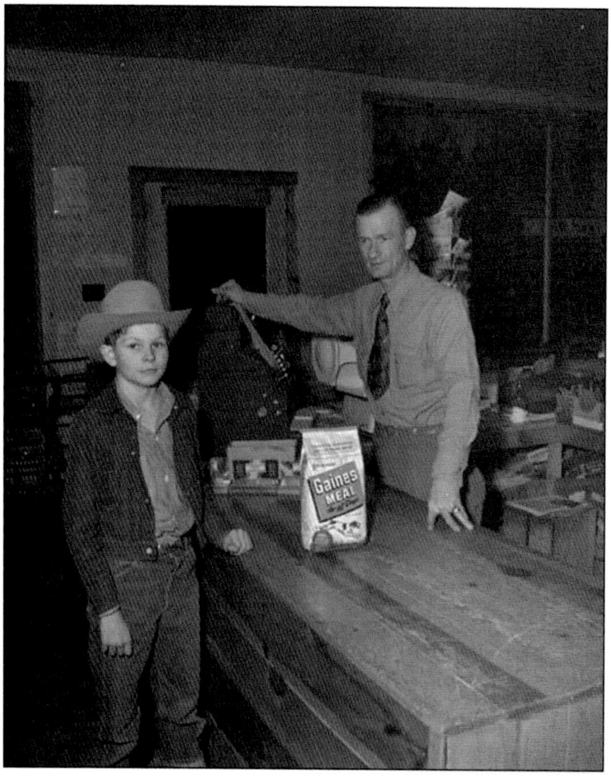

The store, as well as its clerk and customer, are unidentified in this 1948 photograph, which is representative of the typical commercial establishments in early Ruidoso.

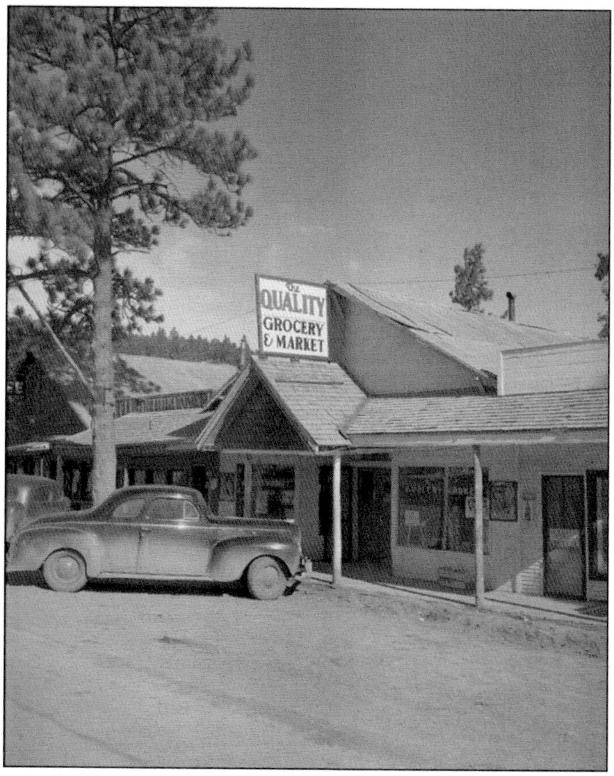

The Quality Grocery & Market was located in what was known as the Wingfield Block, also the home of Ike Wingfield's general store and post office. The Pine Tree Square shopping complex occupied this site in 2014.

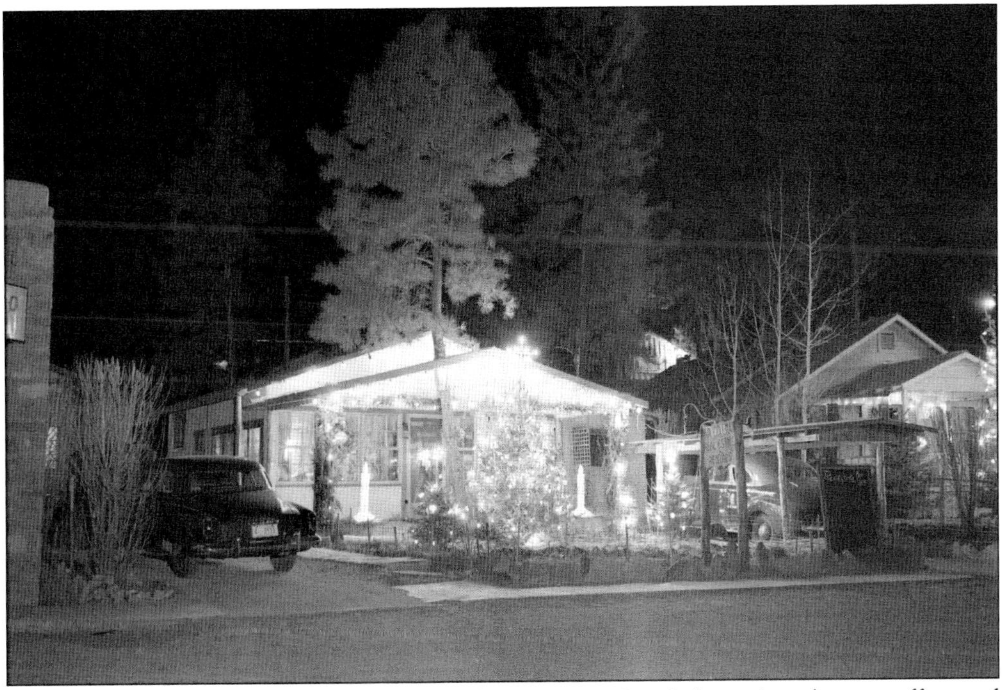

Located in a building on Sudderth Drive, what was once Iva Coleman's real estate office and residence is now, as of 2014, the Rocky Mountain Christmas Shop, a strong contender in the annual Christmas decorating contest.

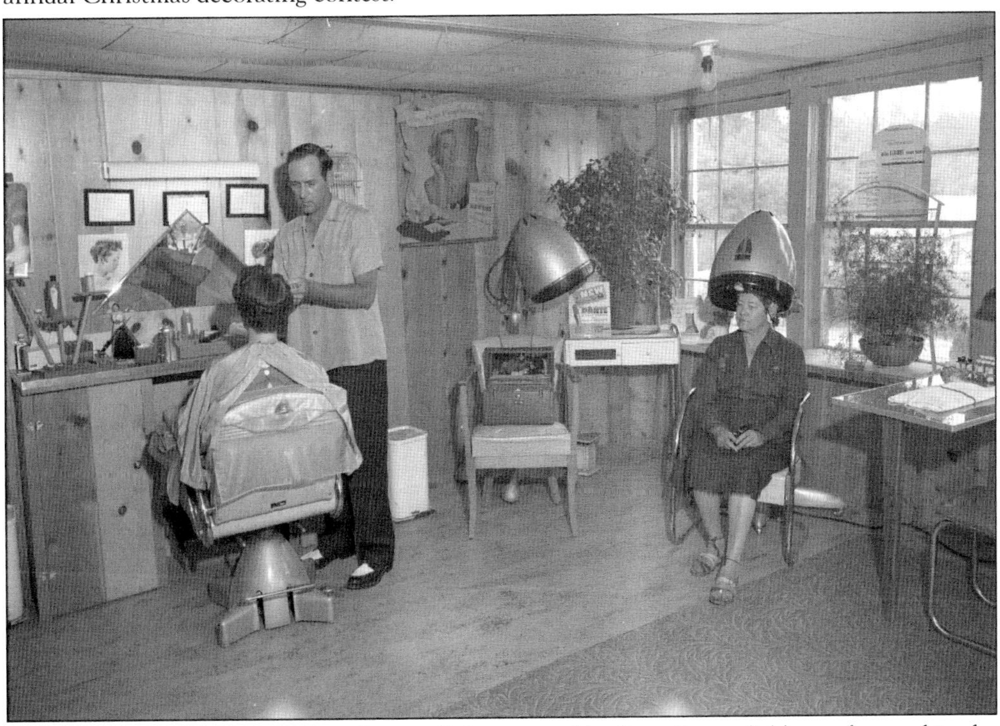

The newly remodeled Gena Rose Beauty Salon, owned by Rose Brownfield, was featured in the *Ruidoso News* in 1954. Bob Hollis is the hairstylist; the customers are unidentified.

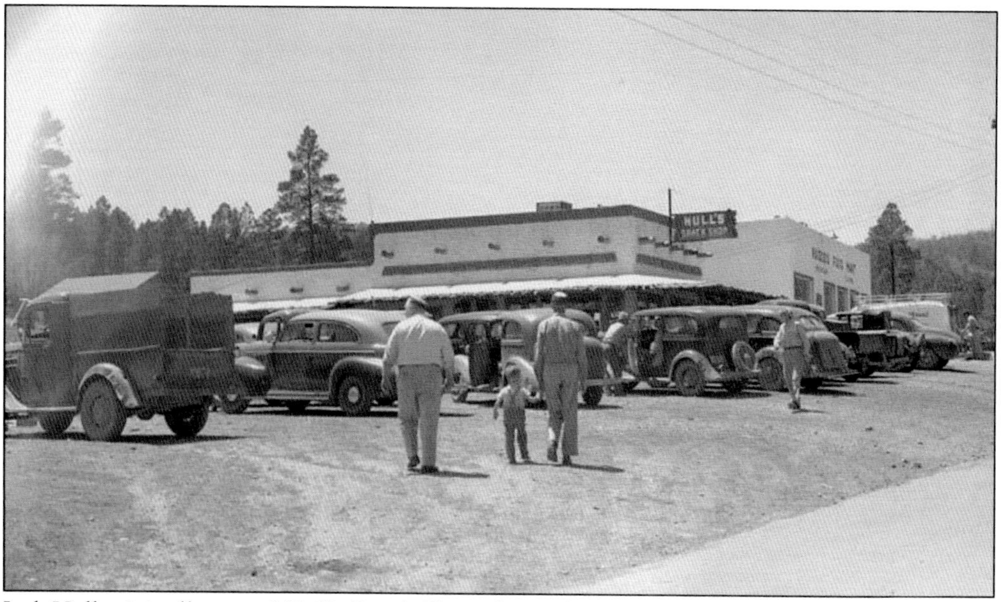

Jack Hull originally owned Hull's Snack Shop, then sold it to the Furrys, who moved to Ruidoso from San Antonio, Texas, in 1947. The building stood approximately where the Great Wall of China restaurant was located today, in 2014.

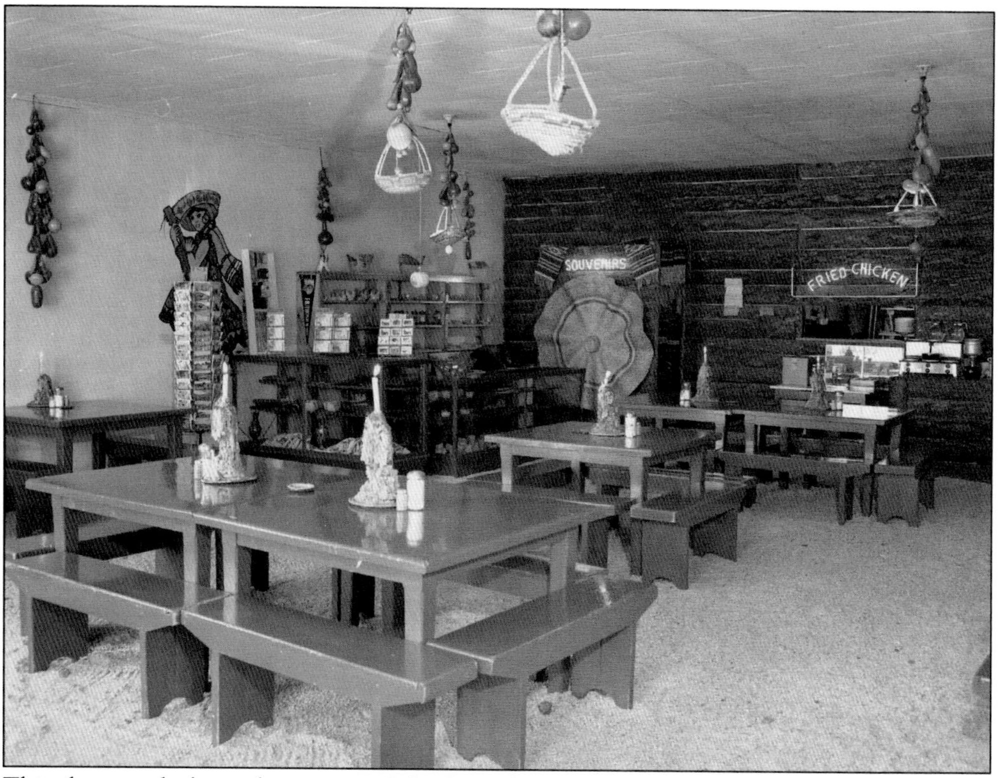

This photograph shows the interior of the Spanish Nook Mexican restaurant, which opened in 1946. In addition to the Buckaroo Lounge, it occupied the same building that housed the shop Candle Power in 2014.

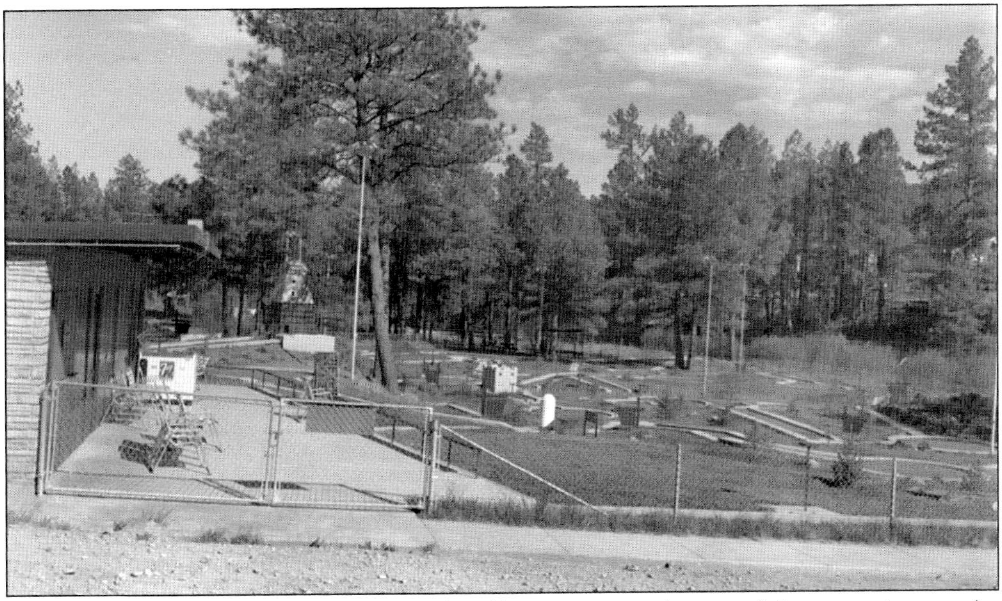

The Pan-O-Rama miniature (or "carpet") golf course was only one of the attractions at the amusement center built by Cap Arrington in 1950. In 1963, it also boasted a 40-foot Ferris wheel and a ride called The Astronaut, with eight space capsules that were "duplicates of the one John Glenn rode in." The Ruidoso River Resort had replaced the golf course by 2005.

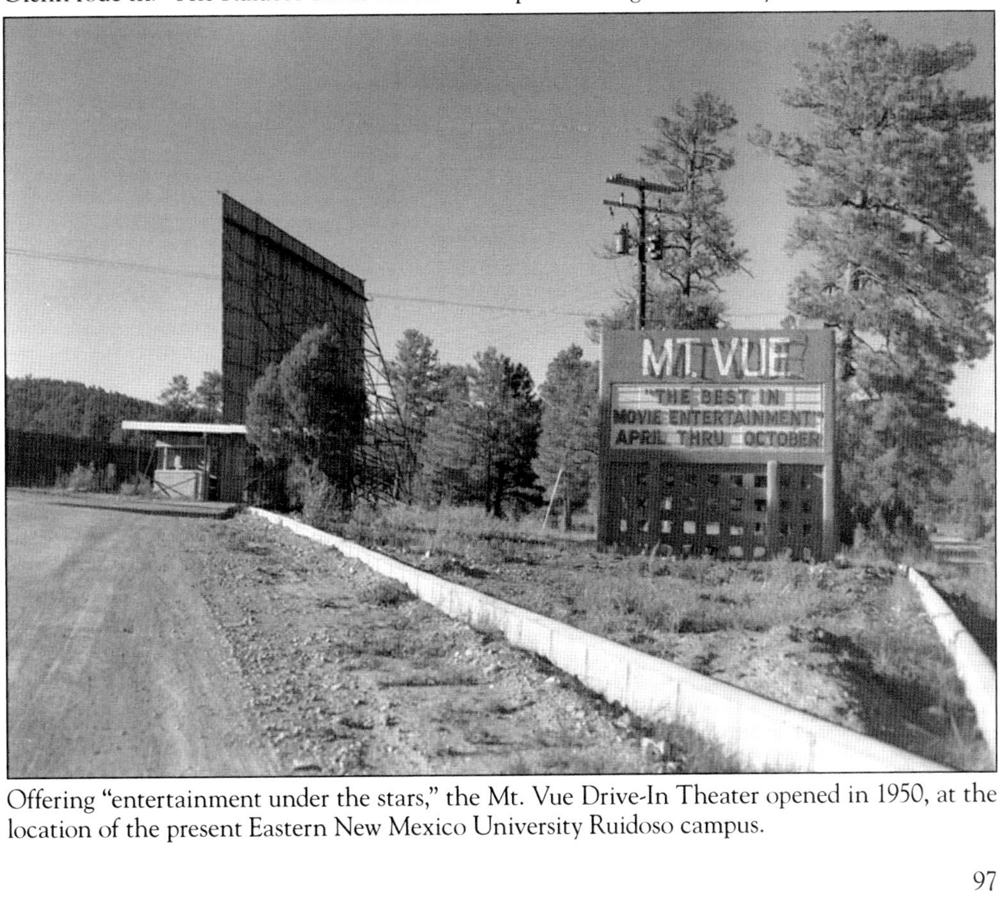

Offering "entertainment under the stars," the Mt. Vue Drive-In Theater opened in 1950, at the location of the present Eastern New Mexico University Ruidoso campus.

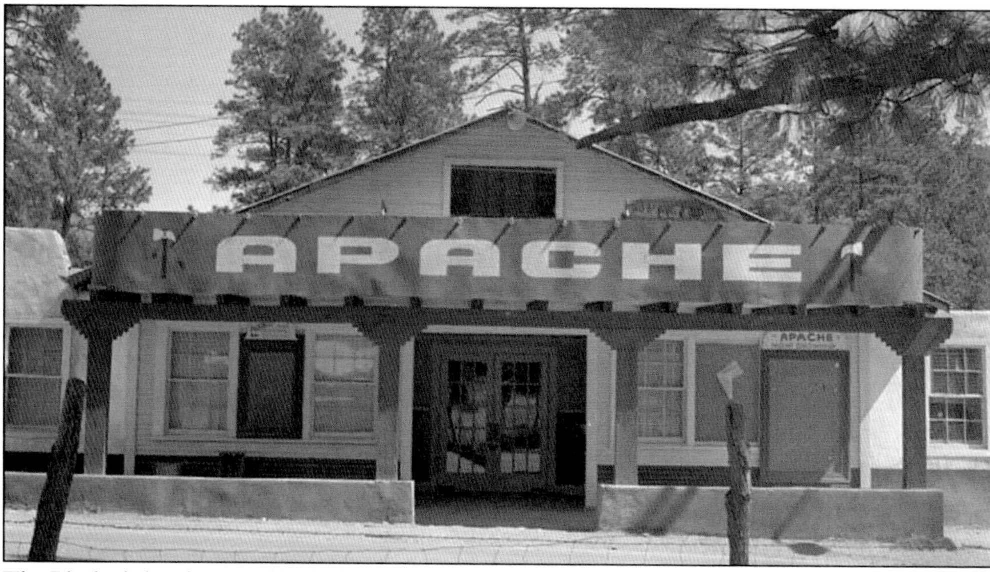

The Blaylock family owned both the Apache Theater and the Pueblo Theater. The Apache Theater was sold to R.A. Coker in the 1940s, and a lively competition developed between the two theaters.

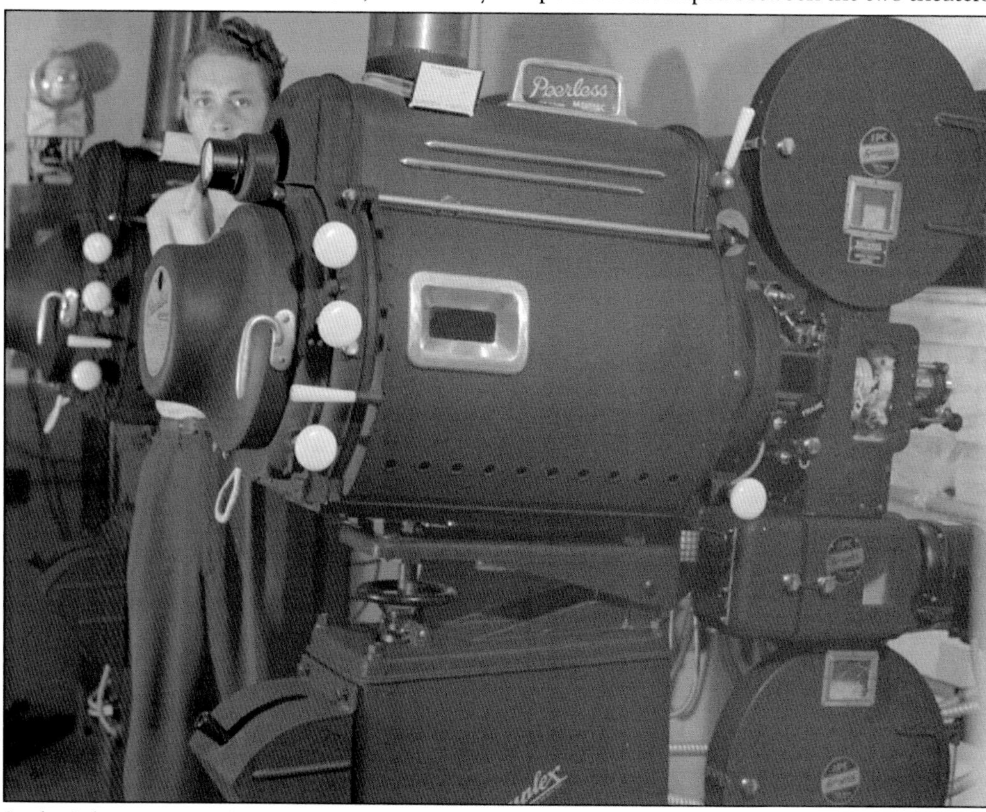
In the July 30, 1946, edition of the *Ruidoso News*, Jennings Blaylock announced that $9,000 worth of modern projection equipment had been installed in the Pueblo Theater. When Dean Holman worked as a projectionist during junior high school, he had to stand on wooden crates to be tall enough to reach the top reel.

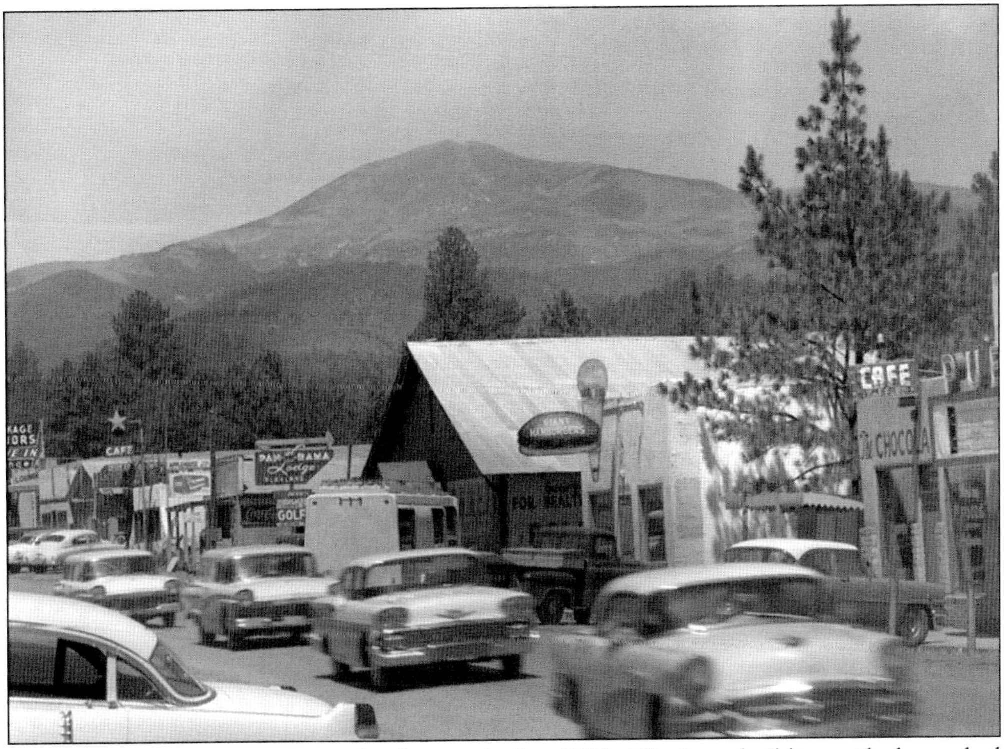

This photograph shows midtown Ruidoso in the late 1950s. The large building with the peaked roof held the roller skating rink, now the location of Lucy's Mexican Restaurant, in 2014. The sign for the Pan-O-Rama is seen just beyond it.

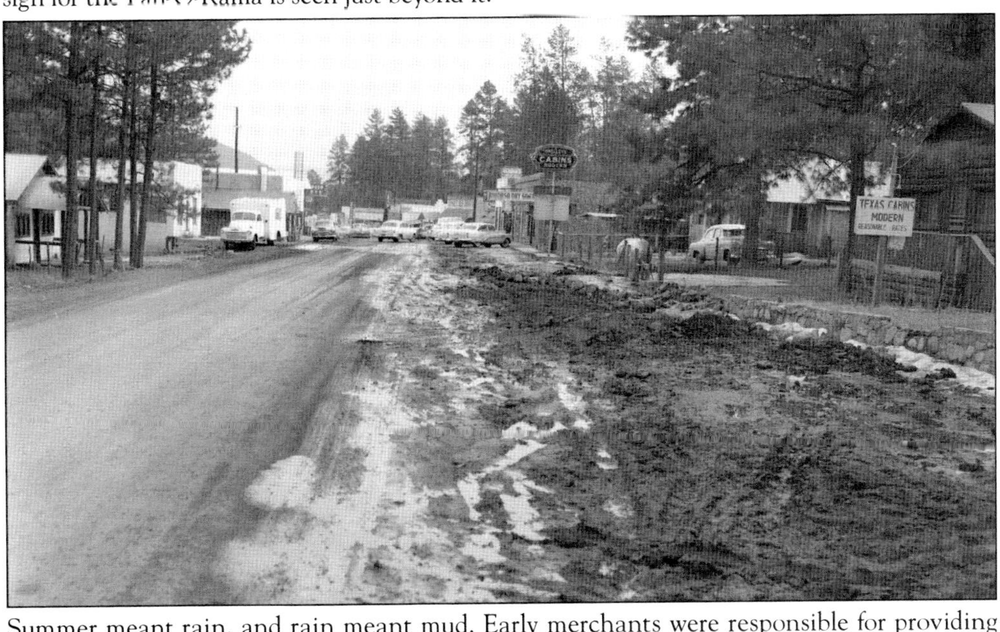

Summer meant rain, and rain meant mud. Early merchants were responsible for providing sidewalks in front of their stores, but many opted to let the pedestrians fend for themselves. This photograph appeared in the *Ruidoso News* in 1954. By 1970, only 62 of the 212 miles of Ruidoso streets were paved.

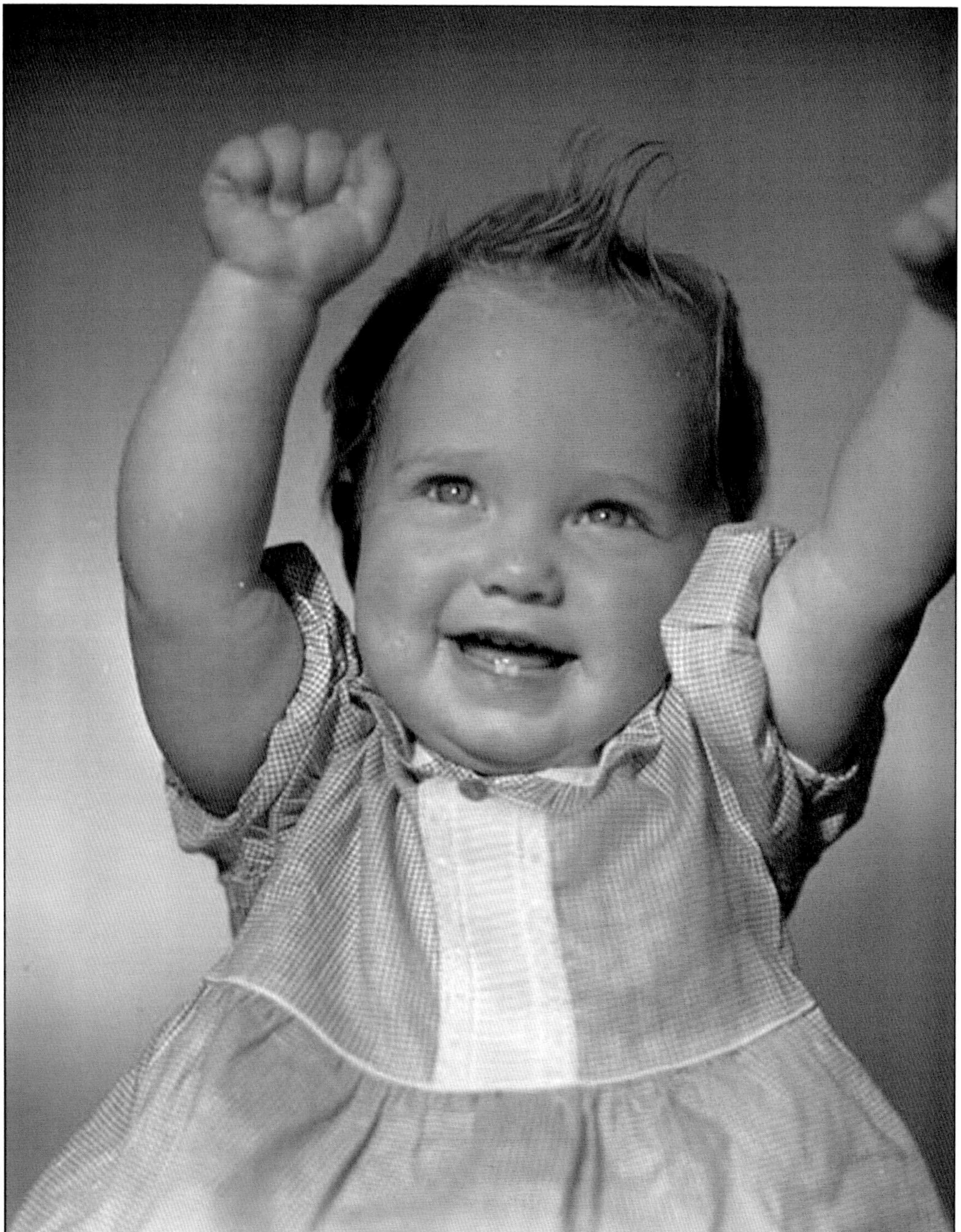

Carmon Phillips probably did not have to coax this subject to smile. Portrait photography was a luxury for many Ruidoso families, and Phillips made sure his customers were satisfied.

Eight

Say "Cheese!"

Making a living in Ruidoso has always been a challenge. "In the early days people would do just about anything," Phillips remembered. "They would raise chickens and sell the eggs. Some people would sleep in their cars so they could rent their houses out to visitors."

Over the years, Phillips would sell film, cameras, postcards, books, records, tape recorders, souvenirs, perfume, jewelry, clothing, flour, cornmeal, and novelty items like a hat with a battery-powered fan.

In addition to the gift shop and photograph processing he offered, Phillips sold images to magazines for articles that promoted Ruidoso. Using a 4x5 Speed Graphic camera, he took photo-finish shots of the horse races at the Hollywood Park racetrack, which was later renamed Ruidoso Downs.

He set up a portrait studio in the front room of his house, where he would photograph babies, politicians, engaged couples, graduates, and aspiring beauty queens. Leona Mae would hand-color the large portraits. Carmon also went on site to photograph weddings, anniversaries, conventions, birthday parties, athletic events, Christmas mornings, and, on at least one occasion, funerals.

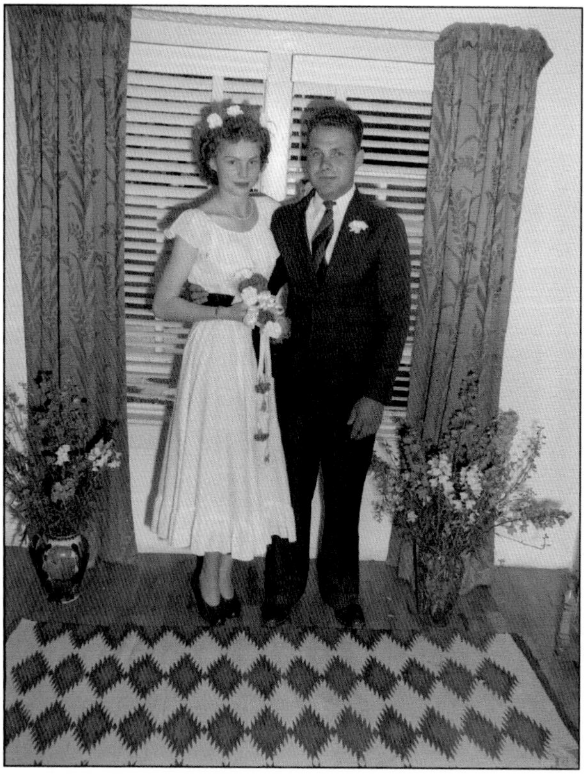

Weddings are a large part of any commercial photographer's work. Carmon Phillips photographed Lloyd Perry and Dora Parnell (left) and Dorsey and Suzie Bonnell (below) as they began their new lives together.

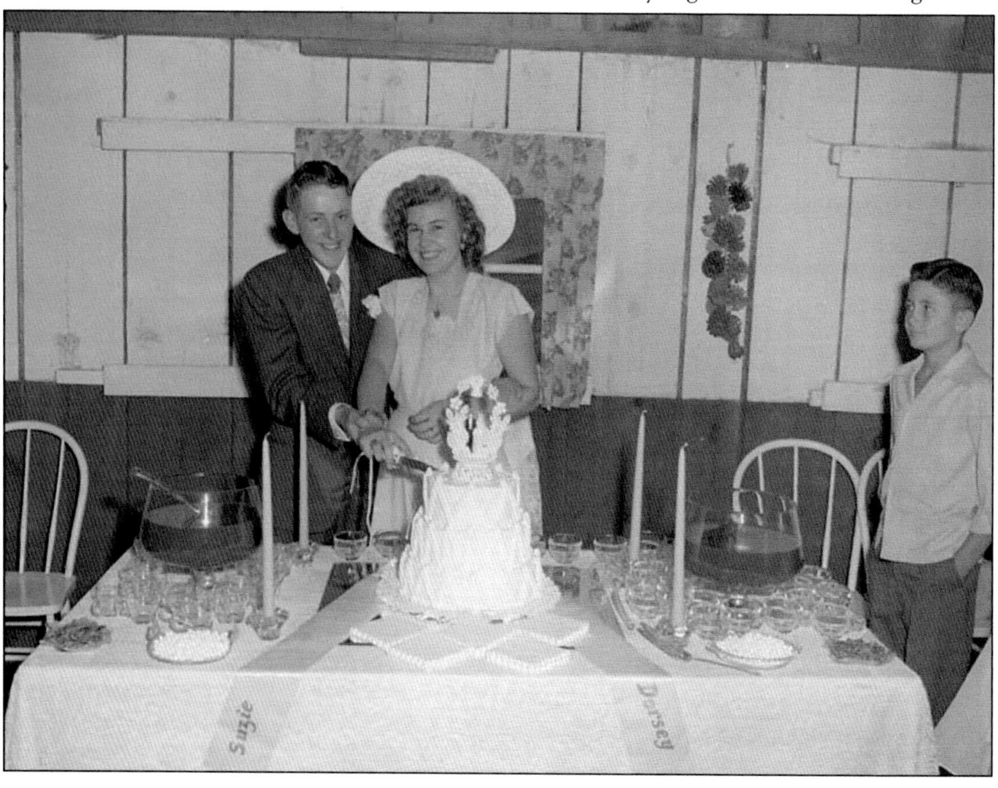

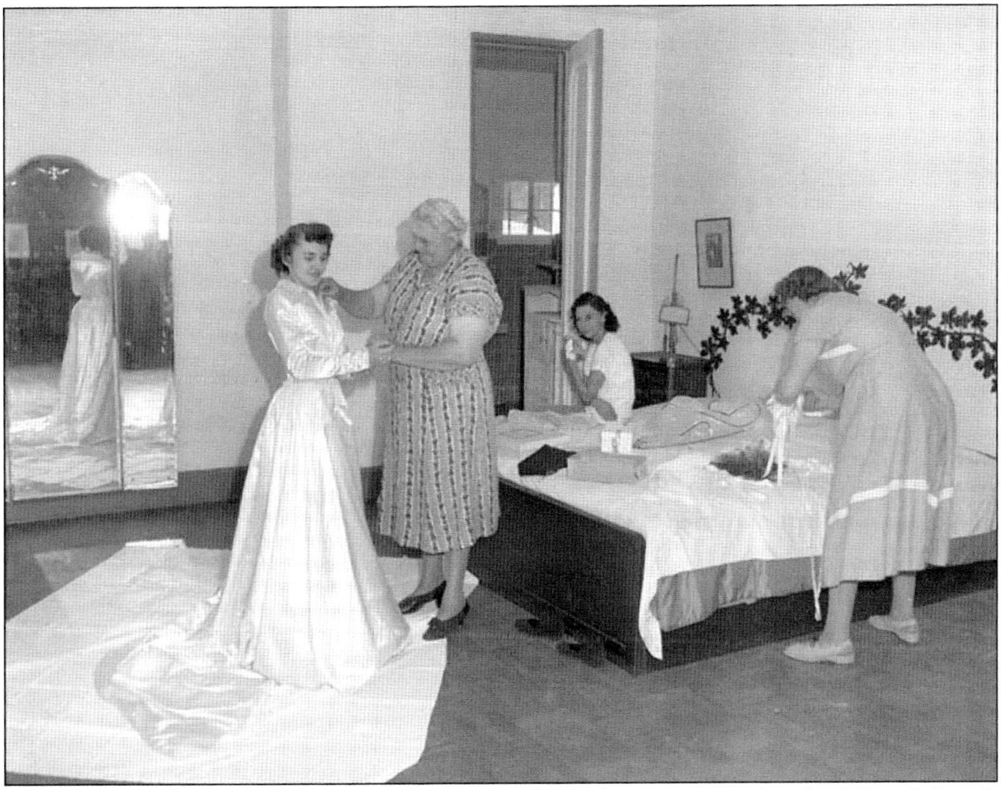

Ted Bonnell of Alamogordo and Mary Glenda Shook of Alto were married at the O-Bar-O Ranch near Carrizozo in 1949.

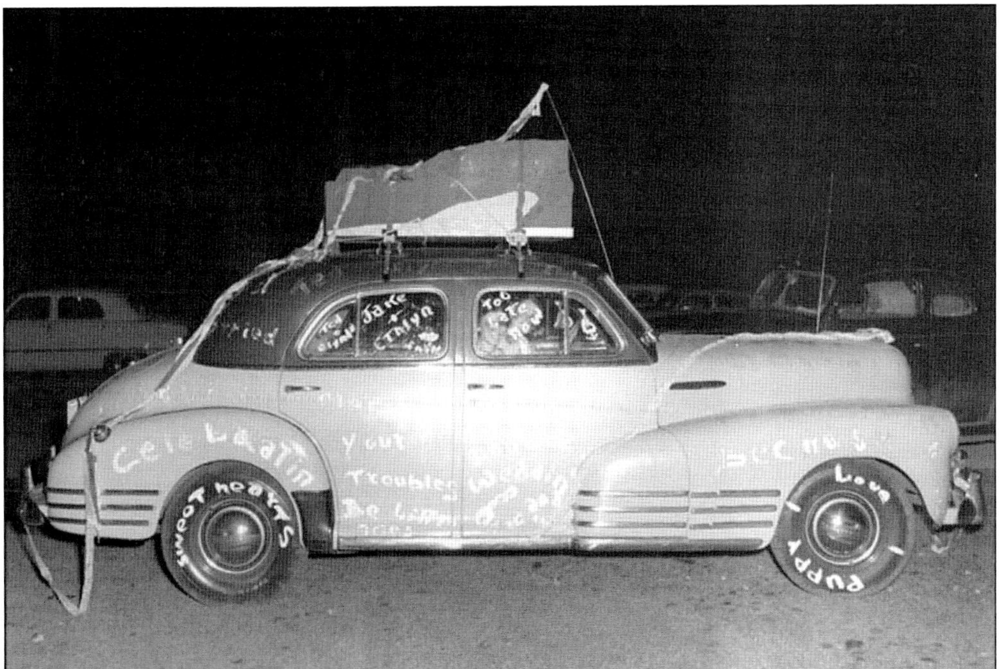

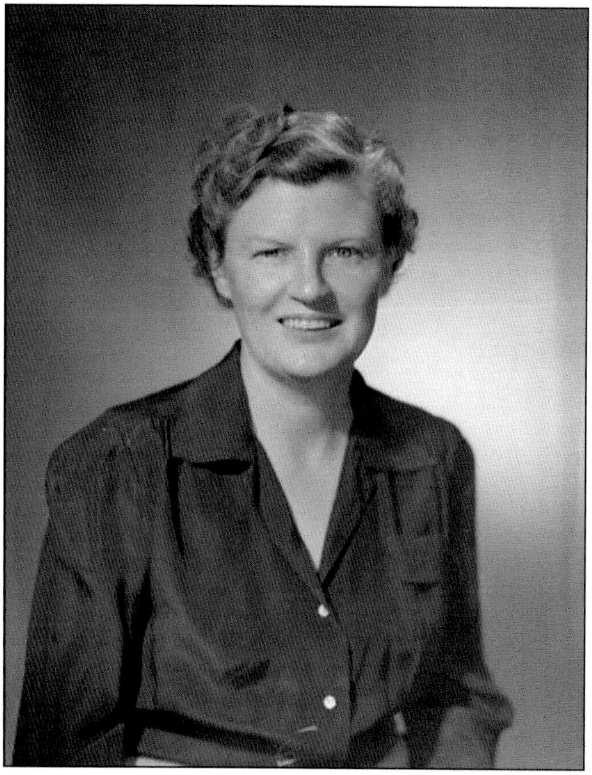

In 1950, Lorine Samelson, an elementary school teacher, ran for superintendent of schools—and won. This was her campaign portrait.

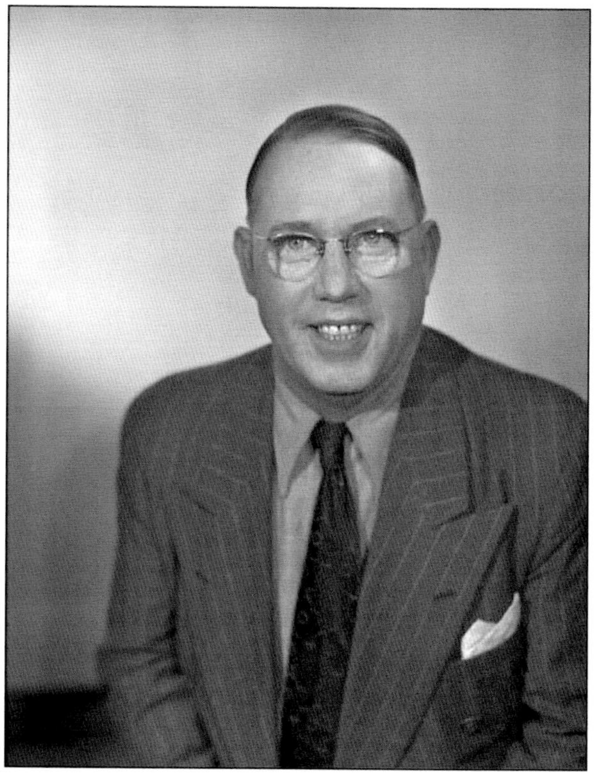

In March 1948, Lloyd Bloodworth, first publisher and editor of the *Ruidoso News*, announced his candidacy for governor of New Mexico. In spite of an enthusiastic send-off, including a barbecue attended by 1,500 people, he did not win.

Jan Randle, sponsored by the Women's Club, represented Ruidoso in El Paso's Sun Carnival, which is held every year between Christmas and New Year's Day. In the October 25, 1946, issue of the *Ruidoso News*, an unidentified reporter wrote, "I saw her in Carmon Phillips's studio having some pictures made and she is luscious!"

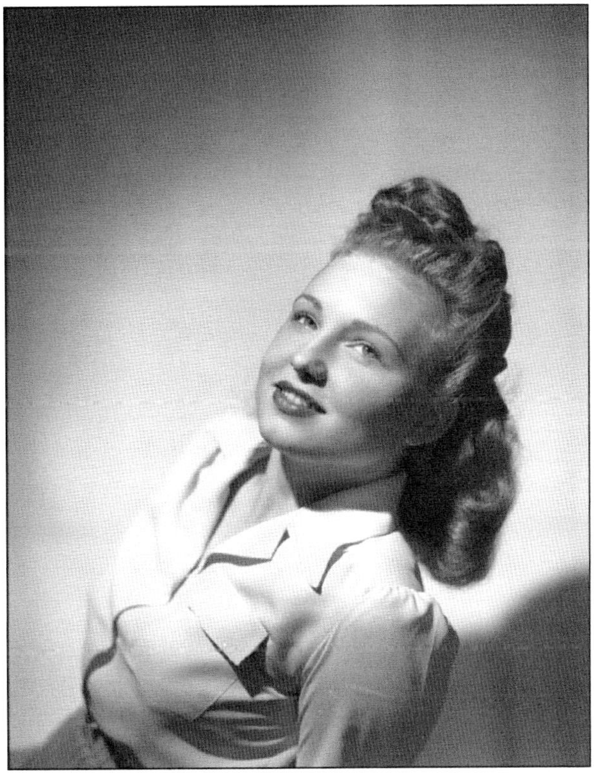

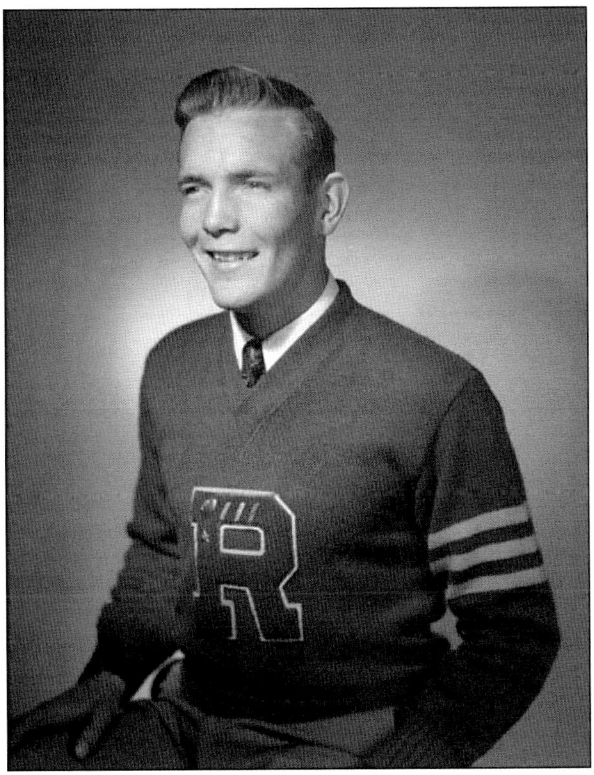

Wade Hedgecoke graduated from Ruidoso High School in 1950. He attended Texas Western College (later renamed University of Texas El Paso) on a football scholarship. His father, R.H. "Coke" Hedgecoke, drove the school bus for 13 years and operated Coke's Shooting Gallery in Midtown.

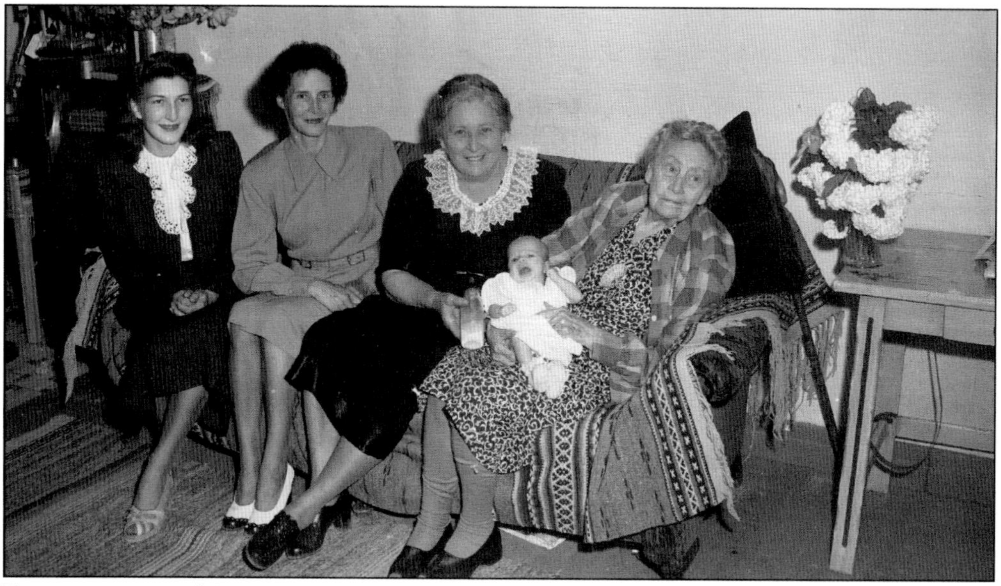

Five generations of Coe women pose for a group portrait. They are, from left to right, Eleanor Bonnell McClendon, Jewel Bonnell, Sydney Coe Bonnell, and Helena Tully Coe, holding Linda McClendon. Cousins Frank and George Coe settled in the Hondo Valley in the early 1870s. They left their ranch during much of the Lincoln County War in an attempt to stay neutral, but they had been friends of Billy the Kid. The Coe family descendants still live in the Hondo Valley.

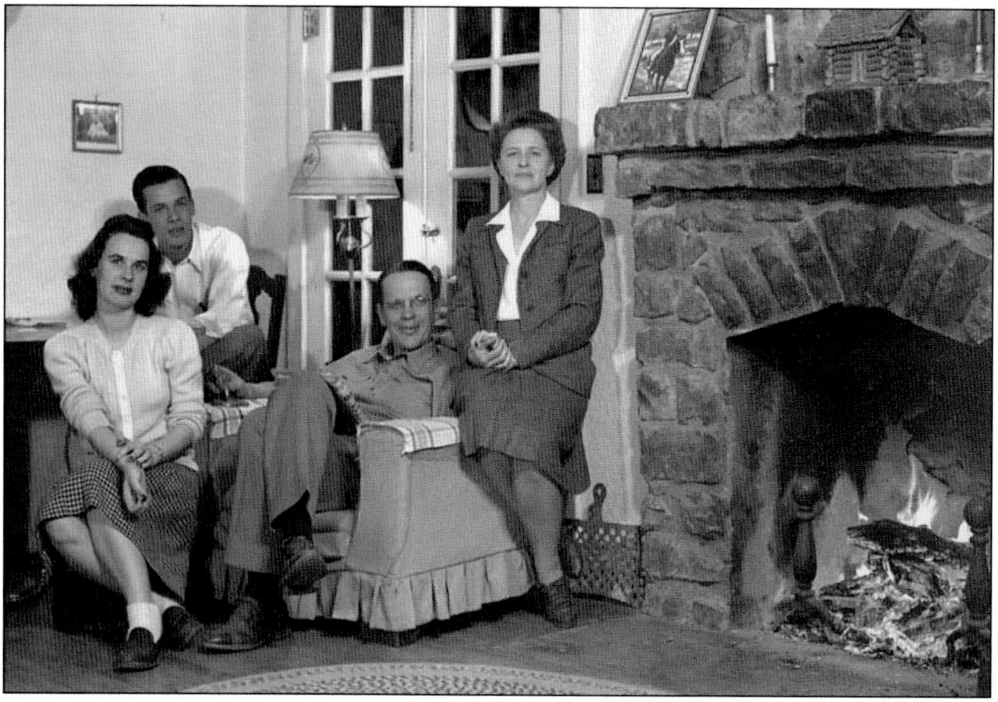

The Palmer family poses at home. Joe Palmer was one of the original partners in the White Mountain Development Company, which bought large tracts of land once owned by James Cree. The Palmer Gateway area, which was annexed by Ruidoso in 1954, was named after him. In the photograph are, from left to right, Sarah Louise, Joe Max, Joe Palmer, and his wife, Delsey.

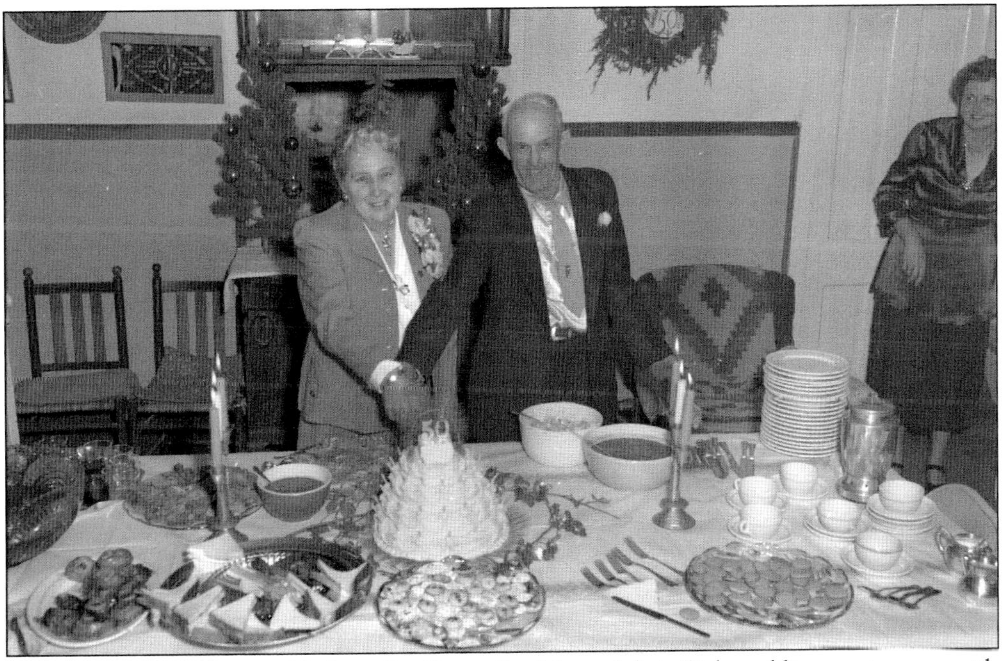

In December 1950, Bert and Sydney Coe Bonnell celebrated their 50th wedding anniversary with a large gathering at the Bonnell Ranch in Glencoe. Bert's family came from Kansas to White Oaks when he was a child. He worked as a cowboy on the V.V. Angus ranch for Lord Cree, then came to work for Frank Coe in 1889, at which time he met Frank's daughter Sydney. In 1930, Bert and Sydney opened a dude ranch at their 1882 family home in the Hondo Valley, east of Ruidoso. In addition to welcoming guests from all over the country, the ranch served as a social center for local residents. Sydney's younger sister, Edith Boyce, opened the Navajo Lodge, which held a similar position in Ruidoso.

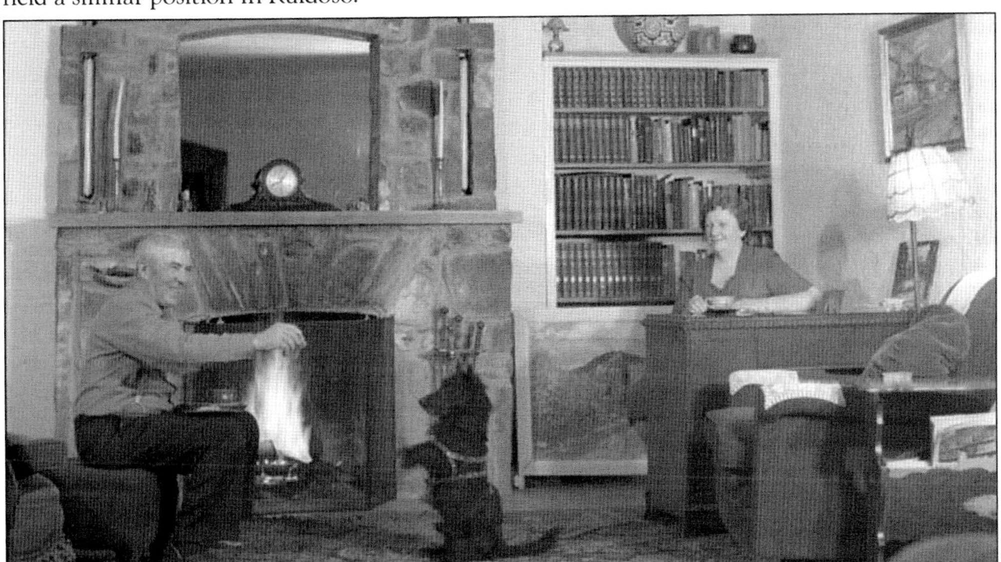

Harry and Tippy Fairbanks pose with their dog in their Ruidoso home. Fairbanks built several homes in Ruidoso and was the contractor who built the jail—for $1,168—and the first Ruidoso High School in 1946.

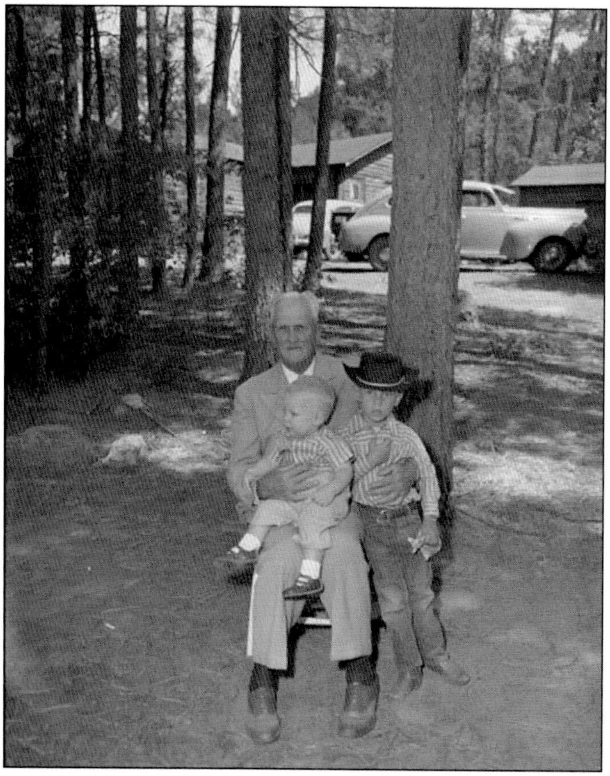

Ruidoso has always been a popular place for family reunions. The oldest and youngest members of the large clan below appear to be featured in the photograph at left.

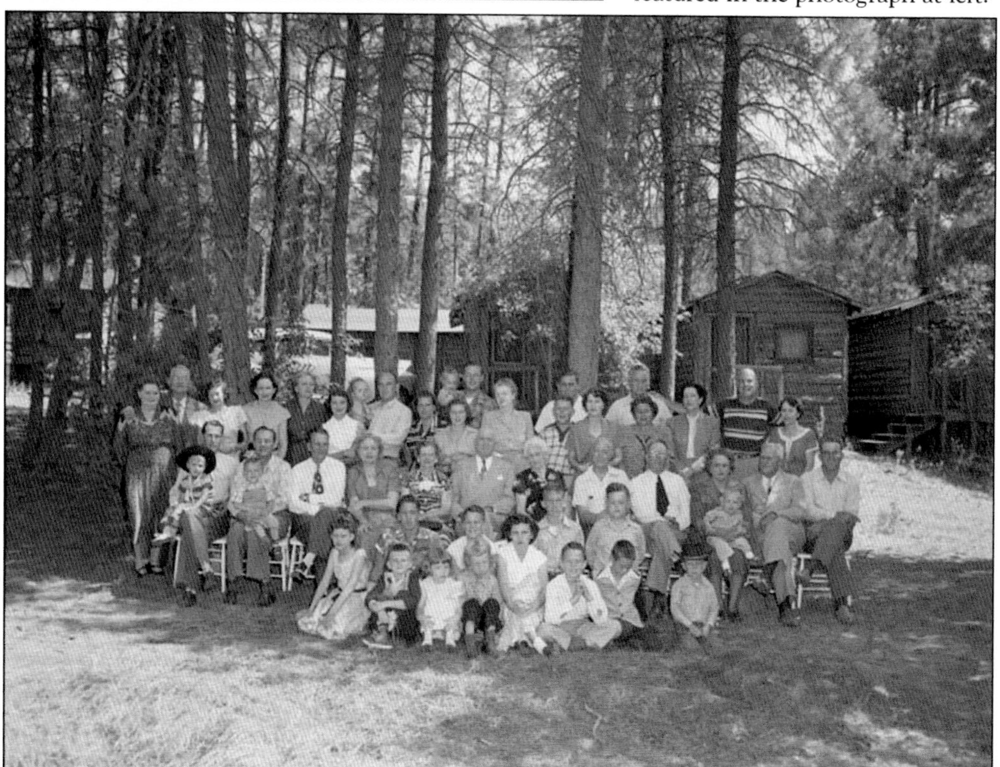

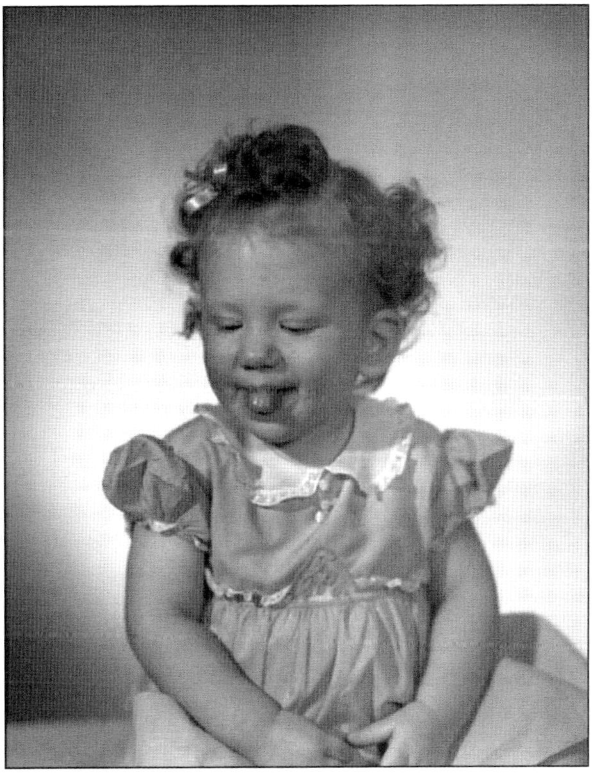

Carmon Phillips photographed many local children, who met the experience with varying degrees of enthusiasm or distaste. In the photograph at left, Leroy Wayne Perry, of Glencoe, tries to restrain his uncooperative sister, Janice.

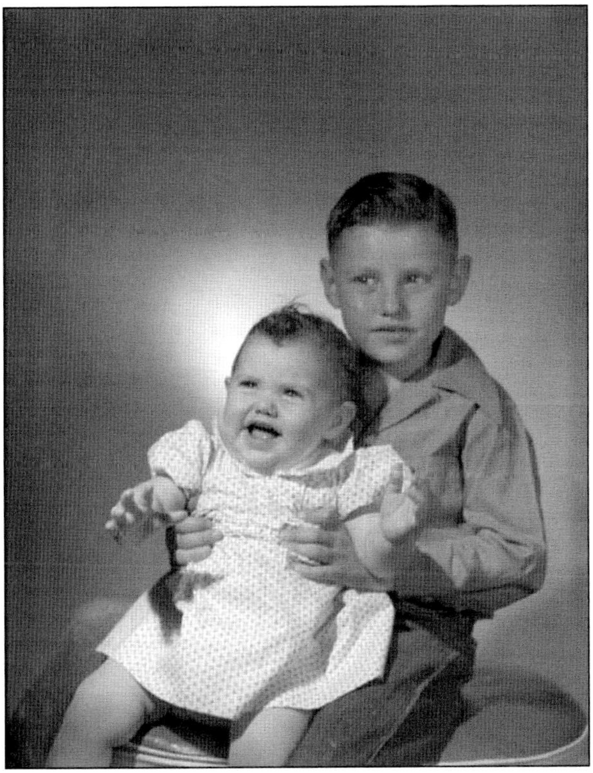

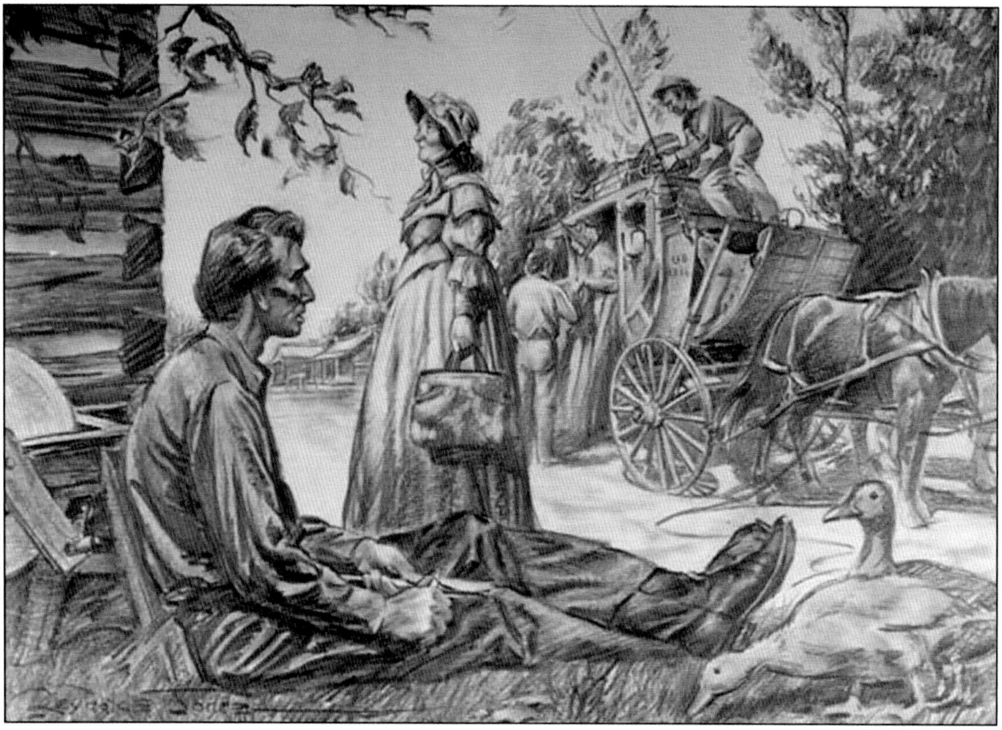

Carmon Phillips photographed his friends' work, including that of artist Reynolds Jones. Originally from Illinois, Jones's artwork depicted scenes from the life of Abraham Lincoln for a series of calendars for the Chicago and Illinois Midland Railway Company. The company, a short line system that shipped coal in central Illinois, commissioned the calendars from 1931 to 1955, with Jones creating the calendars from 1947 to 1955. Eight of Jones's original paintings from the series are now found in the Abraham Lincoln Presidential Library in Springfield, Illinois. This painting titled *Lincoln and Mary Owens* is from the 1951 calendar.

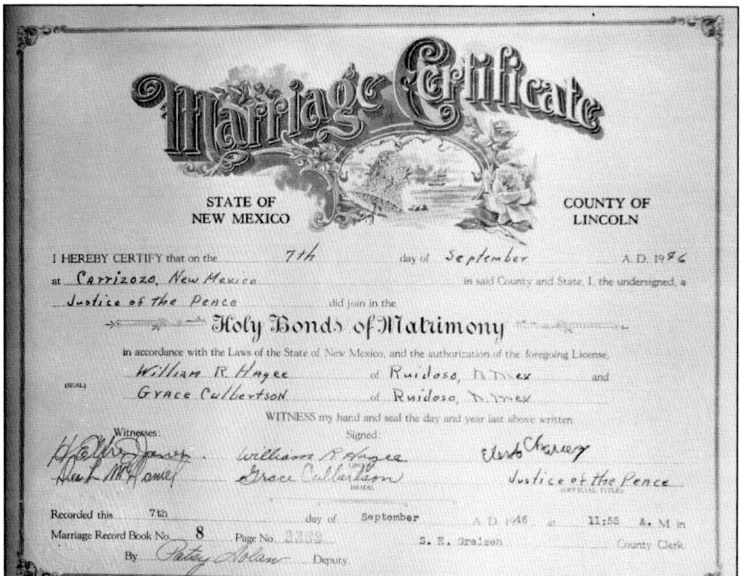

Marriage Certificate

STATE OF NEW MEXICO

COUNTY OF LINCOLN

I HEREBY CERTIFY that on the 7th day of September A.D. 1946 at Carrizozo, New Mexico in said County and State, I, the undersigned, a Justice of the Peace did join in the

Holy Bonds of Matrimony

in accordance with the Laws of the State of New Mexico, and the authorization of the foregoing License,

William R. Hagee of Ruidoso, N. Mex and

(SEAL)

Grace Culbertson of Ruidoso, N. Mex

WITNESS my hand and seal the day and year last above written.

Witnesses:

Signed:

William R. Hagee

GROOM

Grace Culbertson

BRIDE

Justice of the Peace

(OFFICIAL TITLE)

Recorded this 7th day of September A.D. 1946 at 11:55 A.M. in Marriage Record Book No. 8 Page No. [illegible]

S. E. Graisen County Clerk

By Patsy Nolan Deputy

Before photocopying, documents were safeguarded by photographing them. Carmon provided this service for marriage certificates, military discharges, birth certificates, and diplomas.

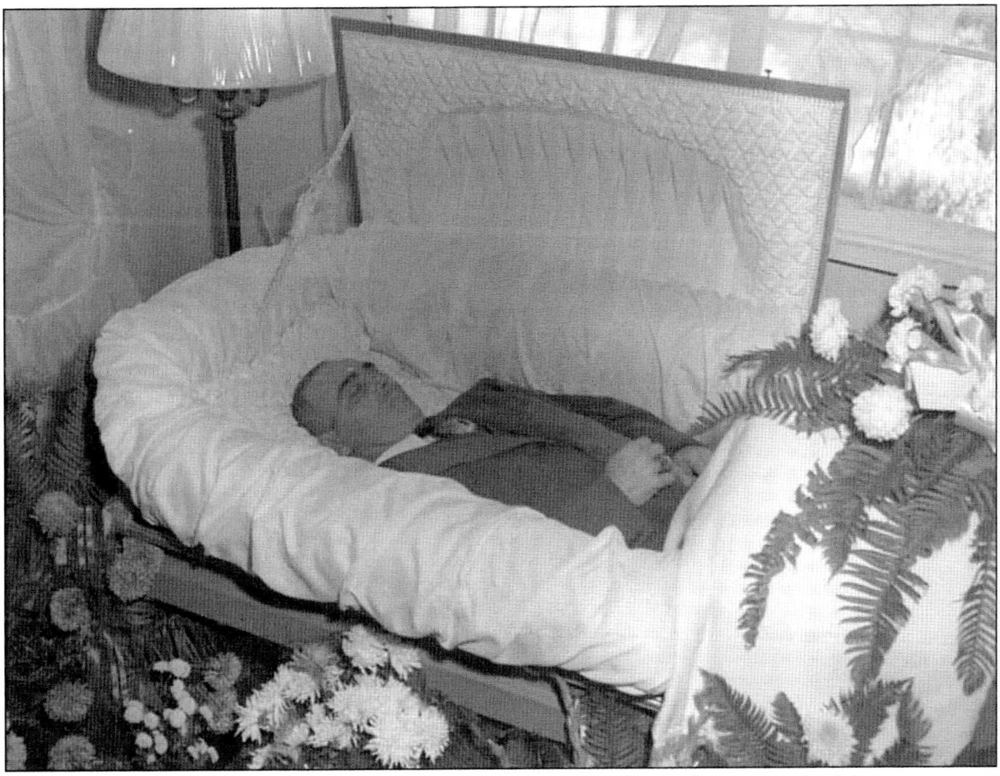

This unidentified man at his home funeral was undoubtedly well respected, if the amount of flowers is any indication.

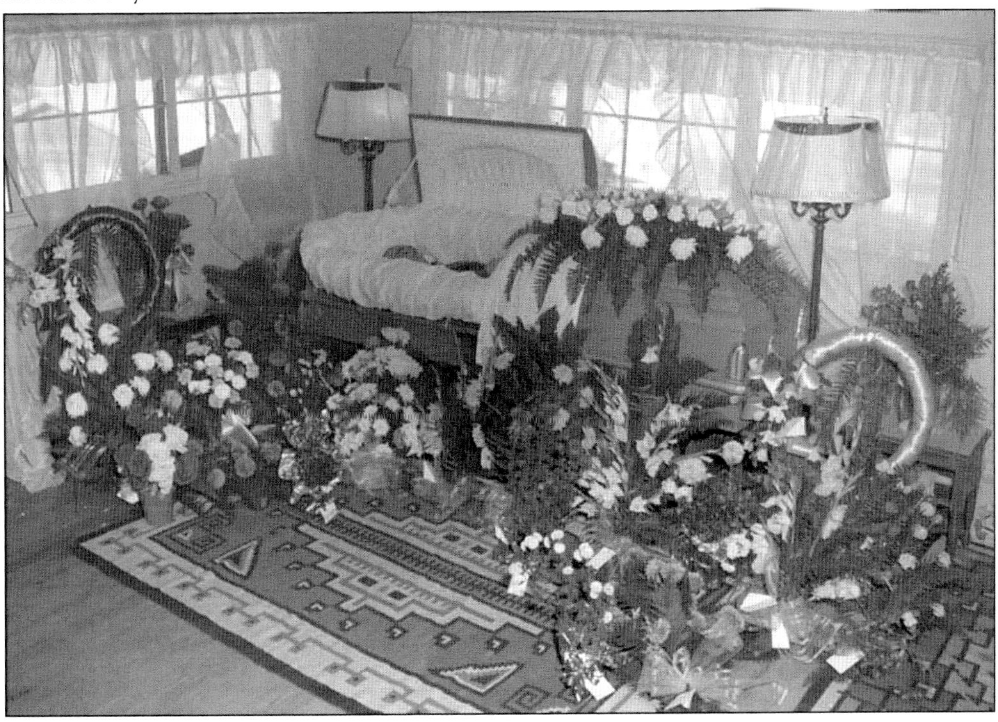

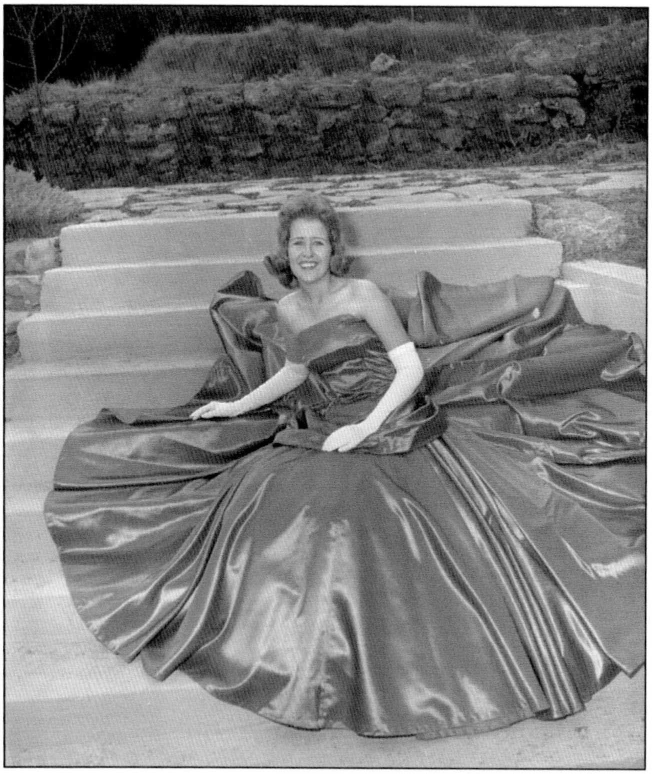

Denese Short poses in her dress for the senior prom in 1961. Her mother, Dema Short, had designed and fashioned the red satin gown. "It was definitely a show-stopper," Short remembered.

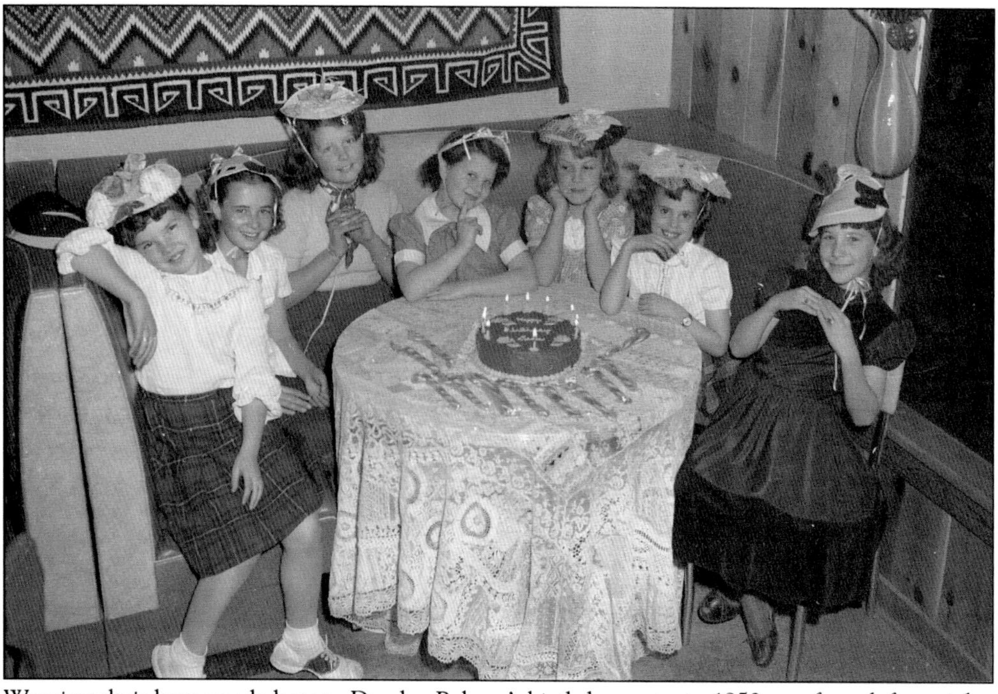

Wearing their homemade hats to Deedee Palmer's birthday party in 1950 are, from left to right, unidentified, Jo Betty Reese, Joan Marie Poteet, Deedee Palmer, Jeanene Carpenter, Bertha Reese, and Ricki Carroll.

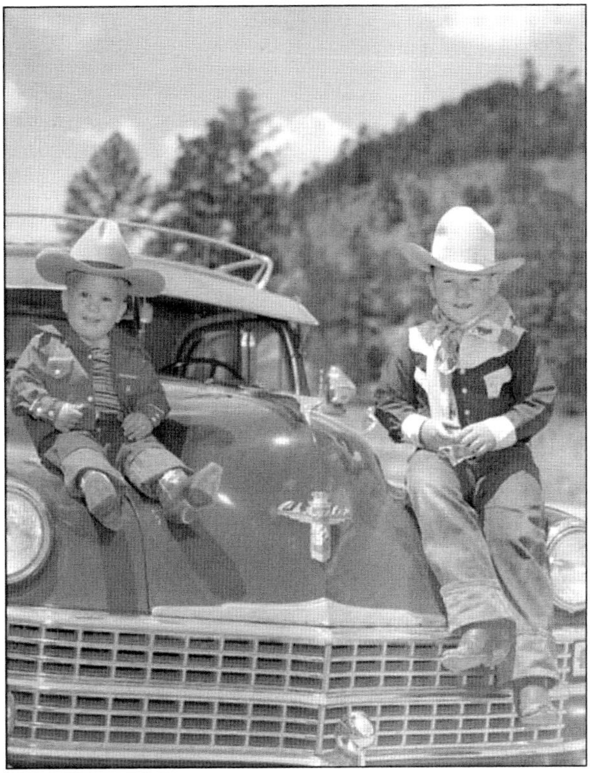

Two boys pose in their cowboy outfits, the older of whom is Pat Rooney.

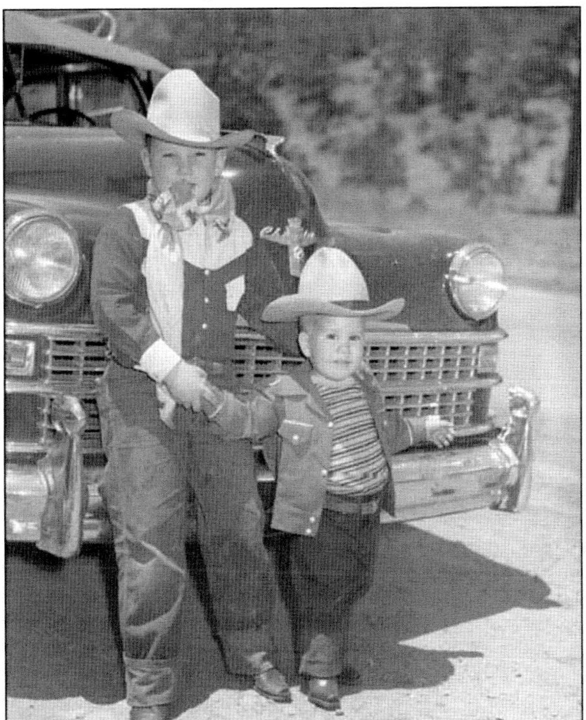

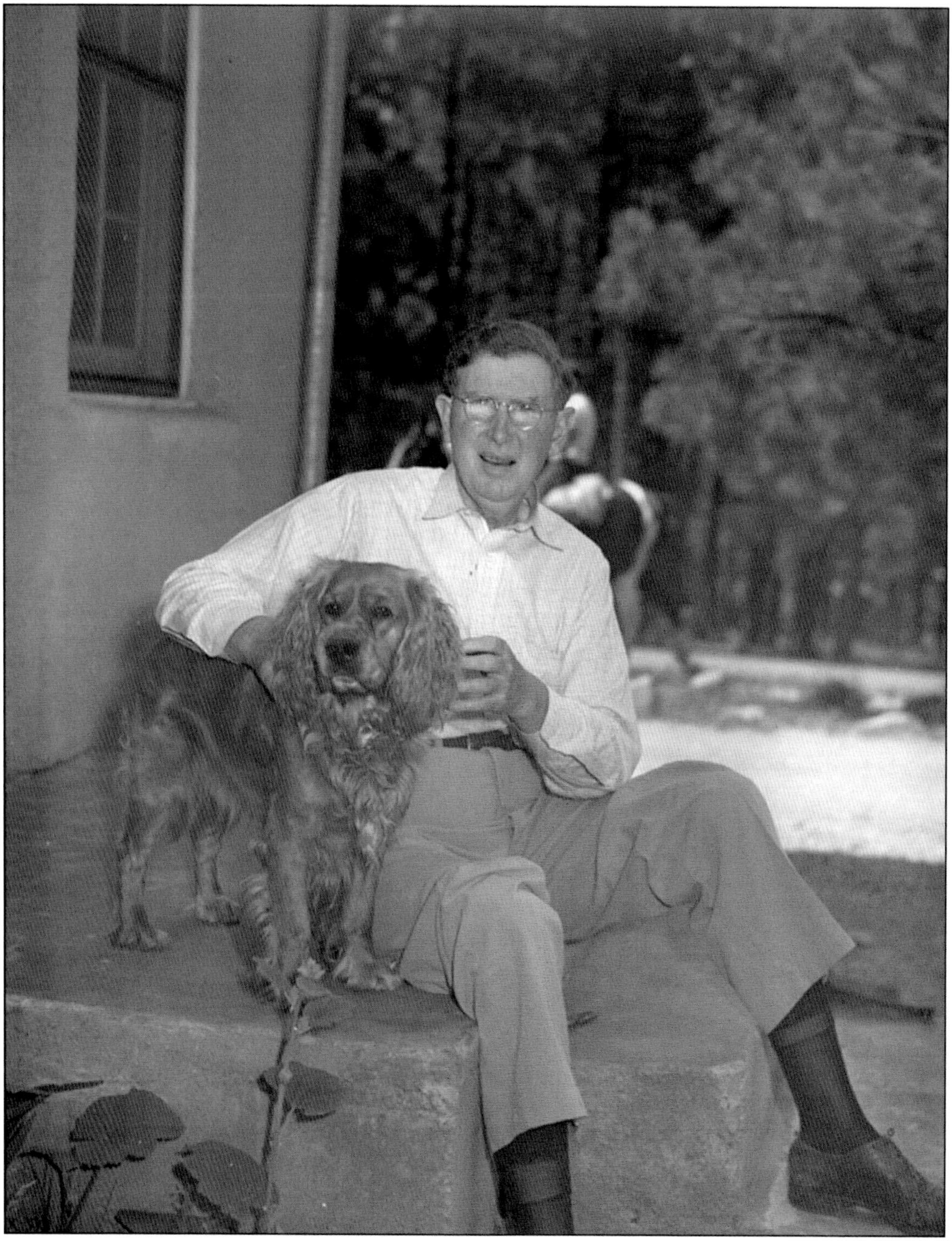

Clarence Cornell "CC" Chase (right) and his dog Barney pose on their front steps. Chase and his company, Ruidoso Realty, were instrumental in the early development of Ruidoso. Chase was also chairman of the hospital board in the early 1950s.

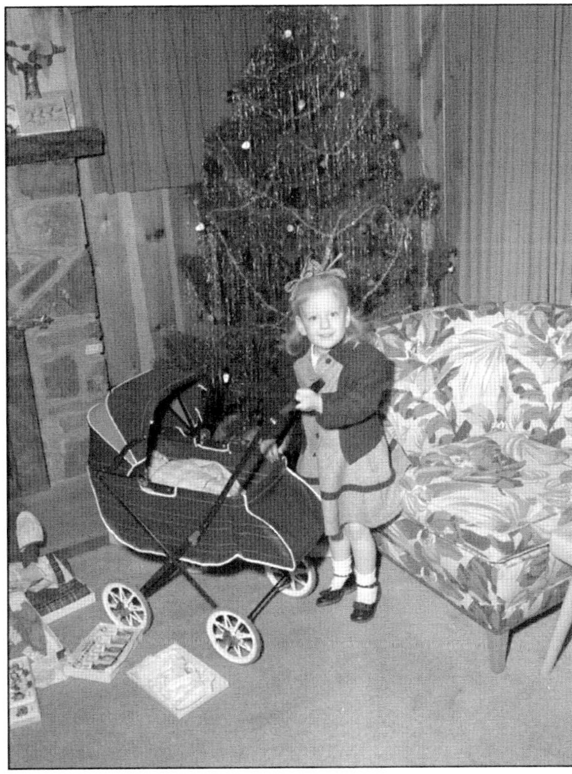

Carmon spent Christmas morning 1947 photographing Sandra Jones, daughter of his friend artist Reynolds Jones, as she opened her presents.

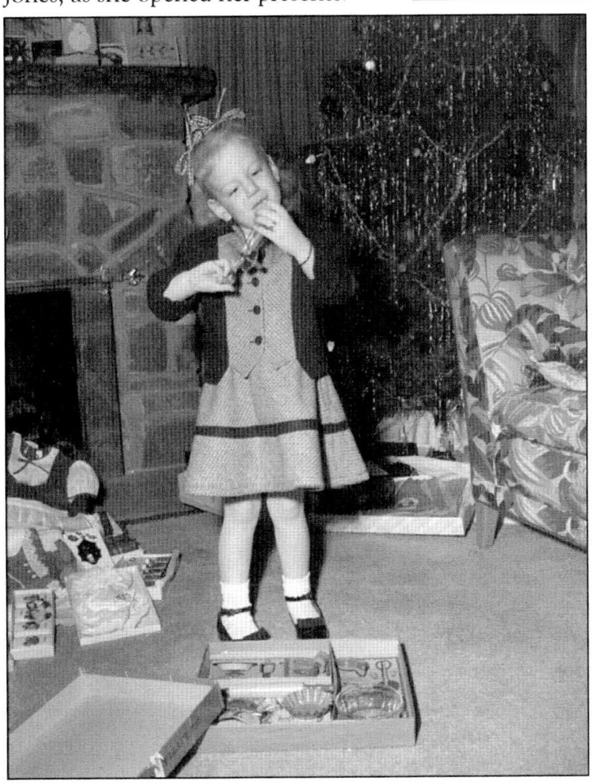

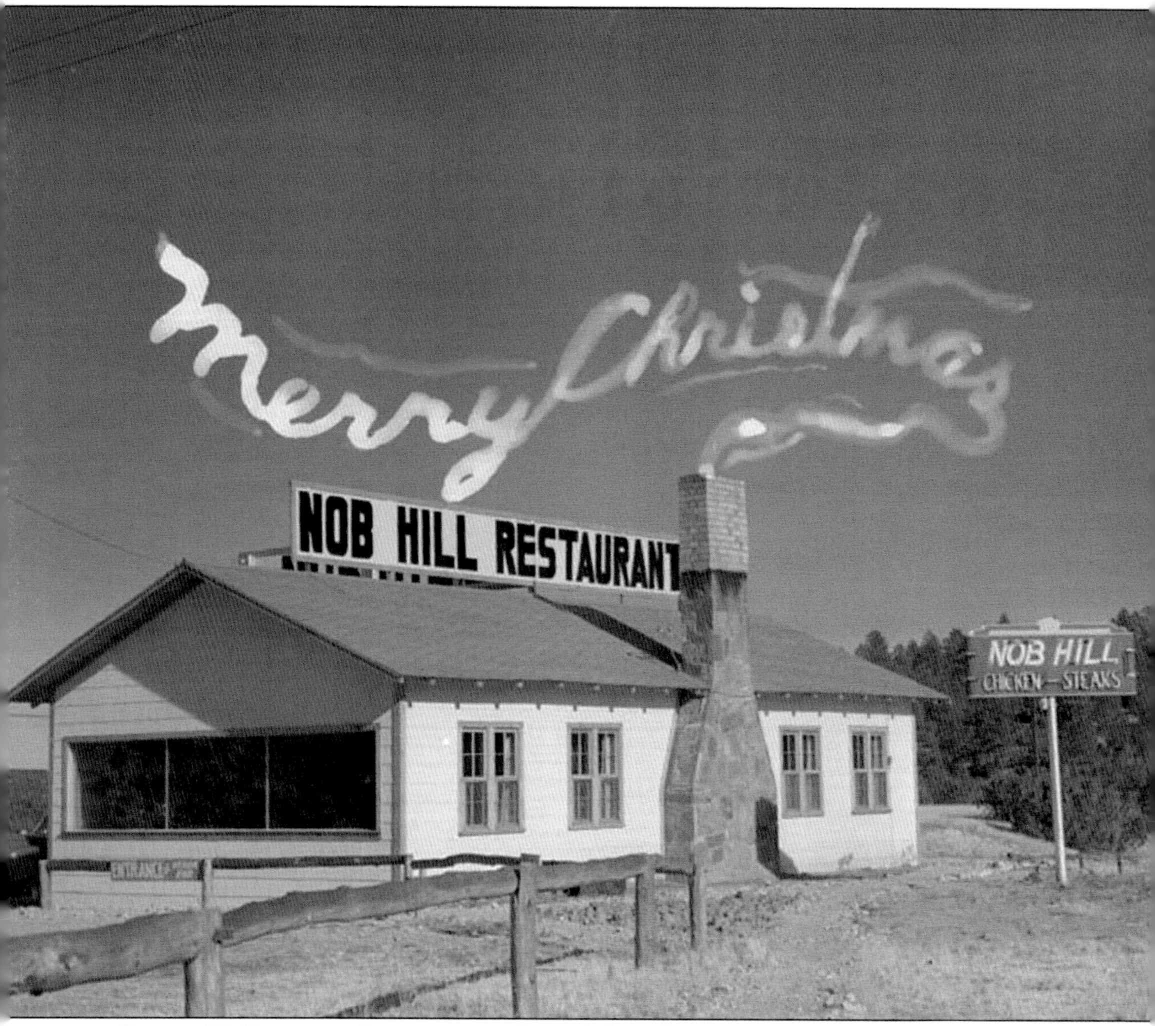

Carmon Phillips created many postcards, including this Christmas greeting from the Nob Hill Restaurant, whose dining room offered a beautiful view of Sierra Blanca.

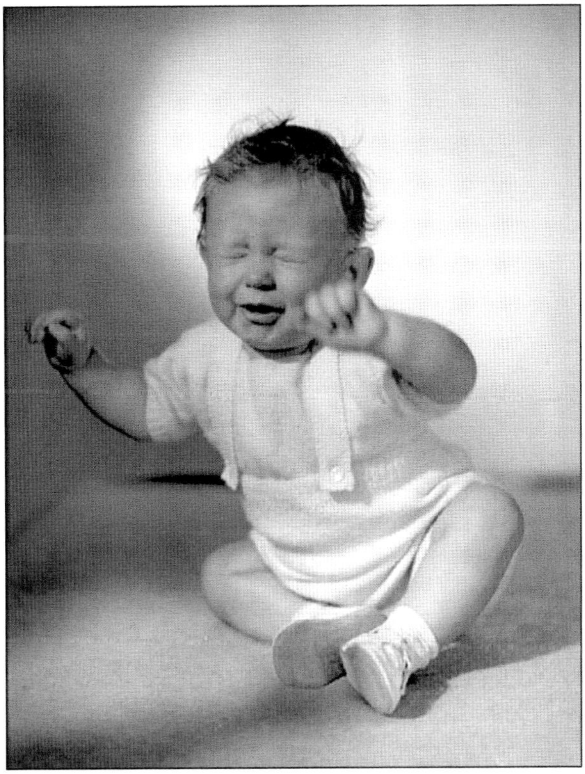

A few more of Carmon's portraits are seen here. The leather-covered ottoman, below, appears in many portraits and was also part of the Phillips' household furnishings.

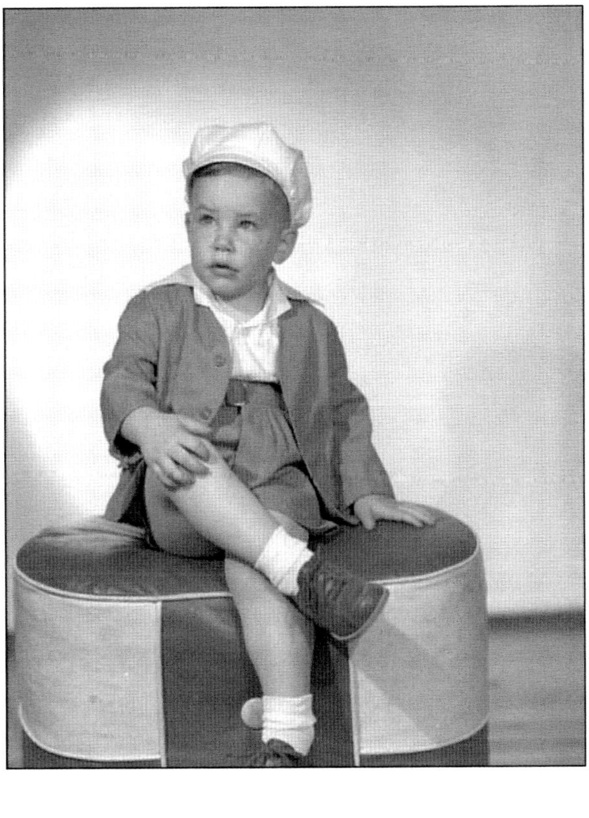

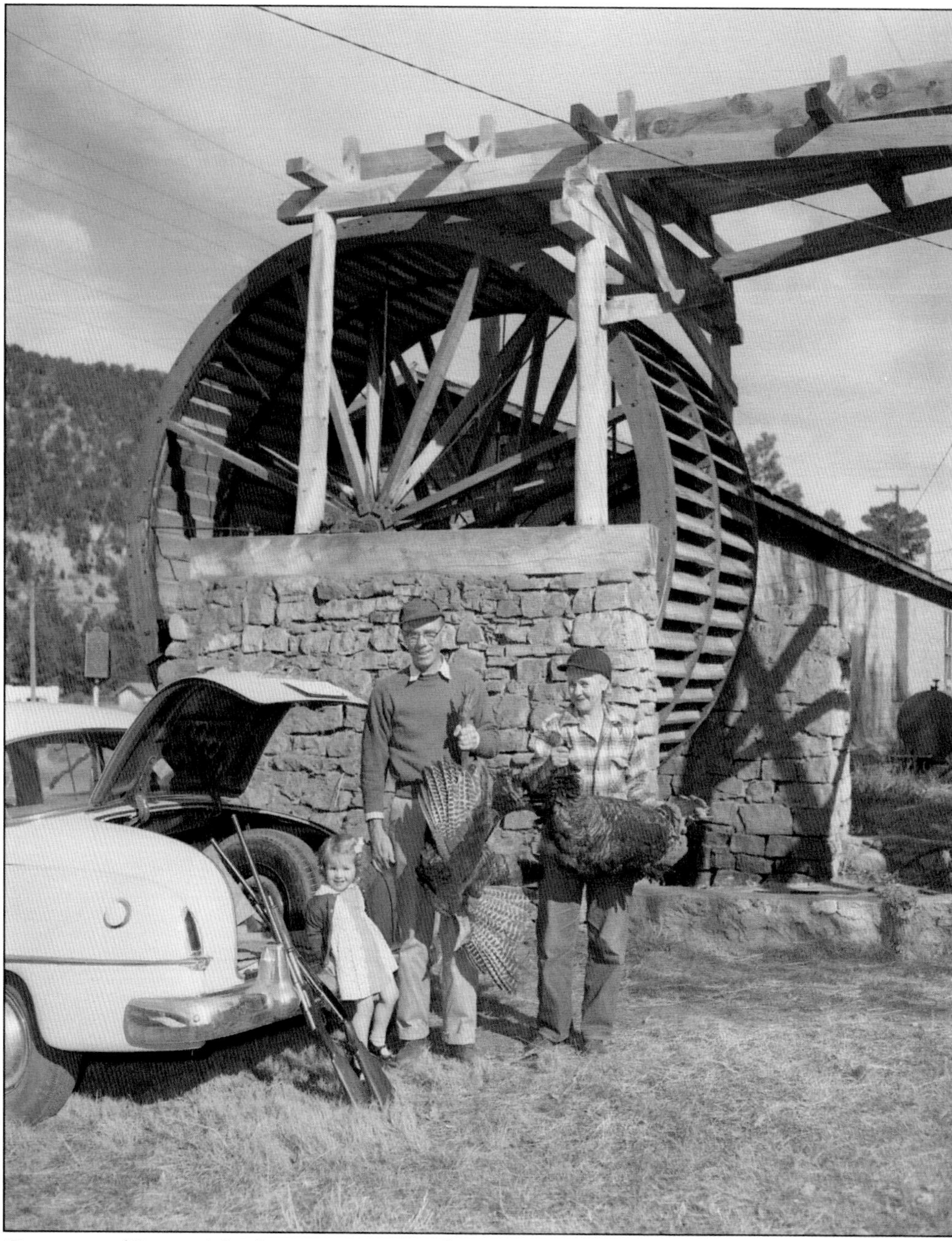

Carmon and Leona Mae lost no time in making new friends and settling into their life in the mountains. Like many Ruidoso residents, they took advantage of the abundant game in the surrounding forests.

Nine

Family Life

In the midst of all his attempts to make a living—his active involvement in community organizations and his apparent goal of photographing everything in Ruidoso—Phillips managed to make time for family and for a creative life.

"Carmon was active in the community, but he never got into politics," Mary Lou Gooch remembered. "He was a good family man—a good man." Mary Lou Gooch moved to Ruidoso with her husband, Leroy, in 1953 and met the Phillips shortly after. Like many people who knew Carmon and Leona Mae, she described them as her "best friends."

"Carmon and Leona Mae lived in that little building next to the mill," she remembered. "Carmon had his studio in the front room. Their bed was built in, sort of in the kitchen, and Delana had a little closet just big enough for a baby bed. And that was the whole house."

Leroy Gooch and Carmon formed a band, the Mellotones, which kept busy playing for dances at the Navajo Lodge and Noisy Water Lodge. Carmon sang and played the drums, in addition to writing several of the songs they performed.

Phillips was a man of many interests. He studied astrology and learned to calculate astrological charts. He traveled to Santa Fe to research the geology of Sierra Blanca. In an article in the *Ruidoso News* in 1954, he reported that the mountain was a 20-million-year-old remnant of volcanic rock. He also noted that the Sacramento Mountains were the southernmost point of glaciations during the last Ice Age.

He was one of the founders of the First Christian Church, for which he was occasionally called on to preach a sermon.

"He was a lot of fun to have as a dad," his daughter Delana remembered. "I would tag along when he went out to photograph people and places. He had a good sense of humor—he and I would imitate people and animals, and my mother would pretend to be annoyed. He and I would go roller skating—he was a good skater and dancer."

In the New Year's Eve 1955 issue of the *Ruidoso News*, there was an advertisement for the Old Mill. Above the usual promotional information was a message from Carmon: "Let's make cheerfulness our way of life this year."

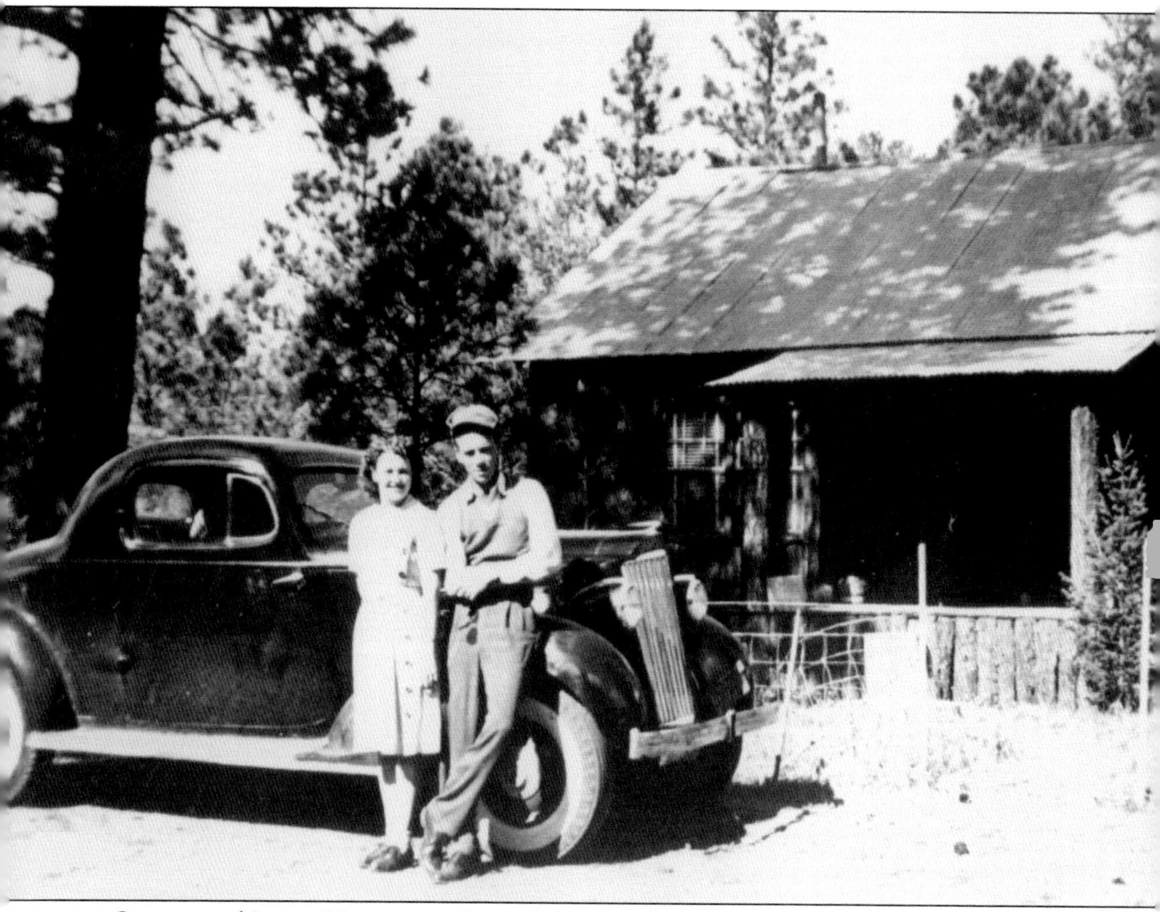

Carmon and Leona Mae pose in front of their first home in Ruidoso, a cabin owned by Leona Mae's parents. The cabin still stands on Ruidoso's Fifth Street today, in 2014.

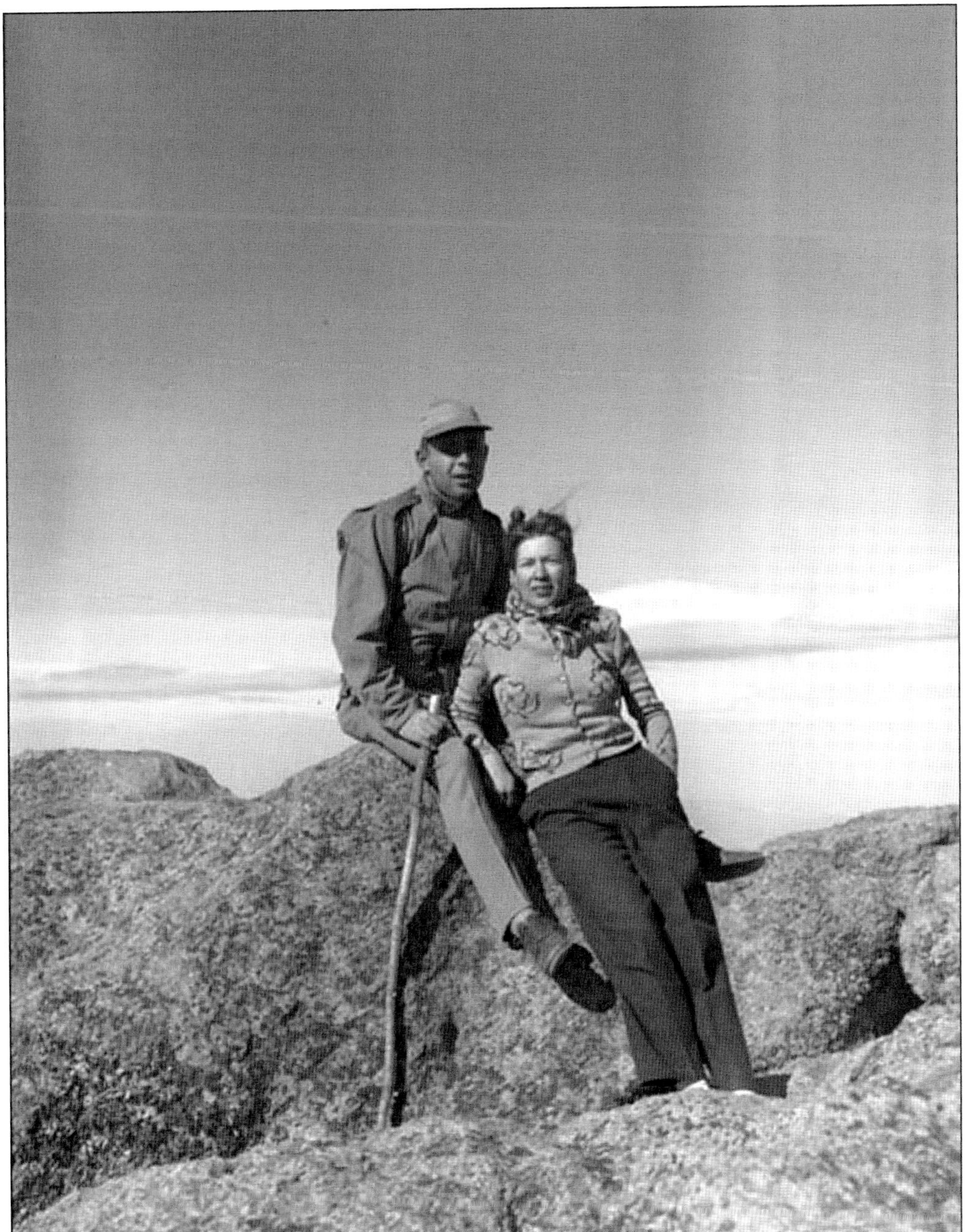

Wilford "Doc" and Lou Horton, friends of Carmon and Leona Mae, pose on the 12,000-foot peak of Sierra Blanca on October 11, 1947. "There were six of us that started, including Leona Mae," Lou Horton remembered. "Carmon, Doc and I were the only ones who made it to the top, and the last half hour, we'd take a few steps and then stop to catch our breath. But it was a gorgeous fall day and the view was wonderful."

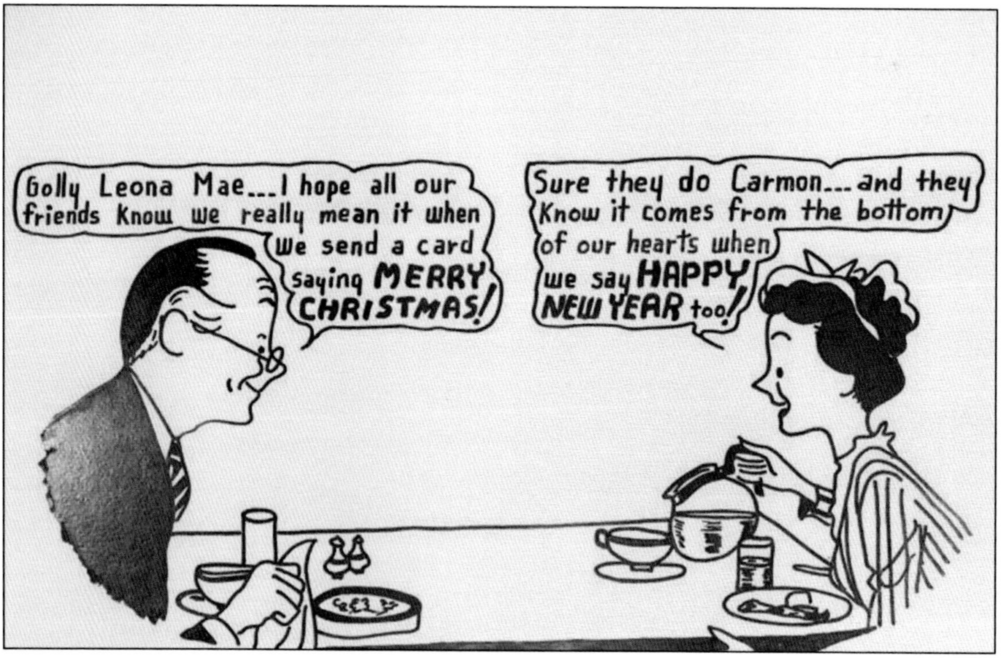

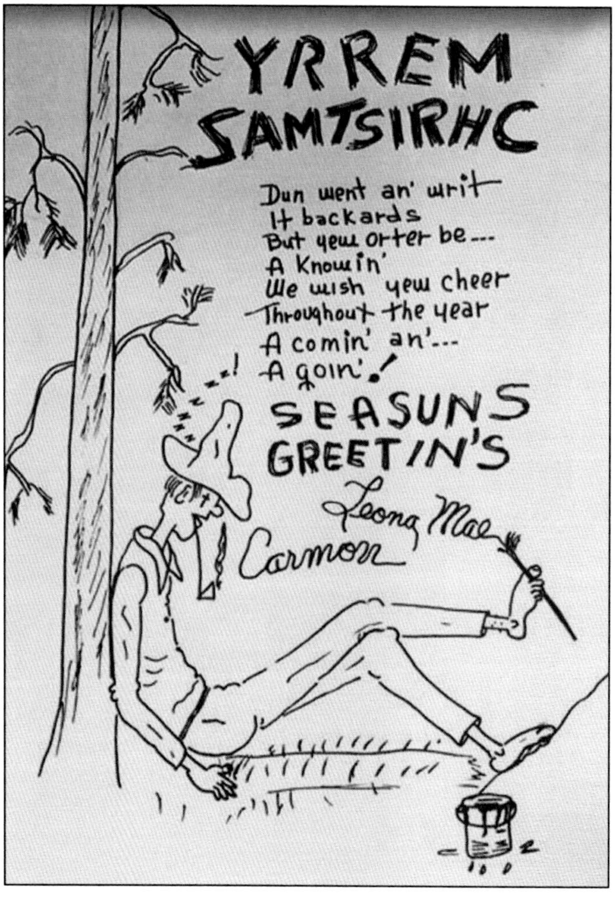

Although Carmon and Leona Mae's homemade Christmas cards are undated, they were probably sent between 1945, the year the couple moved to Ruidoso, and 1950, the year their daughter Delana was born.

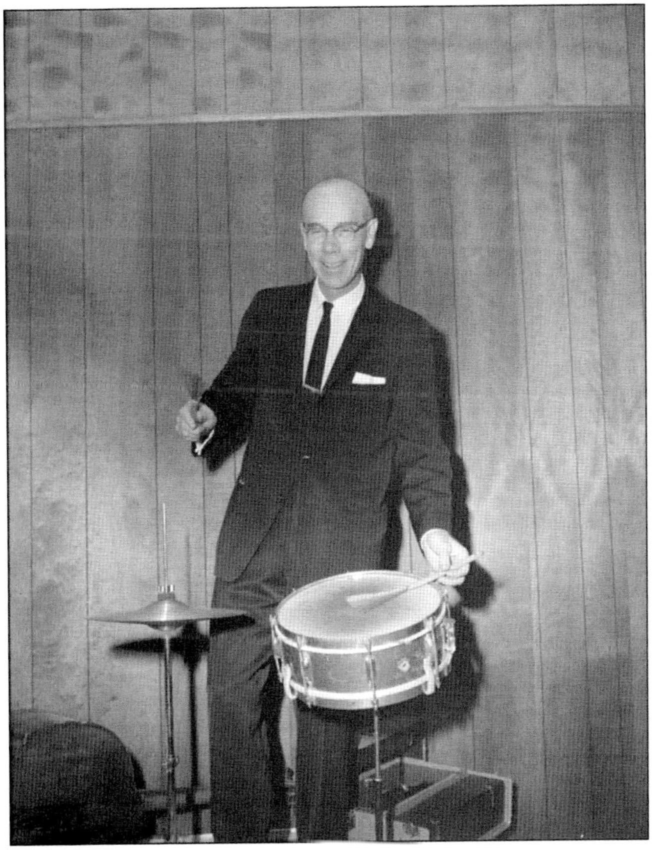

The Mellotones prepare for a performance at the Navajo Lodge. Carmon Phillips (in front of the camera rather than behind it) poses with the drums at right. In the photograph below are, from left to right, Bob Kauffman, Mariana Christian, Carmon Phillips, Leroy Gooch, and Lou Dodson.

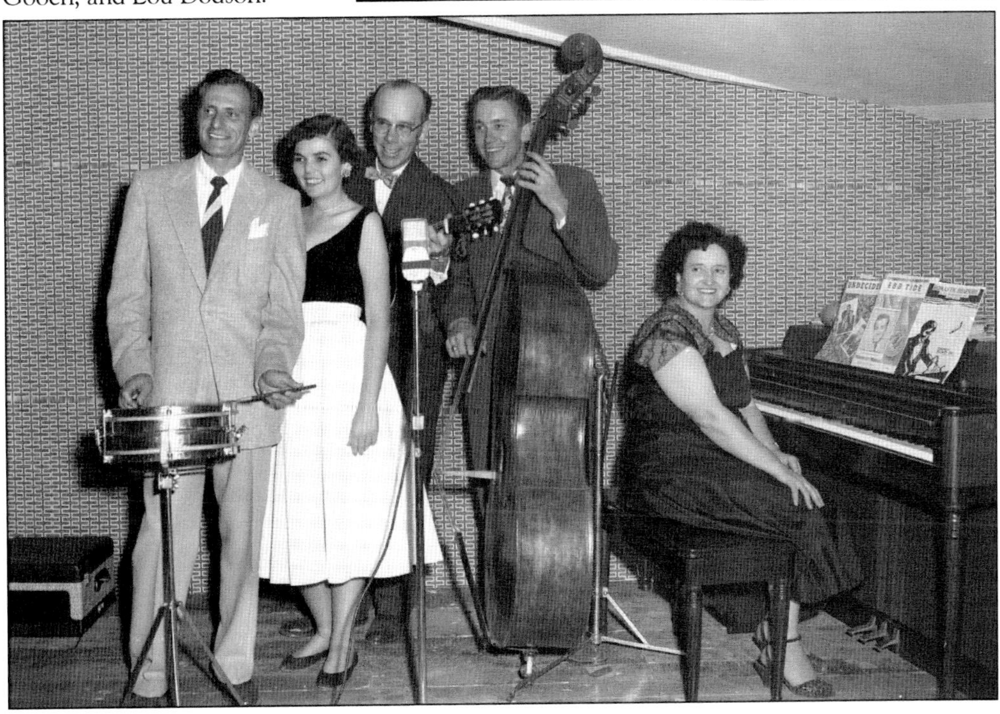

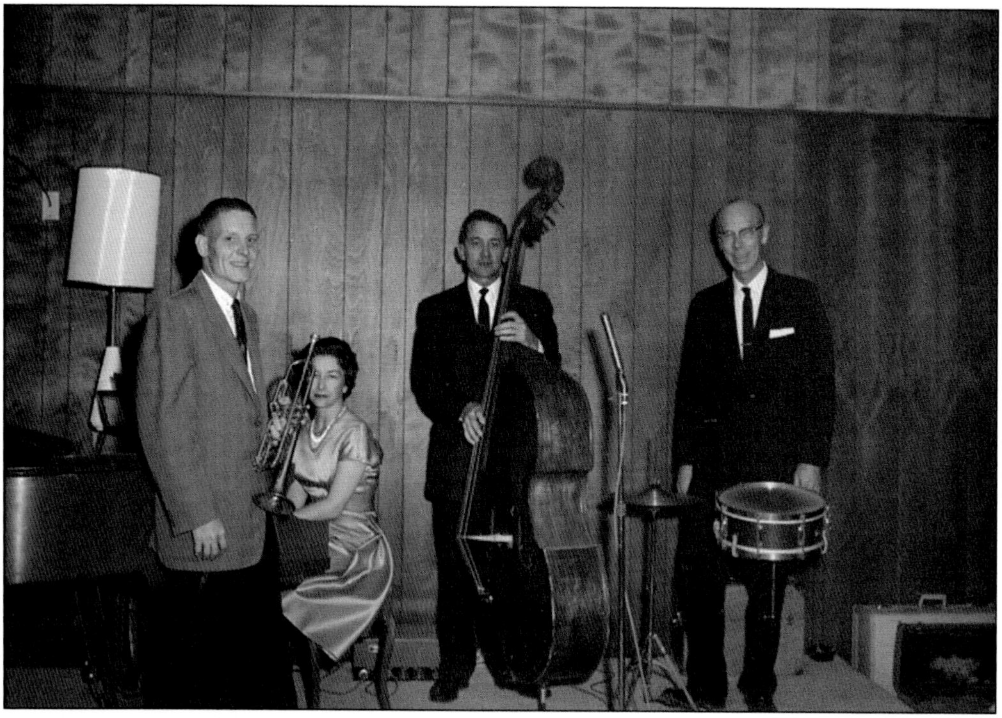

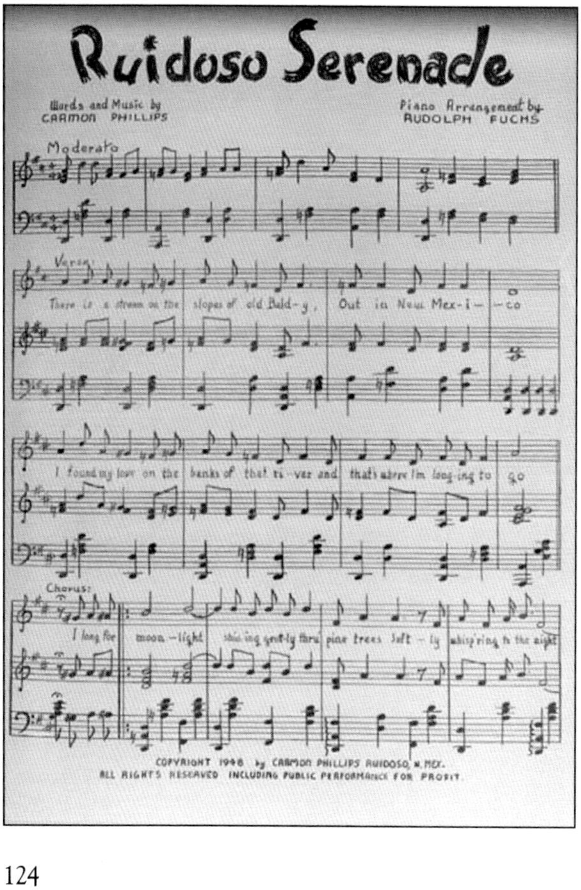

The composition of the band changed from time to time. In this photograph are, from left to right, Art Holt, Lou Newton, Leroy Gooch, and Carmon Phillips.

In January 1948, Carmon Phillips announced that, after three months of work, his song "Ruidoso Serenade" was complete. He planned to publish the song and market it, packaging it with promotional materials about Ruidoso. Among the other songs he wrote were "Summer," "Afterglow," and "Peel Me off the Ceiling, Baby."

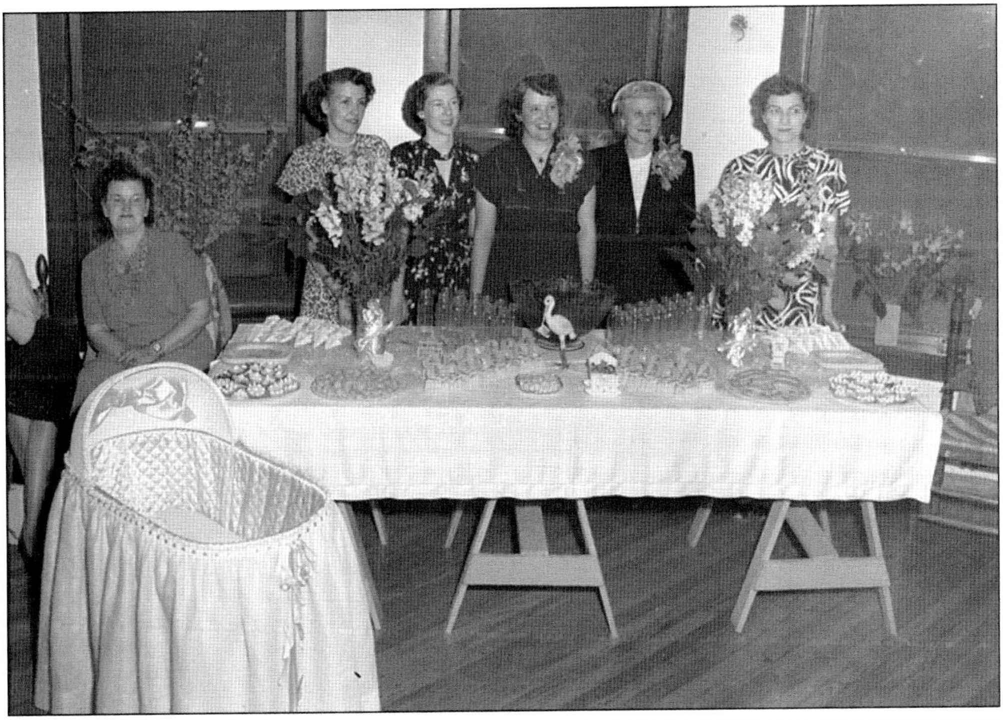

The imminent arrival of a new family member was celebrated with a baby shower in 1949. Leona Mae is fourth from left; the others are unidentified.

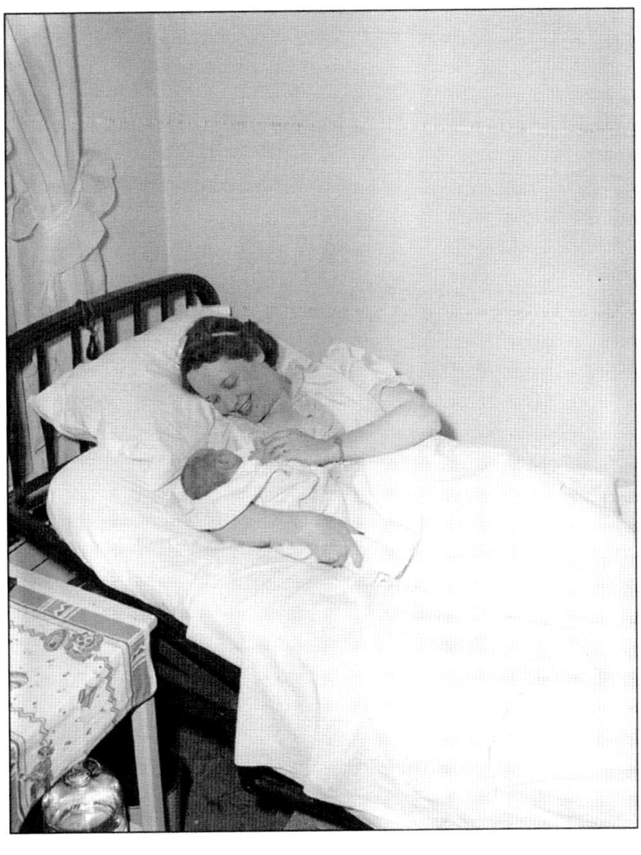

The Ruidoso Hospital was nearly ready to open, but Delana was born in Roswell on May 7, 1950, with Dr. Willie Horton in attendance.

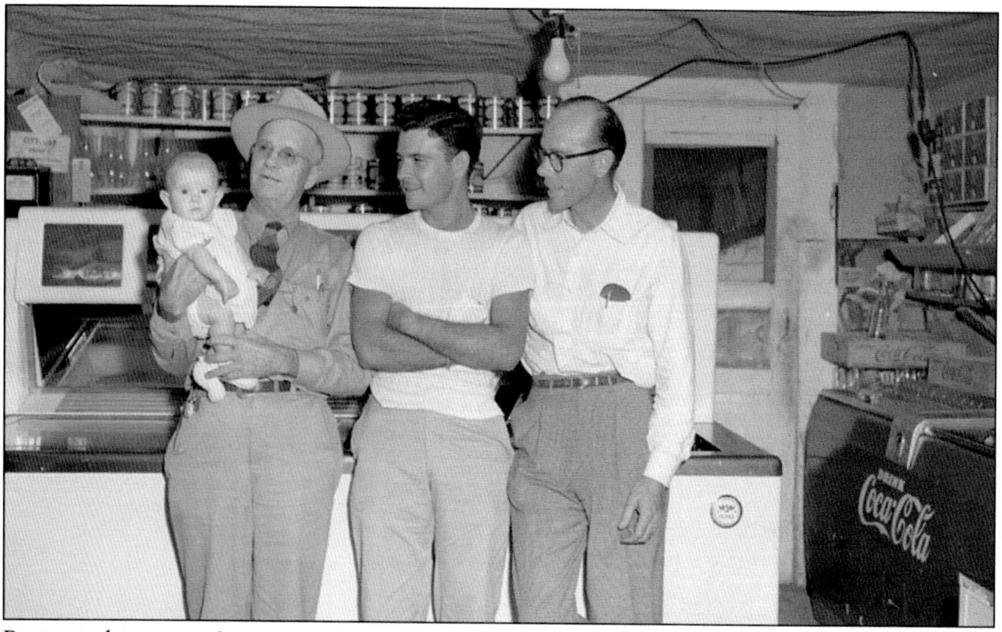

Posing in his parents' grocery store in Shamrock, Texas, are, from left to right, Carmon's father, William, holding Delana; Carmon's brother Don; and Carmon Phillips. As a teenager, Carmon worked in his father's store in Erick, Oklahoma. He developed his salesmanship skills while selling ice cream, entertaining the customers by juggling bottles and learning to flip a scoop of ice cream in the air and catch it in the cone.

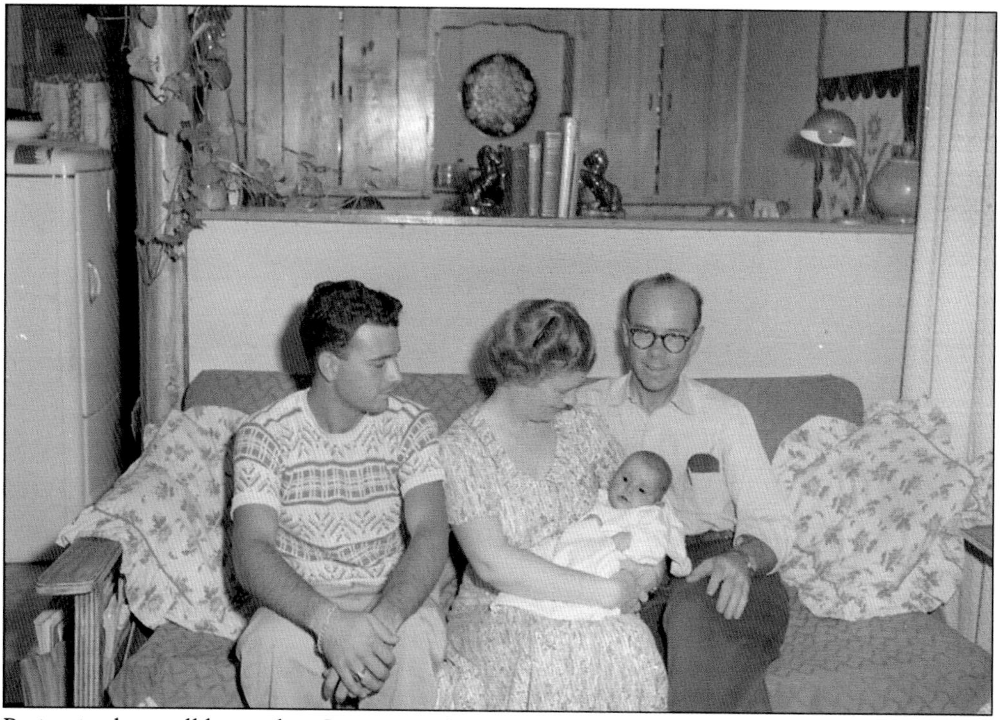

Posing in the small home that Carmon and Leona Mae built next door to the mill are, from left to right, Don Phillips, Leona Mae with Delana, and Carmon Phillips.

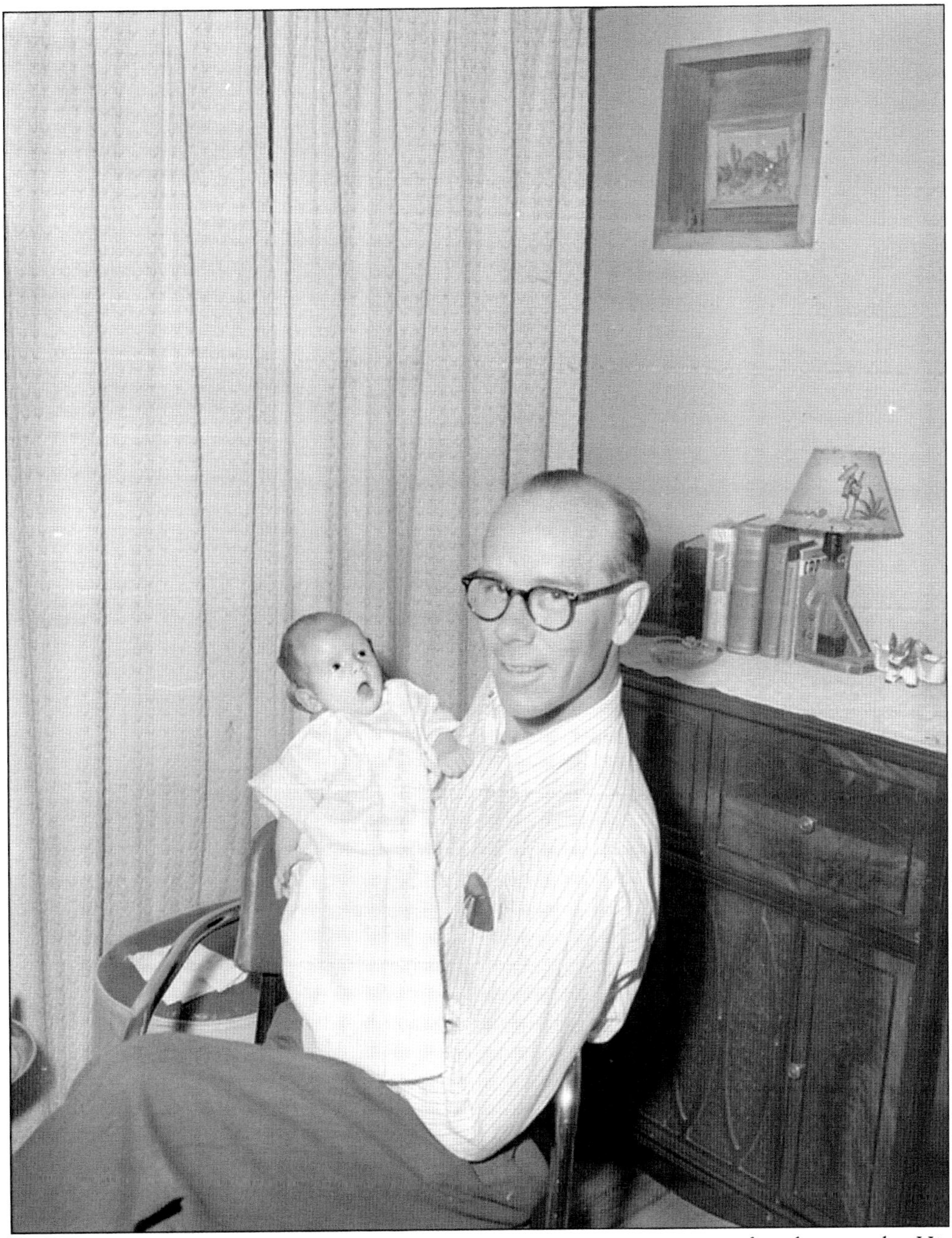

Carmon assumes a new role—that of proud father. Carmon appears in very few photographs. His place was always behind the camera.

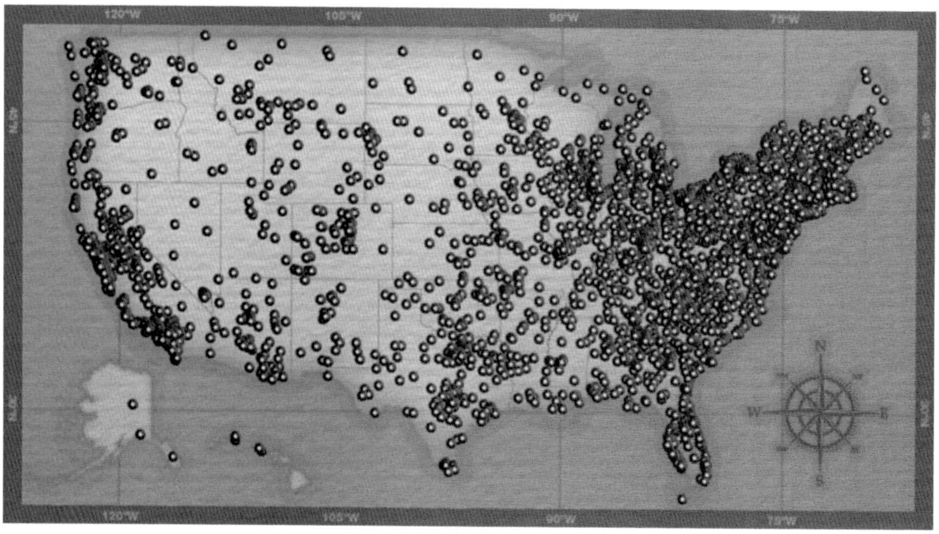